encountering feminism

intersections between
feminism and
the person-centred approach

edited by
gillian proctor and mary beth napier

PCCS BOOKS
Ross-on-Wye

First published in 2004

PCCS BOOKS Ltd
Llangarron
Ross-on-Wye
Herefordshire
HR9 6PT
UK
Tel +44 (0)1989 77 07 07
www.pccs-books.co.uk

**Encountering Feminism: Intersections between feminism
and the Person-Centred Approach**

A CIP catalogue record for this book is available from the British Library

ISBN 1 898059 65 9

Cover design by Old Dog Graphics
Printed by Bath Press, Bath, UK

CONTENTS

SECTION III AN INTELLECTUAL UNDERSTANDING. NEW
THEORIES TO GUIDE OUR ACTIONS

SECTION IV PRACTICAL APPLICATIONS AND SUCCESS STORIES

ACKNOWLEDGEMENTS

We believe that the journey of producing this book would not have been possible if there were not many women before us who forged a path for us to follow. These include unknown women who have suffered at the hands of the mental health system and sexist societies and who have fought back and offered alternatives to 'power over' structures. It includes women who have lovingly and persistently kept the ideas of feminism alive in the person-centred community. Some of these women we have never met. Some of these women are contributors to this book. We have personally been touched by the strong and powerful voices of Carol Wolter-Gustafson, Gay (Swenson) Barfield, Maureen O'Hara, Peggy Natiello, Natalie Rogers and Marge Witty. We have also been supported by those closest to us. Mary Beth is blessed to share her life and love with her partner Joanne Davis who provides constant encouragement for her ideas and projects. Gillian has been supported to get to this point by her parents, who gave her the confidence and education to have the ability and privilege to be involved in this project; by Sheila Youngson, with whom she was first able to explore these ideas and who has been a continual support, mentor and friend and by her partner Bernadette Tuohy, who provides support, encouragement and stimulating discussions of ideas. We dedicate this book to all of these individuals and thank them for lighting our path and walking with us on this journey.

FOREWORD

PEGGY NATIELLO

During the 1970s I decided to go back to school. I was an impassioned feminist, raising four sons and a daughter, and inspired by my person-centered work with groups that included Carl Rogers. I considered a doctoral degree in Psychology, but, when I reviewed the curriculums of traditional programs, it became clear that none of them addressed issues of gender or the impact of sexism on psychological development. In addition, each one relied heavily on the expert, medical model for diagnosis and treatment. The field was pervaded with male-dominated values. A doctorate in Human Development, an interdisciplinary degree, with a specialization in the Person-Centered Approach and feminism, seemed more appropriate.

Today, with many years of experience coupled with that doctorate, I introduce myself as a *feminist person-centered practitioner*. And now, in this bold collection of writings, I have come face-to-face with the complexities of that identity.

Between these covers, the reader will find person-centered and feminist theory articulated, crystallized, defended, and challenged. Has Rogers' approach sufficiently accounted for self-in-relationship as well as the organismic, essential self? How much are conditions of worth socially constructed, and how does gender and sexism contribute to them? Do person-centered therapists who consciously abdicate power over the client unwittingly ignore the structural power they have over a client and the consequences of that power? Is the commitment of most feminists to teach and engage in social action in conflict with the non-directiveness of the Person-Centered Approach? Does feminist theory enhance or intrude upon person-centered therapy with women? Can person-centered work with women be effective without it? Where does client and clinician's spirituality fit into the therapy relationship? These questions, and others that we are not accustomed to considering, are guaranteed to engage the reader and expand the mind.

In addition to raising such questions, there is an insider's look at feminist struggles in the 70s and 80s that rattled the foundations of The Center for the

Studies of the Person and some staff persons including Rogers himself. There are contributions by men who acknowledge the changes in society perpetuated by feminist theory, and find possibilities for their creative, expanded selves in the new order of things. Several contributors investigate other approaches to human development compatible with the Person-Centered Approach and feminist theory. They argue for convergence rather than competition in order to strengthen the challenge to authoritarian power. The feminist exposure of the disempowerment and 'blaming the victim' that often occur for women who have been abused in a sexist culture, is fierce and articulate in this book! The writers of these stories are often survivors themselves, and their voices reveal the intimate world of personal experience that best informs all theory and practice.

I recommend this book to all students and practitioners of person-centered and feminist theory—actually for all helping professionals. It expands the discussion of person-centered theory by its in-depth look at the wounds suffered under sexism, and, thus, illuminates some aspects of the wounding of all victims/survivors of oppression in any form. It revitalizes the crucial importance of seeing clients in their wholeness, and being able to connect empathically with the reality of their experiences around race, gender, culture, religion, sexual preference, class, and other identities that social forces demean and penalize. It reminds us that we need to learn from those with whom we work by listening curiously and carefully to things we may not fully understand rather than trying to 'fix' them. It opens out the possibilities of enhancing our pedagogy and practice by dialogue with others on similar paths, working together for a more responsive and inclusive world.

This is a theoretically powerful, thought-provoking book that brims over with compassion, integrity, original thinking, and courage. Prepare yourself to feel stimulated and drawn into the discussion. Gillian Proctor and Mary Beth Napier have brought to fruition a long overdue conversation about feminism and the Person-Centered Approach. Thanks to them and to each of the contributors for their enlightened participation.

Peggy Natiello, PhD
Sedona, Arizona

INTRODUCTION

GILLIAN PROCTOR AND MARY BETH NAPIER

THE JOURNEY OF CREATING THIS BOOK

The idea for this book did not originate from one moment in time but from a process, or journey. We (the editors) first met in 2000 during the time of the 5th International Conference for Client-Centered and Experiential Psychotherapy (ICCCEP) conference in Chicago. On meeting, we immediately found several points of connection in the doctoral theses that we were involved in. Gillian had just completed hers on the dynamics of power in therapy and Mary Beth was midway through hers on an analysis of the Stone Center model of therapy and how the client-centred concepts of genuineness, mutuality and non-directivity could be incoporated into the Stone Center's theory. We soon realised that we shared not only a foundation and firm political and ethical belief in Person-Centred/Client-Centred Therapy but also in the theory and political practice of feminism. Early discussions focused on issues of power and mutuality in therapy and how Person-Centred Therapy and feminism informed our ethical dilemmas. Our connections and discussions continued over email after these first meetings.

At the same time, there were several presentations at the ICCCEP conference around the theme of feminism and Client-Centred Therapy (CCT) and a group of delegates created an email list to try to continue discussions. The presentations included Gillian Proctor's 'Power in Person-Centred Therapy', Sarah Hawtin's 'The Organismic Valuing Process and Ethics in Person-Centred Theory', and Ann Lovering's 'Person-Centered and Feminist Theories: How we connect them in our work with groups of Mexican women' (all published in Watson, Goldman and Warner, 2002) and Carol Wolter-Gustafson's 'The Power of the Premise: Reconstructing gender and human development with Rogers' theory' (published in Fairhurst, 1999). The following year Gillian and Beth met again at Warm Springs encounter group in February. Here we had five days to continue our discussions

1

and apply them in the real situation of interactions within a group. Our discussions at this stage were that these interactions in a person-centred group of 'equal' people were informed by the inequalities of gender expectations and sexism. We were surprised how discussions about gender differences did not take place within the encounter group and we experienced at times not only a lack of understanding, but a resistance to understanding from some participants when we tried to bring up issues of gender and sexism. There were varying responses from men. Some men had educated themselves about gender expectations and dynamics and were open and supportive to our discussions. Others were dismissive and hostile.

In 2002, Gillian spent seven months in the US, mostly in Chicago. Mary Beth and Gillian met early during this period to discuss what modules of teaching we wanted to offer jointly to the Doctorate in Clinical Psychology program at Illinois School of Professional Psychology (ISPP, now Argosy University), and decided to offer two modules as part of the Client-Centered stream. One of these was on trauma and CCT and the second on feminism and CCT. The amount of material we covered and the interest generated by this 11-hour course was the final catalyst to inspire us to co-edit this book. Later that summer (of 2002) we facilitated workshops on feminism and CCT at the Carl Rogers Centenary Conference in La Jolla and at the Association for the Development of the Person-Centered Approach (ADPCA) conference in Cleveland. On returning to the UK at the end of the summer, Gillian facilitated a workshop in Durham at the British Association for the Person-Centred Approach (BAPCA) conference. Much enthusiasm and interest in the subject at both of these conferences confirmed our feelings that this book would be of interest to many. At Cleveland, a larger group of us who had met due to a common interest in this subject at previous conferences met again to discuss how to take these issues forward. Carol Wolter-Gustafson, who had been trying to put feminism on the agenda in the client-centred world for decades, wanted to concentrate on organising a stream on feminism at the next ICCCEP conference in Holland, in 2003. Wade Hannon and Jeff Cornelius-White expressed interest in contributing chapters, and all were pleased to hear that Gillian and Mary Beth committed to begin the process of editing a book about the intersections of these two bodies of knowledge.

Before Gillian left the US at the end of August 2002, Mary Beth and Gillian had put together a proposal to email as many groups, lists and individuals as possible to ask for chapter proposals by the following spring. We were extremely excited to receive over 20 proposals in time for our next meeting in 2003. Clearly this subject had touched a chord for many people. Throughout the editing process, we have worked as collaboratively as possible within editing limitations (such as word counts) and have worked together as editors. We have always aimed to work with our person-centred and feminist principles of respect and empowerment at the heart of our interactions. And now we have the result.

INTERSECTIONS OF FEMINISM AND THE PERSON-CENTRED APPROACH

Both feminism and the Person-Centred Approach are responses to societies that structure personal and institutional relationships so that one group or individual has power over another. They are reactions against authorities and hierarchies of power which give some people the power to tell others what to do. Instead of trusting in outside authority, the Person-Centred Approach believes in the trustworthiness and potential for growth of each individual, relying on an individual's own internal sense of what is right for them (see Proctor, Chapter 3). The Person-Centred Approach challenges us to develop facilitative and connecting relationships where each individual is respected and valued. Feminism arose as a response to the systemic and systematic oppression of women in society. Feminism questioned the notion of women as second-class citizens and of the 'natural right' of men to have power over women. Feminism (originally called the Women's Liberation Movement) aims to liberate women from their oppressed status and to release women's real potential to make choices about their own lives rather than accept dependence on men. Feminism prioritises connections and relationships as the starting point, rather than the traditionally masculine goals of individual autonomy and independence. Already, the connections between these two theories and approaches are evident in the questioning of taken-for-granted authority and what, for centuries, was seen as the 'natural order' of society.

Each approach discusses how control of an individual within society affects each individual internally. The Person-Centred Approach focuses on how 'conditions of worth' are internalised by people, so that we change ourselves to please others and 'do the right thing' whether or not it is our 'real self'. Feminism concentrates on how oppression is internalised and how assumptions and stereotypes affect those who they are supposed to describe. We believe that feminism's notion of internalised oppression is the concept of conditions of worth at a societal level. They are messages from society about who we are and how we should behave. Within both theories, these messages within individual relationships (as in person-centred conditions of worth) or at a broader societal level (as in feminist internalised oppression) have the effect of limiting our potential for growth. Both approaches are about liberating us from the damaging effects of these methods of control.

Both feminism and the Person-Centred Approach share a stance with regard to power (see Proctor, Chapter 11). Both feminist theorists and person-centred theorists have critiqued the damaging effects of 'power-over', authority or coercion. Both approaches instead advocate the potential of 'personal power' (the Person-Centred Approach) or power-from-within (feminists), each of these concepts referring to an internal sense of agency, a trust in oneself. Both approaches also advocate the potential of 'power-with' (feminists) or the power of people in groups (Person-Centred Approach). These both refer to the positive potential of people working together with mutual respect for the benefit of all. Working together in groups has been a big part of the development and history of each approach, with feminist consciousness-raising groups and person-centred encounter groups.

Both feminist and person-centred theory have critiqued the dominant constructions of 'madness' and distress. Both offer alternative viewpoints to the dominant medical model's understanding of diagnosis and treatment which rest on the assumption that distress and madness are always the result of internal pathology. Feminist and person-centred theories provide different epistemologies from the medical model (see Wolter-Gustafson, Chapter 9) that suggest that much distress is the result of relational dysfunction, whether that be on a personal or societal level. Both theories stress the importance of mutual and genuine relationships as the key to establishing and maintaining psychological well-being.

Each shares a critical approach to education, and the mainstream educational methods of teaching as control rather than encouragement of critical thinking and positively relating to others (see Cornelius-White and Godfrey, Chapter 14).

Additionally, feminist and person-centred practitioners view the importance and role of spirituality in a person's life in a way that does not pathologise a person for having spirituality as a value or an aid in life. Both approaches are more open to the experience of a spiritual dimension within the person, and clinicians who practice both approaches are likely to be more accepting and comfortable discussing spiritual issues and assisting clients to use their spiritual beliefs as forms of knowing. This is in direct contrast to scientific models that value rational thinking that can be quantified and objectified as the only reliable sources of information. Some feminist theory and some person-centred theory explicitly discuss the impact and relevance of spirituality (see Steele, Chapter 8).

We, and many others, believe that each approach has much to offer in our understanding of our world and human relationships, and that each can learn from the other. Whereas the Person-Centred Approach gives us a model for individual relationships, feminism adds an understanding of wider societal structures of power and influence on the individual. Feminism gives us a model to criticise patriarchy and many patriarchal practices and institutions, and the Person-Centred Approach, coupled with awareness of feminist theory, gives us a model to build up different relationships and structures based on principles of equality and respect rather than hierarchies and authority. Dominant models of feminist therapy can learn from the principles of person-centred therapy to make

4

their therapy relationships more consistent with their theories of mutuality and collaboration (see Napier, Chapter 10). Person-centred therapists can learn from feminism to improve their understanding of how individuals are affected by societal structures and appreciate commonalities in experiences within oppressed groups (see Proctor, Chapter 11). This is particularly the case for therapists working with women who have experienced the effects of patriarchal oppression in traumatic ways such as rape, sexual abuse and domestic violence (see Hill, Chapter 18; Shaw, Chapter 12; Smailes, Chapter 17; Davis and Bird, Chapter 16).

POINTS OF CONFLICT BETWEEN THE PERSON-CENTRED AND FEMINIST APPROACHES

Perhaps the biggest point of conflict between the two approaches is the focus of study. For person-centred theorists, the focus is always on the individual man or woman. There is no systematic analysis of gender dynamics when attempting to understand the person. For feminist theorists, the gender of a person is considered the most defining feature of that person and, therefore, an analysis of gender and the effects of sexism and patriarchy must always be considered when attempting to understand the individual's experience. After the focus on the difference between men and women's experience, a feminist theorist would consider differences between groups of women, such as women of colour versus white women or differences between the experiences of lesbians and heterosexual women. A person-centred theorist would focus on the uniqueness of each individual and study those aspects of the particular person that the person deems important. A person-centred approach does not include gender analysis or analysis of any other societal factors unless an individual specifically mentions them as being personally relevant.

Although there are many points of intersection and commonalities between person-centred and feminist therapies, each approach is critical of the other. Person-centred theorists criticize feminist therapy because a feminist therapist has a particular agenda for every client that is in addition to whatever the client's initial agenda is. For example, feminist therapy often has a teaching component to it that is used to empower a woman and to assist her in locating the source of her distress in societal factors such as sexism rather than seeing distress as something that is solely an intrapsychic event. A therapist's agenda is outside the client's frame of reference and is not in keeping with a non-directive approach. Person-centred theorists argue that psychological healing occurs when the therapist offers certain facilitative conditions for the client that allows each client a strong sense of autonomy and self direction. A therapist's agenda can undermine client autonomy and self-direction. It also puts the therapist in an expert role that undermines mutuality between client and therapist. Person-centred therapists experience women as feeling powerful and gaining a sense of empowerment and connection, not because they educated the women about sexism, but because they provided a supportive environment where each woman could find and listen to her own voice.

Feminist theorists criticise Person-Centred Therapy because in PCT, the source of distress is located wherever the client experiences it. This is seen as unwittingly assisting the client to blame herself for distress that is caused by societal or relational factors rather than intrapsychic dysfunction (e.g., see Shaw, Chapter 12). Another criticism is that the Person-Centred Approach was developed before gender analysis informed social sciences. Therefore, a person-centred therapist would not necessarily have training in gender or cultural analysis and could be operating from unchallenged, unevaluated sexist, 'racist' and classist assumptions (e.g., see Ehrbar, Chapter 13; Napier, Chapter 2).

There are other differences in the theories in addition to the criticisms they have of each other. For example, the goal of person-centred therapy is the development of the self. Feminist therapy often emphasizes the development of relational capacities within the client. All of these differences and critiques are addressed in the chapters of this book. Some 'differences' and criticisms seem to us to be valid, others seem to be more misunderstandings than true differences, and still others provide places of intersections where the two theories together may be stronger than either theory alone. As the reader will discover, the chapters in this book offer a wide spectrum of how these two bodies of knowledge have been used to guide many of us in our work and personal lives.

ARE THE PERSON-CENTRED APPROACH AND FEMINISM RELEVANT TODAY?

It seems that today is an historical time when neither the Person-Centred Approach (PCA) nor feminism are on the agenda in most contexts. Since the heyday of both approaches in the early sixties and seventies when the values and ethics of each fit with the political climate at the time, interest and enthusiasm in what these values can bring to human relationships and existence has waned (e.g., see Barfield, Chapter 4 and O'Hara, Chapter 5). At the same time, hostility and a backlash to these ideas has increased, and conflict within the world continues (see Hopkins, Chapter 6), with continuing aggression always failing to end wars. Many argue that individual freedom has never been higher and that women have never before had so many choices. However many inequalities between men and women remain unchanged and ideas of individual growth and creativity are low on the political agenda.

To say that we live in a male-dominated society usually provokes a lot of reactions. People like to point out how much things have changed in the past few decades for women. Yet many things remain the same. In the Western world, women still earn much less than men; are overwhelmingly found in low paid, low status or part-time work; are massively under-represented in structures of power; are still largely responsible for childcare and housework; are sexually objectified in the media and the ever increasing pornography industry; are told how our lifestyles, bodies and appearances should meet up to a feminine norm, and stigmatised and excluded if we 'fail'.

Globally, the statistics for violence against women are frightening. At the Vienna Human Rights Conference and the 4th World Conference on Women, priority attention was given to violence against women, characterised as 'the most pervasive yet least recognised human rights abuse in the world.' (Heise, 1993: 171). In many countries, women are victims of 'Honour' killings, defined as acts of murder in which a woman is killed for her actual or perceived 'immoral behaviour'. Such 'immoral behaviour' may take the form of marital infidelity, refusing to submit to an arranged marriage, demanding a divorce, flirting with or receiving phone calls from men, failing to serve a meal on time, or—grotesquely—'allowing herself' to be raped. Such killings have been reported in Afghanistan, Bangladesh, Britain, Brazil, Ecuador, Egypt, India, Iran, Iraq, Israel, Italy, Jordan, Pakistan, Morocco, Sweden, Turkey and Uganda (Ahsan, 2003). 120 million women and girls worldwide have suffered Female Genital Mutilation with a further 2 million girls at risk from this practice each year, mostly in African, Middle Eastern and Asian countries (UNFPA-SWP, 1997). Trafficking women and children for sexual exploitation generates more than 8 billion dollars each year with two million girls aged five to fifteen being introduced to the commercial sex market annually (UNFPA-SWP, 1997). Ninety per cent of pregnant girls between the ages of 12 and 16 years in Peru are pregnant as the result of rape, often incest. In Costa Rica, Peru and Uruguay, rapists are not convicted under law if they agree to marry their rape victim and the woman agrees. Domestic violence is documented in most societies where the question is examined, although some peasant and small-scale societies are reported to be 'essentially untroubled by family violence' (Heise, 1993). A US study estimates that between 21 and 30 per cent of women are beaten by a partner at least once in their lives and that over half of these women are beaten at least 3 times a year (UNFPA-SWP, 1997). Each year in the US alone 700,000 women and girls are raped or sexually assaulted. This is the highest percentage in western countries and only 16 per cent of women report the rape (UNFPA-SWP, 1997) In conflict situations globally, the rape of women has long been used as a weapon of war. Clearly, it's a dangerous business to be born a woman in this world.

Men's control of women within heterosexual relationships, the workplace and in education, continues through violence, rape, sexual harassment, and the perpetuation of gender stereotypes. These dynamics are perhaps sometimes more subtle and less overtly acceptable since feminist analyses of the sixties and seventies. However, whilst some behaviours have become more unacceptable, the same attitudes affect women's lives in more insidious ways. At the same time, it has become more unacceptable for women to challenge these attitudes and behaviours as the backlash to feminism continues.

Feminism has challenged men and there continues to be varying responses by men to this challenge. Some men are horrified to learn how they gain their power at the expense of women and are concerned about the effects of patriarchal expectations on men and women. Some men educate themselves about gender stereotypes and the dynamics between men and women and increase their awareness of their own behaviour in an effort to not be personally part of the oppression of women (e.g., see Hannon, Chapter 7). However, as long as feminism has existed, there has been a backlash and fear by men of losing their power and the status quo of gender expectations and relationships being challenged. Backlash reactions are taken from the usual range of ways that men have power in relationships with women, particularly in heterosexual partnerships. These reactions range from violence (including sexual violence) perpetuated against feminists, and women who question the patriarchal status quo, to attempts to demean, degrade and criticize women who speak out against men's naturally assumed status and power. In the UK, the latest manifestation of the backlash in the media seems to be men attempting to gain sympathy from women about the difficulty men have in dealing with women's changing expectations and how they can react to feminism. Often this response does succeed in gaining the sympathy of women, who then continue their role as care givers in looking after these 'poor men'. In these ways, the gender dynamics within relationships are used to attempt to undermine women's increasing power and increasing demands for equality, and it is as common to find women undermining feminism as it is to find men, as they continue to play their expected roles within patriarchy of defending and looking after their men.

Of course, feminism *is* challenging for men and women. It requires us to be more creative in how we live our lives, being unable to respond to a pattern or blueprint of how to have relationships that patriarchy has provided (e.g., see Schmid, Chapter 15). It is dangerous for those in power who rely on others' acceptance of the right to that power. It confronts women who have relied on men taking responsibility, and men who have relied on women to look after them. It requires us, as a society, to rethink notions of the traditional family and gender divided roles and responsibilities.

As feminist theory continues to provide fresh insights into societal injustices and personal pain, and as feminist therapy continues to provide a safe haven for women and men who wish to claim their own voices of strength and compassion, feminism will continue to provide a guiding light to a hurting world. Our foremothers guide our path as we join with our sisters and brothers to continue their legacy to work for a world that is more just and compassionate for all. A large number of feminist theorists continue to demand that feminism expand its analysis to include more voices from women's communities other than white, middle-class. These theorists suggest that for the majority of women worldwide the effects of sexism cannot be separated from the effects of racism and classism. They challenge us to broaden our naming, understanding and analysis of the kinds of oppression that impact women worldwide.

Similarly, the Person-Centred Approach continues to be challenging. It challenges the authority of those in power, and suggests that each individual can create their own path in life. The Person-Centred Approach, with its goals of empowerment and growth for each individual, man or woman, provides a model through which we can communicate with respect about how to respond to the challenges that feminism provides. The PCA provides a framework for creating more mutual relationships where the goal is to understand, not control, the other. It can inform the practitioners of feminist therapy about the attitudes and behaviours that promote collaboration and mutuality between people that goes beyond the therapist as teacher and guide. It provides a well-researched, extensively studied body of knowledge of how to deeply respect the unique, phenomenological process of each client. On a societal level, it has brought together and continues to bring together vastly different groups in ways that promote understanding and compassion across differences. It challenges the medical model of mental health.

It is our hope that the readers of this book will come away with more tools and a greater understanding of how to improve their own relationships—whether with partners, family members, friends or clients. We hope that by providing the reader with examples of how to combine these theories, that we have provided a window into new possibilities of theory, therapy and justice-making on a personal and societal level.

FORMAT OF THE BOOK

The book is divided into 4 sections. The first section contains the introductory chapters. The aim of these chapters is to introduce readers unfamiliar with either person-centred theory or feminist theory to the main concepts within these theories. These chapters should provide enough of a foundation to make the following chapters understandable.

The second section is entitled 'The Personal is Still Political—and Healing. Personal Reflections of Using Person-Centred and Feminist Theories in Work' and presents personal stories and reflections. In Chapter 4, Gay Swenson Barfield shares how both the feminist movement and the person- centred movement shaped and changed her life. It is a beautiful 'herstory' of her life as well as a chronology of the growth of both movements. Maureen O'Hara is interviewed by Gillian Proctor in Chapter 5 and discusses the influences of the Person-Centred Approach and feminism on each other and on her career, going though facilitating person-centred groups in Brazil to becoming president of Saybrook University. In Chapter 6, Rosemary Hopkins tells the story of her journey to becoming an activist against chronic global 'terror' and inhumanity as her response to the events of 9/11. In Chapter 7, Wade Hannon presents his personal perspective on why and how to be a feminist man. This chapter includes practical suggestions for how men can increase their awareness of their part in oppressing women. Deb Steele (Chapter 8) presents her personal experience of spirituality and the interweaving of feminist and person-centred ideas within this area.

The third section 'An Intellectual Understanding: New theories to guide our actions' includes chapters that focus predominantly on theory. This section commences with Carol Wolter-Gustafson's overview of the historical and epistemological roots of feminism and the Person-Centred Approach (Chapter 9). She highlights the similarities between the two and then urges theorists and practitioners in both areas to engage in dialogue and exploration with each other. In Chapter 10, Mary Beth Napier examines how incorporating a client-centred non-directive attitude into the Stone Center's model of Relational-Cultural Therapy will enhance and deepen the connections between therapist and client, and decrease therapist disconnections from the client's experience. In Chapter 11, Gillian Proctor argues that person-centred therapists can improve their practice with an understanding of feminist theory to consequently extend their empathy to better understand the social and political context of each client's life. In Chapter 12, Clare Shaw discusses the psychiatric and person-centred responses to women survivors of sexual abuse from a feminist perspective. She suggests that although a Person-Centred Approach is a distinct improvement on the diagnostic psychiatric approach, particular knowledge and understanding of the social context of abuse is necessary for practitioners not to collude in further individualising the relational and societal problem of abuse. Randall Ehrbar, in Chapter 13 considers Rogers' theory of therapy with reference to working with clients from a non-dominant culture. He discusses what person-centred therapists need to consider in this context using feminist theory to inform his understanding. In Chapter 14 Jeff Cornelius-White and Phoebe Godfrey consider the area of education by comparing and contrasting a Person-Centred Approach to education with feminist approaches. They suggest that each could learn from the other to benefit the political aims of both. Finally, Peter Schmid examines the area of gender differences and the importance of gender as a defining factor in what it means to be a person (Chapter 15). He considers in detail the areas of sexuality and aggression for men, and challenges men to begin to create positive ways of being men in society rather than reacting to changes initiated by women including feminism.

The final section of this book 'Practical Applications and Success Stories' discusses the practice of therapy, particularly with women and in relation to causes of distress that have been long-emphasised by feminists. In Chapter 16, Edna Davis and Margaret Bird discuss their work using person-centred psychodrama with women and children who are survivors of sexual abuse. Sophie Smailes presents her work in Chapter 17 with female survivors of domestic violence, talking in detail about her work with two particular clients and how she interweaves her feminist understanding with person-centred therapy. Finally, in Chapter 18, Monica Hill presents the work of Rape Crisis from her personal perspective of working with women survivors of sexual abuse and rape in individual and group therapy. She describes how her feminist understanding informs her Person-Centred Approach to therapy.

LIMITATIONS OF THIS COLLECTION

Unfortunately, we have not been able to present the breadth of contributions and voices that we would have liked and tried to seek. We particularly lack representation from women of colour, working-class women and women who have experienced distress. We also wanted to include a chapter that addressed the unique issues of lesbian women. We hope to fill some of these gaps in a future volume if further interest is generated. This volume is the first attempt to bring together the two bodies of knowledge, theory and experience of feminism and the Person-Centred Approach in the hope that each will be mutually enhanced. We hope to reach interested readers in the person-centred and feminist worlds and to strengthen each approach in the process. We very much welcome feedback, dialogue and further conversation. Come join us on this exciting journey.

REFERENCES

Ahsan, MH (2003) *'Honour' killings of women*. Dhamaka News. See www.dhamakanews.net/archives/honorkilling.htm

Heise, L (1993) Violence against Women: The missing agenda, in M Koblinsky, J Timyan and J Gay (eds) *The Health of Women: A global perspective*. Boulder, Colorado: Westview Press.

UNFPA-SWP (1997) see www.unfpa.org/swp/1997

Watson J, Goldman, R and Warner, M (2002) *Client-Centered and Experiential Psychotherapy in the 21st Century: Advances in theory, research and practice*. Ross-on-Wye: PCCS Books.

Wolter-Gustafson, C (1999) The Power of the Premise: Reconstructing gender and human development with Rogers' theory, in I Fairhurst (ed) *Women Writing in the Person-Centred Approach*. Ross-on-Wye: PCCS Books, pp. 199–214.

INTRODUCTION TO FEMINIST THEORY AND THERAPIES

Mary Beth Napier

Although the political movement of feminism has been felt around the world since the 1920s, people are often confused about what feminism is and what it is not.[1] Many women still refuse to claim the label 'feminist' citing that they do not hate men and have never considered burning their bras to protest against sexist behaviors. Women (and men) who do call themselves feminist vary in some of their beliefs and in the social action that springs from their feminist beliefs. This pluralism extends into the field of feminist therapy. There are numerous feminist therapies that vary in their goals for clients. This chapter will highlight some of these similarities and differences in feminist thinking and therapy. It will briefly recount the origins of contemporary feminist thought, discuss main themes in feminist theory and therapy, and discuss continued development of feminist thought and ongoing questions and concerns. Of special importance to this book, this chapter will also present feminist critiques of the Person-Centered Approach.

Feminist thought began as a political statement and stance on gender inequality. It studied the uses of power and how status hierarchies deprived women of their freedom and equality (Worell and Remer, 1992). It is based on the belief that in societies that divide sexes into differing cultural, economic or political spheres, women are less valued than men. Feminism also rests on the belief that women can consciously and collectively change their social place (Humm, 1992). It challenged the sex roles that were considered the norm and helped open up more possibilities for women's lives. Feminism also encouraged the belief that women's experiences are important and that a woman's distress is never purely intrapsychic but must be understood in a social context.

The development of feminist thought and action has been described chronologically as different 'waves'. First-wave feminism (1890–1920) was concerned

---

[1.] For an excellent historical perspective of the international roots and development of feminism, see Ballou and Gabalac, 1985.

primarily with equality. Second-wave feminism (1960 to today) uses women's differences to oppose the 'rule' of patriarchy.[2] In first-wave feminism, women challenged commonly held beliefs about women's psychological make-up and abilities, as well as their place in society by using the strength and wisdom of their own experiences. First-wave feminism challenged institutions, whereas second-wave feminism also challenges the invisibility of patriarchy that occurs in the more personal spheres of relationships and their everyday lives. This represented a move from materialism to the dynamics and psychological aspects of women's lives (Humm, 1992). Recently, young feminists have begun writing about the tasks and sensibilities of third-wave of feminists (Bruns and Trimble, 2001). They discuss the ramifications of growing up when feminism was already a part of academic curriculum and access to more resources and opportunities were open to them as white, middle-class, educated women. They see the challenges of their generation of feminists as 'the loss of subversive stories from young feminist memories, the tendency to believe [they] are the end product of the feminist fight rather than part of a continuing process and disregard the political activism aspects of feminist psychology, and the tendency to be blind to the undertow of the backlash [against progress in women's issues and lives]' (p. 20). They seek to continue the dialogue on using power as 'relational power', finding ways of including more diverse voices within feminist analysis, establishing mentoring relationships with second-wave feminists and continuing to remain open to listen for the areas in our lives and in the world community where societal change is still needed. They hope to use their privilege and new freedoms to help others—both men and women—who are still in the struggle for equality.

MAIN THEMES OF FEMINIST THOUGHT

Feminist psychological therapy springs from feminist thought. Consequently, it is imperative to identify some key concepts in feminist thought before exploring feminist therapy. This section discusses some of these concepts.

THE PERSONAL IS POLITICAL

A rallying cry and major tenet of feminist thought is that 'the personal is political'. This statement encompasses feminist beliefs about sex-role stereotyping, institutionalized sexism, and oppression. It highlights the negative consequences of

---

[2.] Patriarchy is the way society is structured with men holding power. It refers to both concrete systems of power and to the ideology and generally understood attitudes and assumptions that go along with the structures—such as different sex roles and expectations for men and women (Proctor, 2002b).

these phenomena and concludes that the external environment is considered the main source of women's problems (Worell and Remer, 1992). This protest from feminists challenged the historical assumption that politics was the world of men, the public world. Feminists argued that *all* of life was political including the everyday reality of women's lives. At this time, women's lives, which had been seen as 'private' and 'personal', became public and open for debate and discussion. This rallying call was the signal for entry of women into the political arena. It also gave feminists and women a platform from which to speak, that of their own personal experience.

Feminists began to challenge the traditional 'ways of knowing' that were based solely on the experiences of men (Belenky et al., 1986). They came to see that women's sensibilities, values and lived reality were valid sources of knowledge and challenged the epistemological base of western modernist ideas of science. Feminism brought back phenomenology into the field of knowledge by emphasizing the importance of women's lived experience. Thus what women said about their experiences of being a woman was the bedrock from which feminist theories about being women grew.

FEMINIST DEFINITIONS/ANALYSIS OF POWER[3]

Feminist theorists questioned the assumptions in society that allowed men to remain in powerful positions that allowed them to have overt and covert control over women's lives. There has been much written about definitions of power and whether or not power is something that women, who have been oppressed by patriarchy, should aspire to. If so, what would that power look like? Feminist theories of power are generally based in a structural model of power. In this model, power is seen as monolithic, unitary (held by men) and unidirectional (exerted by men over women) (Proctor, 2002a). Hence, power is always seen as negative and oppressive. Structural notions of power have yielded greater understanding of how racism, classism and other forms of oppression affect people. It has also furthered our understanding of the relationship between oppression and psychological distress. However, this understanding of power is limited in its ability to predict and address the power dynamics between two individuals in a relationship.

Other theorists have proposed dynamic post-structural perspectives on power. French (1985) is often cited for her definition of power as an interaction rather than a substance. She proposes that there are different kinds of power that point to different ways of relating to others. She introduced the concept of a person having agency to change the power dynamics in a relationship. Starhawk (1987) identified three categories of power that further delineate how power can be used to oppress or used to empower and provide agency to individuals and groups to share power

---

[3.] For a more through study of power see Gillian Proctor's Chapter 11 in this volume and Proctor, 2002a.

between them. Power then is not a unitary concept that only leads to oppression of one individual or group over another.

SPECIFIC SOCIAL CONCERNS ADDRESSED BY FEMINIST THINKERS

Since feminism is rooted in women's real life experiences, the development of feminist thought was closely aligned with exposing the circumstances in women's lives that were keeping women oppressed as a group and as individuals in the unique circumstances of their lives. The sexual objectification of women was defined in pornography, prostitution and compulsory heterosexuality including compulsory marriage and childbearing. This objectification extended into violence against women that includes rape, domestic violence and incest. Naming these forms of violence and supporting women survivors of them has been, and continues to be, a major activity of feminist theorists and activists. Subsequent generations of feminists also added an analysis of race, class, religious beliefs, sexual orientation and other oppressed categories as ways in which individual women have been marginalized.

THE DEVELOPMENT OF FEMINIST PSYCHOLOGICAL THEORY AND THERAPY

In the 1970s, women began to study traditional forms of therapy and found that women were invisible in psychological theory and that there was no recognition of the oppression of women in society (Wyche et al., 1997). Feminist therapy was developed in reaction to these factors. There are many therapists who call themselves 'feminist therapists'. These include women and men who use varying criteria for using this definition. Clinicians who use person-centered, psychodynamic, cognitive-behavioral, family systems, trauma work, and other approaches to therapy all claim to provide feminist therapy. Although feminist therapists may use many different techniques in their work and come from a number of different theoretical orientations, it is the commitment to address women's subordination and disadvantaged status in society that serves as the unifying thread linking all feminist psychologies and therapies (Wyche et al., 1997). Wyche et al. (1997) believe that this commitment provides a philosophical approach that guides how therapy is conducted and how the client is viewed by the therapist. Feminist therapists practice on a continuum from conducting therapy solely from a therapy based on feminist principles to 'hybrid' models that apply a feminist lens to the theory and practice of another theoretical orientation.

Worell and Remer (1992) state that the base of a feminist stance is the conviction that women's problems cannot be solved in isolation from the gender politics of the larger social structure. Some common themes of feminist therapy are described below.

REDEFINING THE CAUSES OF DISTRESS AND 'PATHOLOGY'

Traditional therapy models ignored the role that clients' social, political, economic and cultural environments play in the problems that clients are experiencing. They tended to focus solely on the client's intrapsychic make-up, locating the problem in how the client is feeling, thinking and/or behaving (Greenspan, 1983; Sturdivant, 1980). Often, when the client's external environment is not taken into account when searching for the source of a client's distress, the therapist can blame clients for aspects of their problems that are socially induced (Greenspan, 1983). This is called 'blaming the victim' because the individual is blamed or held responsible for displaying behavior, thoughts, and feelings that were developed to cope with a restricting and oppressive environment (Worell and Remer, 1992). In feminist psychology, it is recognized that the primary source of a client's pathology *is not intrapsychic or personal*, but rather *is social and political* (Gilbert, 1980). The acknowledgment of the societal sources of women's problems is the core of feminist therapy (Sturdivant, 1980).

As early feminist thinkers and activists were identifying the conditions in a woman's life that left her with few options, feminist activists and therapists were working to change societal conditions to assist women in addressing and recovering from abuses that left women psychologically vulnerable. Feminists set up services for women so that women could receive support and an escape from abusive experiences with men. These included the genesis of domestic violence shelters/ refuges and education, rape crisis counseling and advocacy, and support groups for women survivors of sexual crimes including child sexual abuse.

An underlying value in this feminist activity is to emphasize that societal change is needed rather than 'adjustment' to unjust and unhealthy situations in which women find themselves (Gilbert and Scher, 1999; Worell and Remer, 1992) Gilbert and Scher explain that societal changes are needed to bring about egalitarianism and to decrease the amount of gender-biased conditions that leave women at a disadvantage emotionally as well as financially. For example, glass ceilings are still in place in most major companies that prohibit women, particularly mothers, from obtaining top management positions.

Some feminist theorists suggest that therapists need to be involved in changing these systemic problems in addition to helping clients deal with the aftermath of violence, discrimination and sexism that is still codified into law and promoted by societal institutions.

REDEFINING PATHOLOGY

Feminist theory has challenged notions of mental health and pathology. Instead of pathologizing a woman's emotional response to sexual, physical and psychological violence, feminist theorists have shed light on how women's reactions to these events are normal and healthy reactions to incidents of abuse. Chesler's (1972) groundbreaking work on definitions of madness uncovered how society, and the medical professional in particular, had the power to define what constituted emotionally healthy or sick women. For example, a woman's depression over the continued physical abuse at the hands of her husband was defined as an intrapsychic deficit rather than as a healthy, adaptive way of dealing with this abuse when the woman had nowhere to escape such treatment.

This kind of analysis continues today as clinicians are challenging such diagnostic categories as borderline personality disorder that has been predominantly diagnosed for women who are survivors of abuse (Shaw and Proctor, in press). This is just one example of how traditional therapists have applied different diagnostic categories and labels for females and males (Ford and Widiger, 1989). Rather than using current diagnostic methods of labeling a person, based on the DSM-IV (American Psychiatric Association, 1994), many feminist therapists seek to understand and offer assistance to a client without labeling the client's thoughts, beliefs, and emotions as abnormal (Caplan, 1995; Kaplan, 1983; Lerman, 1995).

REDEFINING THE NATURE OF THE THERAPIST-CLIENT RELATIONSHIP

Following Chesler's (1972) comparison of the therapy relationship with the patriarchal, authoritarian relationship between a father and daughter, feminists have taken the role and consequences of power in the therapy relationship very seriously. There has been much discussion about how to transform a therapy relationship in which the roles of therapist and client are inherently unequal into an egalitarian relationship. Although there is still debate about how to achieve this end, practitioners of feminist therapy agree that the therapist has a responsibility to consciously attempt to establish the most egalitarian relationship possible with each client. One particular area of concern is how to allow the therapist to be a 'real person' in the therapy relationship rather than remaining in an aloof, expert role. Therapists are encouraged to be more self-disclosing and to work towards a collaborative relationship in which both therapist and client make decisions about number of sessions, cost of therapy, and contact outside of planned session time, to name a few potential areas for consideration.

At the beginning of the development of feminist therapy it was an important consideration that women be seen in therapy by women only. This was seen as necessary in order to ensure that a woman client did not have to contend with the power dynamics between herself and a man, who was seen as not being able to provide a woman with an experience that would be empowering rather than pathologizing.

In her 1997 foreword to a new edition of *Women and Madness*, Chesler reviews what has changed since 1972 and delineates what is considered 'feminist therapy'. She describes the features of 'feminist therapy' as follows:

17

Feminist therapy:

1. Tries to believe what women say.

2. Helps women to understand 'that it is normal to feel sad or angry about being overworked, underpaid, underloved; that it's healthy to harbor fantasies of running away when the needs of others … threaten to overwhelm her' (p. 22).

3. Believes that women need to hear that men do not love enough and that fathers are equally responsible for children's problems, that self-love is the basis of love for others and that it's hard to break free of patriarchy.

4. Tries to listen to women respectfully rather than in a superior or contemptuous way. Not minimizing wounds but being optimistic.

5. Does not label women as 'mentally ill' because they are at odds with their feminine role.

Chesler (1997) quotes Janet Surrey who says that 'The work of feminist healers is to integrate our minds and our bodies, ourselves and others, human community and the life of the planet'.

SPECIFIC FEMINIST THEORIES OF THERAPY

Worell and Remer (1992, Chapter 2) provide an excellent history and analysis of the different kinds of feminist therapies. For the purposes of this chapter, I will briefly discuss two prominent and well-developed sets of feminist therapy. They are the empowerment model (Worell and Remer, 1992), and the Stone Center's relational cultural model of therapy (Jordan, 1997; Jordan, et al., 1991; Miller, 1976; Miller and Stiver, 1997).

EMPOWERMENT FEMINIST MODEL OF THERAPY

Empowerment feminist therapy was the first form of feminist therapy (Gilbert and Scher, 1999). It was developed in the 1960s and 1970s by clinicians and theorists (Gilbert, 1980; Lerman, 1976; Sturdivant, 1980) and further developed by Brown (1994) and Worell and Remer (1992). Empowerment therapy challenged the existing models of therapy. It focused on the woman's actual life and the events in her life that caused distress rather than making the assumption that a woman's distress was caused by her intrapsychic deficits. It challenged the medicalization of women's problems and major definitions of madness (Chesler, 1972). It also challenged existing mental health and pathology models, especially psychoanalytic and psychodynamic models that helped a woman adjust to her proper role in life as wife and mother.

Empowerment therapy helped women to identify society's definitions about women as weak, emotional and dependent. It also assisted women to challenge narrow and sexist notions of a woman's mental health and assisted women in claiming their own power in their lives including defining themselves from internal standards rather than prevalent societal notions of what a woman should be (Worell and Remer, 1992). This also was embodied by new ways for a therapist to form an egalitarian relationship with clients (Marecek and Hare-Mustin, 1987).

Worell and Remer (1992) believe that few women can attain equality alone and, consequently, that feminism requires both individual and collective action for social and political changes. They explain that feminist counseling seeks a dual outcome: 'assisting the woman toward empowerment in her own life, and seeking change in the social power structure that forms the basis of many of her problems' (p. 17).

THE STONE CENTER'S MODEL OF RELATIONAL CULTURAL THERAPY

The Stone Center's model of relational cultural therapy began in the 1970s with a group of women clinicians and academics who realized that existing models of mental health and therapy were not based on women's actual experience. They theorized that for therapy to be helpful to women, that therapy must embody values that are important to women. A key value was women's natural tendency to work at preserving connection with others. In contrast to Erickson's view of moral development where autonomy was seen as the pinnacle of moral development, with thinking about others being viewed as immature, Gilligan (1982) redefined moral development for women, prioritizing women's emphasis on relationships and connections. The work of the Stone Center helped shift a woman's desire for connection from pathology to a natural, healthy orientation to life. The Stone Center's model of relational cultural therapy rests on the belief that therapy has to provide the client with a new relational experience and that the particular quality of the therapist-client relationship is the key to healing (Miller and Stiver, 1997). According to Stone Center theorists, a healing therapeutic relationship is one in which the therapist is with a client in ways that promote a growing sense of mutuality between them. It is this connection between the client and the therapist that produces psychological healing for the client.

In this model, differences between the therapist and client are honored and the therapist seeks to understand the client's unique experiences through the client's eyes in order to share the inner world of the client. As the Stone Center theoreticians continued to develop this theory they began to realize that their understanding of women's mental health and psychopathology can be applied equally to men. They have continued to expand their understanding beyond therapy to workplace issues of power and collaboration (Jordan, 1997; Jordan et al., 1991).

FEMINIST CRITIQUES OF HUMANISTIC AND
PERSON-CENTERED THEORIES

Since the focus of this book involves the intersections of the Person-Centered Approach and feminist theory and thinking, I will only specifically mention critiques of person-centered and humanistic models of therapy. For critiques of other forms of therapy, see Brown and Ballou (1992).

Lerman (1992) explains that early in feminist theory, the humanistic branch of psychology was seen as being in harmony with much feminist thought (also see O'Hara, Chapter 5, this volume). However, as feminist thinking became more focused and advanced, there were differences in the two camps that lead feminist thinkers to distance themselves from the humanistic theorists. Lerman explained that Rogers' emphasis on the internal perspective of the client in his phenomenological approach to therapy does not acknowledge the external factors that cause a client's distress. She stressed that Rogers believed that there was no such thing as objective reality but rather that internal perceptions create a person's psychological make-up. Lerman argues that reality is not solely determined internally but is impacted by outside forces that contribute to the person's view of the world. For example, Lerman (1992) states: 'feminist psychologists and sociologists, in their studies of the real lives of women, have demonstrated that patriarchal institutions limit and severely constrict the possibilities for women—regardless of whether the women involved believe themselves to be oppressed or not' (p. 13).

As feminist thinking became clearer about the role that external factors such as societal sexism played in a woman's psychological health and distress, feminist thinkers abandoned the humanistic camp to further develop their own theories that had gender analysis as a core tenet of their approach. Lerman wonders if clinicians who practice Person-Centered Therapy will be able to identify and assist the client with sexism if the therapist has not had specific training to develop a feminist perspective on women's daily lives. It is possible that such a clinician could end up blaming the victim for social forms of oppression (also see Proctor, Chapter 11 and Shaw, Chapter 12 in this volume). Greenspan (1983), and Ballou and Gabalac (1985) state their concerns that it would be an easy mistake for a humanistic therapist with no training or awareness of the effects of external oppression to believe that all a women has to do is to change her internal perceptions of herself to achieve psychological health. Lerman (1992) states: 'to imply that such an internal change would eliminate all cultural, economic, legal and interpersonal obstacles to a woman's physical and psychological actualization is absurd' (p. 15).

Lerman is also critical of the humanistic psychologies lack of differentiation between the experiences of men and women, the development of these theories based solely on men's experiences and the development of these theories before the importance of cultural factors was known. She argues that because these theories pre-date the awareness of cultural considerations on clients' well-being, that these theories are not capable of encompassing the diversity and complexities of women and their lives. Lerman (1992) concludes that 'there is little in the humanistic theories that is inherently unsupportive of feminist or nonsexist psychotherapy. In general, the theories were formulated before the present growth of feminist psychology and neither support nor preclude our concepts' (p. 17). She suggests that perhaps humanistic theory and feminist theory could each inform the other in ways that would enhance both to bring about a 'revolution' in how we view reality.

Maureen O'Hara provided a feminist analysis of one of Rogers' demonstration sessions with a client (O'Hara, 1996). In this critique she states that she had known Rogers as a mentor, colleague and friend and continues to have much respect for him and his theories. She uses the Person-Centered Approach as the foundation for her work with others. However, O'Hara is critical of the Person-Centered Approach because of the subtle ways that an uninformed therapist can assist a client in locating oppression as an internal psychological difficulty rather than as a societal force that impinges upon the individual. She also stressed that person-centered theory was developed during a historical time that was not yet informed by a feminist analysis. Person-centered clinicians, in their attempts to understand a client's internal frame of reference as if it were their own, can erroneously believe that they can hear a client's world without being affected by their own bias and prejudices. O'Hara argues that feminist analysis has demonstrated that a person always hears others through an internal lens no matter how diligently the clinician attempts to put aside his or her own beliefs. This is never totally possible and can result in a clinician supporting the client's view of oppression as an intrapsychic problem. She gives many examples of how Rogers' work in a demonstration with a particular woman was filled with examples of how Rogers' choice of words in his responses contained unintended bias. Similarly, theorists have recently critiqued Rogers for his unintended racist bias in *Carl Rogers Counsels a Black Client* (Moodley, Lago and Talahite, 2004). O'Hara believes that in order for Person-Centered Therapy to remain a vital force for change in the postmodern, pluralistic world, it must be able to incorporate the knowledge gained from feminist as well as other forms of analysis that seek to inform a clinician about the ways in which societal forces (such as sexism and racism) hurt people and cause psychological distress. If person-centered therapists were educated in these analyses, it would allow them to better hear their clients with an understanding of the bias they bring to the therapy relationship. This consciousness will assist a therapist in hearing a client's world more accurately and give the therapist a better chance at not responding to a client through lenses that contain unexamined bias and prejudice.

CONTINUED DEVELOPMENT OF FEMINIST THOUGHT AND THERAPY

There has been much scholarship that has advanced our understanding of how women's experience can be honored and individual women nourished and supported. There are also criticisms of feminist thought that continue to challenge feminist theorists and activists.

A prominent criticism of current feminist thinking is that is has not gone far enough in acknowledging that gender is just one piece in the larger issue of diversity (Greene et al., 1997) This challenges the notion that gender is the defining and most important aspect of all women's identities and experiences. It also challenges the notion that there is such a thing as 'a woman' for whom all aspects of feminist theory apply. For example, a woman who is heterosexual has many similar but also many different experiences than a woman who is lesbian. Similarly, a white woman does not have the same kind or level of discrimination as a woman of color. Socio-economic status, physical (dis)ability, intellectual ability, country of origin, and family dynamics all define a particular woman's experience. Feminists struggle with how to honor all of these particulars of a woman's life without losing the importance of the gender analysis that guided feminist thinking for the last two decades.

Feminist theorists also struggle to articulate a more unified theory of feminist therapy so that an individual clinician can know whether she or he is actually practising feminist therapy. It has been suggested that since feminist therapy must always be rooted in a person's actual lived experience, that there can never be a unified, one-size-fits-all feminist therapy (Brabeck and Brown et al., 1997). Each individual client will be responsive to different levels of self-disclosure and need different kinds of interventions depending on life circumstances. An explicit set of guidelines and values for feminist therapists can help determine when a feminist therapist is acting ethically. This is important because feminist principles challenge many 'rules' and therapists' behaviors that are codified in traditional models of therapy. For example, the use of therapist self-disclosure is very different for feminist therapists than therapists who use expert-based models of psychotherapy such as psychodynamic or cognitive-behavioral approaches.

Within the diversity of approaches that are called 'feminist therapies' many ethical dilemmas remain without clear answers. Some examples of areas that still need more thought, analysis and discussion are questions such as: is it considered feminist therapy if a therapist works with a wife and husband from a traditional, patriarchal family to help the husband see how his status in the community will rise if his wife becomes literate? Or is this simply buying into the patriarchal power structure of the family? Is it unethical for a therapist, after much consideration, to invite a suicidal client to spend the night with her family rather than hospitalize her, like some therapists have done? What does it say about yielding power when a therapist refuses to be open to a shift in the therapist/client relationship after therapy solely on the grounds of expert-based therapies that hold that a therapy relationship can never transform into something else? How many feminist therapists diagnose their clients for insurance reimbursement purposes without informing and inviting participation of the client in the diagnosing process? When do our theories and practices benefit us as the more powerful in the therapy relationship and when do they benefit our clients?

Finally, how do the pioneers of feminist thinking and action allow room for the ideas and energy of a new generation of women and men to help shape and sharpen the tenets and understanding of feminist thinking and therapy? How can women who have sacrificed much and been the target of discrimination and prejudice in their personal and professional lives, who have now become the 'powers-that-be' in the feminist community, not use power in a way that is similar to the patriarchal use of power and abuse that began the feminist uprising? There are many student experiences with women professors who call themselves feminist that sound closer to abuse of power rather than power being used to empower all involved. When a group of prominent female feminist thinkers convened to discuss feminist theory and ask how to move ahead the theory and practice of feminist therapy, they asked themselves, 'How do we challenge the system while being paid and rewarded by it?' (Brabeck et al., 1997: 21).

CONCLUDING REMARKS

This chapter was a brief introduction into some of the more prominent tenets, practices and further developments of feminist theory and practice. I have tried to pull together some of the unifying strands in the diversity of feminist theories and therapies. Whereas some people would suggest that we are now in an era of 'post feminism', and indeed first and second-wave feminists have achieved changes for women's lives today, the need for feminism is far from over. As Bruns and Trimble (2001) suggest, there is still much to be done. With our foremothers to guide our path, we join with our sisters and brothers to continue their legacy to work for a world that is more just and compassionate.

REFERENCES

American Psychiatric Association (1994) *Diagnostic and Statistical Manual of Mental Disorders* (4th ed) (DSM-IV). Washington, DC: Author.

Ballou, M and Gabalac, NW (1985) *A Feminist Position on Mental Health.* Springfield, IL: Charles C Thomas.

Belenky, MF, Clinchy, BM, Goldberger, NR, and Tarule, JM (1986) *Women's Ways of Knowing—Development of self voice, and mind.* New York: Basic Books.

Brabeck, M and Brown, L (1997) Feminist theory and psychological practice, in J Worell and NG Johnson (eds) *Shaping the Future of Feminist Psychology: Education, research and practice.* Washington, DC: American Psychological Association, pp. 15–35.

Brown, LS (1994) *Subversive Dialogues: Theory in feminist therapy.* New York: Basic Books.

Brown, LS and Ballou, M (1992) (eds) *Personality and Psychopathology: Feminist reappraisals.* New York: The Guilford Press.

Bruns, CM and Trimble, C (2001) Rising tide: Taking our place as young feminist psychologists. *Women and Therapy, 23*(2): 19–36.

Caplan, P (1995, August) The DSM-IV and gender issues. Paper presented at the 103rd Annual Convention of the American Psychological Association, New York.

Chesler, P (1972/1997) *Women and Madness.* New York: Four walls eight windows.

Ford, M and Widiger, T (1989) Sex bias in the diagnosis of histrionic and antisocial personality disorders. *Journal of Counseling and Clinical Psychology, 57,* 301–5.

French, M (1985) *Beyond Power: On women, men and morals.* London: Jonathan Cape.

Gilbert, LA (1980) Feminist therapy, in AM Brodsky and RT Hare-Mustin (eds) *Women and Psychotherapy: An assessment of research and practice.* New York: Guilford Press, pp. 245–65.

Gilbert, L and Scher, M (1999) *Gender and Sex in Counseling and Psychotherapy.* Boston: Allyn and Bacon.

Gilligan, C (1982) *In a Different Voice: Psychological theory and women's development.* Cambridge: Harvard University Press.

Greene, B and Sanchez-Hucles, J (1997) Diversity: Advancing an inclusive feminist psychology, in J Worell and NG Johnson (eds) *Shaping the Future of Feminist Psychology: Education, research and practice.* Washington, DC: American Psychological Association, pp. 173–202.

Greenspan, M (1983) *A New Approach to Women and Therapy: How psychotherapy fails women and what they can do about it.* New York: McGraw-Hill.

Humm, M (1992) *Feminisms: A reader.* London: Harvester Wheatsheaf.

Jordan, JV (1997) *Women's Growth in Diversity: More writings from the Stone Center.* New York: Guilford Press.

Jordan, JV, Kaplan, AG, Miller, JB, Stiver, IP and Surrey, J (1991) *Women's Growth in Connection: Writings from the Stone Center.* New York: Guilford Press.

Kaplan, M (1983) A woman's view of DSM-III. *American Psychologist, 38,* 786–92.

Lerman, H (1976) What happens in feminist therapy, in S Cox (ed) *Female Psychology: The emerging self.* Chicago: Science Research Associates.

Lerman, H (1995, August) A critical look at the DSM-IV. Symposium presented at the 103rd Annual Convention of the American Psychological Association, New York.

Lerman, H (1992) The limits of phenomenology: A feminist critique of the humanistic personality theories, in LS Brown and M Ballou (eds) *Personality and Psychopathology: Feminist reappraisals.* The Guilford Press: New York, pp. 8–19.

Marecek, J and Hare-Mustin, RT (1987, March) Feminism and therapy: Can this relationship be saved? Paper presented at the meeting of the American Orthopsychiatric Association,

Washington, DC.

Miller, JB (1976) *Toward a New Psychology of Women*. Boston: Beacon Press.

Miller, JB and Stiver, I (1997) *The Healing Relationship: How women form relationships in therapy and in life*. Boston: Beacon Press.

Moodley, R, Lago, C and Talahite, A (eds) (2004) *Carl Rogers Counsels a Black Client: Race and culture in person-centred counselling*. Ross-on-Wye: PCCS Books.

O'Hara, M (1996) Rogers and Sylvia: A feminist analysis, in BA Farber, DC Brink, and PM Raskin (eds) *The Psychotherapy of Carl Rogers: Cases and commentary*. New York: Guilford Press.

Proctor, G (2002a) *The Dynamics of Power in Counselling and Psychotherapy: Ethics, politics and practice*. Ross-on-Wye: PCCS Books.

Proctor, G (2002b) Feminist Theory. Unpublished teaching handout. Chicago: Illinois School of Professional Psychology.

Shaw, C and Proctor, G (2004) Women at the margins: A critique of borderline personality disorder. *Asylum (4)*3: 8–10.

Starhawk (1987) *Truth or Dare: Encounters with power, authority and mystery*. San Francisco: Harper and Row.

Sturdivant, S (1980) *Therapy with Women: A feminist philosophy of treatment*. New York: Springer.

Worell, J and Remer, P (1992) *Feminist Perspectives in Therapy: An empowerment model for women*. New York: John Wiley and Sons.

Wyche, KF and Rice, JK (1997) Feminist therapy: From dialogue to tenets, in J Worell and NG Johnson (eds) *Shaping the Future of Feminist Psychology: Education, research and practice*. Washington, DC: American Psychological Association, pp. 57–71.

AN INTRODUCTION TO THE PERSON-CENTRED APPROACH

GILLIAN PROCTOR

INTRODUCTION

The Person-Centred Approach (PCA) refers to Carl Rogers' theories of human growth and interaction. Person-Centred Therapy (PCT) or Client-Centred Therapy was first described by Carl Rogers in the 1950s and was elaborated by him and his colleagues until his death in 1987. He then extended his ideas to a theory of personality, which was more hypothetical and provided a theory of why PCT was helpful. Rogers elaborated these theories throughout his professional life and became increasingly interested in applying his theories in much wider arenas than the individual therapy relationship. He had a profound impact on the world of therapy. Rogers was a psychologist. He developed this way of being with patients (whom he called 'clients') and called it 'counselling', as he was forbidden to use the word 'therapy' because of his lack of medical training. Kirschenbaum and Henderson (1989: xi) suggest that he was responsible more than any other individual 'for the spread of professional counselling and psychotherapy beyond psychiatry and psychoanalysis to all the helping professions—psychology, social work, education, ministry, lay therapy, and others'.

However, his impact was not limited to the world of therapy. Throughout his life, along with his colleagues, he extended his theories of therapy and personality to apply to: education, partnerships, all kinds of human relationships, groups, organisations, the work place and the resolution of international conflict. Bozarth (1998: i) explains that Rogers used the term PCA to 'identify the principles hypothesized in client-centered therapy as they might be implemented in other areas, such as education, business, groups and society'. The PCA continues to be developed and used around the world by practitioners in all of these areas.

The basic message or hypothesis of Rogers' theories are summarised by Kirschenbaum and Henderson and described as both simple and profound.

All individuals have within themselves the ability to guide their own lives in a manner that is both personally satisfying and socially constructive. In a particular type of helping relationship, we free the individuals to find their inner wisdom and confidence, and they will make increasingly healthier and more constructive choices. (1989: xiv)

This hypothesis is a summary of Rogers' (1959) theory of therapy and theory of personality.

THEORY OF THERAPY

The six necessary and sufficient conditions are the theory of therapy and Rogers explains them as follows:

For therapy to occur, it is necessary that these conditions exist:

That two persons are in contact.

That the first person, whom we shall term the client, is in a state of incongruence, being vulnerable or anxious.

That the second person, whom we shall term the therapist, is congruent in the relationship.

That the therapist is experiencing unconditional positive regard toward the client.

That the therapist is experiencing an empathic understanding of the client's internal frame of reference.

That the client perceives, at least to a minimal degree, conditions 4 and 5, the unconditional positive regard of the therapist for him, and the empathic understanding of the therapist. (Rogers, 1959: 213)

The therapist's congruence, unconditional positive regard for the client and empathic understanding are considered the 'facilitative' conditions or facilitative attitudes. As well as these conditions becoming the cornerstone of PCT, Rogers (1957) also describes these conditions similarly in his 'integration statement' (Bozarth, 1998) where he asserts that they are the necessary and sufficient conditions in all therapy. The following is a closer look at all six of these conditions.

CONDITION 1: CONTACT

Rogers further clarifies that the first condition is actually a precondition for the other conditions to be fulfilled. He explains psychological contact as that in which 'each makes some perceived difference in the experiential field of the other' (Rogers, 1959: 221). Basically, this condition means that for therapy to happen, the therapist and client must notice or be aware of each other's presence. Prouty (1994) and others have further developed PCT to elaborate a theory of 'pre-therapy' to work to increase contact between the therapist and client with clients where contact cannot be assumed. Prouty (2002) and Barrett-Lennard (2002) argue that contact is a complex phenomena and exists on continua and in many domains.

CONDITION 2: CLIENT INCONGRUENCE

In the second condition, the state of incongruence refers to the discrepancy between the self-concept and the organismic self.[1] Basically, a person is incongruent when their outer expression is not in tune with their inner feelings or experiences. For example, someone may constantly express that they are totally happy and have had an idyllic life yet be full of distress inside. This connects to Rogers' personality theory of how psychological distress is created. He suggests that all psychological distress can be understood in terms of incongruence. Brodley (2004) has suggested this condition is the least important for the therapy and this is certainly the least often mentioned condition in person-centred theory. Bozarth and Wilkins (2002) suggest that the client needs to be sufficiently aware of their own incongruence and troubled by it to persist in the endeavour of therapy.

CONDITION 3: THERAPIST CONGRUENCE

The third condition requires that the therapist be congruent or integrated. This means that the therapist must be aware of her/his own inner experiencing and must not be presenting a façade to the client. Rogers also clarifies that congruence means an *awareness* of feelings, and not necessarily communicating these overtly to the client. This is a constant process for therapists to aim to be aware of their inner feelings and experiences on a moment-by-moment basis. This condition also refers to the importance in PCT for the therapist to be a real person, not putting on a professional front as a therapist, and not hiding or denying who they are as a person. While Rogers points out that no one individual can be fully integrated at all times, he is referring to the time of the therapy contact:

> It is enough if in this particular moment of this immediate relationship with this specific person he is completely and fully himself, with his experience of the moment being accurately symbolised and integrated into the picture he holds of himself.
> (Rogers, 1957; cited in Kirschenbaum and Henderson, 1989: 215)[2]

---

[1] See below in Theory of Personality for definitions of these terms.

[2] At this point in his career, Rogers used the masculine pronoun to refer to men and women. Later in his career he changed this convention and used inclusive language in his writings and speeches (see his note about this in Rogers, 1978a: ix).

Unlike psychodynamic therapy, PCT does not refer to such concepts as 'transference' or 'counter-transference'. The concept of congruence demonstrates the commitment of a person-centred therapist to a *real* relationship with a client, as a genuine person themselves in the relationship.

CONDITION 4: THERAPIST UNCONDITIONAL POSITIVE REGARD (UPR)

Earlier in the evolution of Rogers' therapy theory, he referred to the importance of the therapist's warmth, acceptance and respect for the client. These characteristics came together following Stanley Standal's doctoral thesis (see Moon, Rice and Schneider, 2002) in the concept of UPR. Rogers (1957) explained that an attitude of UPR from the therapist means caring for the client, but in a non-possessive way, as a separate autonomous person. Rogers also referred to UPR as a deep 'prizing' of the client. An attitude of UPR by the therapist means she/he will aim to value and prize all aspects of the client's experiencing equally. The therapist's acceptance of the client is not conditional on the client having to be or present a certain way. UPR reflects acceptance, care and a non-judgmental attitude. Bozarth (1998: 83) describes UPR as 'the curative factor in client-centered theory'.

CONDITION 5: THERAPIST EMPATHIC UNDERSTANDING (EU)

Rogers explains that to empathically understand is to sense the client's private world as if it were the therapist's own world. Empathic understanding describes the process of the therapist trying to step into the client's world and experience it 'as if' (s)he were the client. It is the therapist following the moment-by-moment experiencing of the client, never trying to be one step ahead of the client but to follow as closely behind as possible and communicate this understanding to the client. Mearns and Thorne (1988) describe this as:

> the counsellor demonstrates a capacity to track and sense accurately the feelings and personal meanings of the client; she is able to learn what it feels like to be in the client's skin and to perceive the world as the client perceives it. (p. 15)

CONDITION 6: CLIENT PERCEIVES THERAPIST'S UNCONDITIONAL POSITIVE REGARD AND EMPATHIC UNDERSTANDING

In the final condition the client must be able to perceive some acceptance and empathy from the therapist. This condition demonstrates the vital importance of the client's perspective in PCT. If the client does not perceive the therapist's attitudes, the conditions are not met; therapy cannot take place. Barrett-Lennard (2002) had this condition at the centre of his research in PCT, recognising that the best person to evaluate the therapist's attitudes was the client.

Rogers emphasises that the extent to which the conditions are fulfilled varies, and he hypothesises that, the more these conditions are fulfilled, the more psychological growth will occur in the client. This suggests that these are conditions to be aimed for by therapists; they are not absolutes. Rogers also claims that these are the necessary and sufficient conditions to work with *any* individual, no matter what problems they may have. He asserts that whenever these conditions are met (whether in formal therapy or outside of it) they are similarly effective.

NECESSARY AND SUFFICIENT

Rogers is clear that these six conditions are *all* that is needed for positive change to take place. These conditions are attitudes, not techniques and if they are fulfilled, no other specific interventions are needed. A further implication of this theory is that 'the techniques of various therapies are relatively unimportant except to the extent that they serve as channels for fulfilling one of the conditions' (Rogers 1957, cited in Kirschenbaum and Henderson, 1989: 233). Specific interventions or techniques may decrease the likelihood of these attitudes being embodied by the therapist.

Moreover, a psychological diagnosis or formulation of problems is not necessary for therapy. PCT is the same with all people, independent of the manifestation of distress within the client. Whatever the diagnosis or specific problem with which a client may come to therapy, the person-centred therapist's job is exactly the same, to convey the attitudes of congruence, empathy and unconditional positive regard.

If these conditions are the necessary and sufficient conditions for all therapy, the facilitative conditions are qualities of experience, not intellectual information, and must be acquired through experiential training: formal qualifications are unnecessary for their acquisition. Academic qualifications or knowledge about personality development or mental health for example, are irrelevant to a person's ability to convey the attitudes of congruence, empathy and unconditional positive regard (Rogers, 1957).

NON-DIRECTIVE ATTITUDE

Intrinsic to the facilitative conditions is a non-directive attitude on the part of the therapist. Brodley explains how this attitude follows from the principle of the self-actualising tendency[3] and the facilitative conditions:

> The nondirective attitude ... influences the therapist to protect the client's self determined processes that promote the client's self-empowerment. And it fosters the avoidance of therapist intentions and behaviors that might disempower the client. (Brodley, 1997: 18)

[3.] See below in Theory of Personality for definition of 'actualising tendency'.

The non-directive attitude is the therapist's discipline to try and inhabit the client's world and understand the client from within the client's frame of reference rather than imposing the therapist's interpretations or explanations. By communicating their empathic understanding to the client, the therapist strives to be with the client's experience and pace without trying to direct content. This attitude reflects the therapist's belief that they are not the expert on each client's world. The therapist does not know what is 'right' or the most helpful way to proceed for each and every client.

THEORY OF PERSONALITY

After arriving at his theory of therapy from research, Rogers then elaborated this to hypothesise a theory of personality, to explain why/how PCT works.

THE ACTUALISING TENDENCY

Central to his personality theory is the hypothesis of the existence of an innate potential for constructive growth in each individual which Rogers termed the 'actualizing tendency' (Rogers, 1959). This concept followed similar hypotheses from biologists such as Goldstein (1939, in Brodley, 1999). Rogers used the analogy of a potato plant to describe this concept. He described finding a potato plant in a dark garage that had grown spindly shoots towards the one high window that gave light, still striving to grow despite the adverse conditions (Rogers, 1978a: 8). He believed in the potential of each living organism to grow to the best of its ability and for humans specifically to grow towards their potential, which is constructive both for each individual and for society as a whole.

CONDITIONS OF WORTH

He hypothesised that this actualising tendency can be thwarted (although never killed completely until the organism dies) by conditions in the environment, specifically when the individual encounters 'conditions of worth'. Conditions of worth are messages that individuals are acceptable only if they think, feel or behave in a certain way. These messages can be cultural (e.g. concerning gender roles) or come from important individuals in someone's life, such as parents. If people receive conditions of worth, they begin to internalise these conditions as a 'self-concept' of what they *should* be, which, over time, can lead the individual to become further and further removed from the 'organismic self'. The organismic self is Rogers' term for the experiencing self within, the messages coming from internal interpretations of perceptions—the inner self or 'real' self. This discrepancy between the self-concept and the organismic self, and the ways that individuals have for coping with this, is hypothesised to be the cause of psychological distress.

Rogers' Personality Theory is very much focused on the development of the individual, and ideas of the 'self'. However, the causes of distress, i.e., the imposition of conditions of worth, and the remediation of this distress (the therapy relationship) are clearly relational. Later, Rogers extended his theories to apply to increasingly larger groups of people and communities.

INFLUENCE OF PERSONALITY THEORY ON THERAPY THEORY

Rogers' personality theory has very little influence on the practice of PCT. Whereas the therapist may use the personality theory to formulate a client's problems outside of therapy, the therapist's aim when with the client is still purely to embody the facilitative attitudes. The therapist still has no aim for the client, and remains non-directive, to preserve the autonomy and uniqueness of the client. Other offshoots of classical or non-directive PCT have developed, such as Experiential Therapy or Focusing that have been more influenced by Rogers' personality theory and have developed aims for the therapist above and beyond the necessary and sufficient conditions of Rogers' therapy theory. These therapist aims are to increase or facilitate the client's depth or speed of processing in therapy. However, when we refer to PCT in this book, we are referring to Rogers' original theory of therapy that is non-directive or classical PCT.

PROCESS OF PERSON-CENTRED THERAPY

Rogers (1959) describes the process that a client who experiences the facilitative conditions of therapy characteristically goes through. It is clear that the characteristic outcomes of therapy do not lead to any aims for the therapist but merely describe changes that are likely to occur as a result of the facilitative conditions. Thus a description of processes that the client may go through does not influence the classical/non-directive person-centred therapist in their practice. In experiential approaches to PCT, personality theory and research about the process of therapy may influence the therapist's aim when with the client. Experiential therapists may use techniques to 'deepen' the client's process or aim to help them go through the following processes more quickly.

Rogers (1959) stated that during the process of therapy, the client is likely to be aware of more of his/her inner experiencing and is able to accurately experience more of his/her perceptions. In reciprocity with the attitudes experienced by the therapist towards the client, the client increasingly feels positive self-regard, is increasingly free to be him/herself and understands him/herself better. In reciprocity with these changes towards self, the client is also likely to experience more positive regard and understanding of others. Rogers describes these changes as follows:

> In such a relationship the individual becomes more integrated, more effective. He shows fewer of the characteristics which are usually termed neurotic or psychotic, and more of the characteristics of the healthy, well-functioning person. He changes his perception of himself, becoming more realistic in his views of self. He becomes more like the person he wishes to be. He values himself more highly. He is more self-confident and self-directing. He has a better understanding of himself, becomes more open to experience, denies or represses less of his experience. He is more accepting in his attitudes toward others, seeing others as more similar to himself. (Rogers, 1961: 36)

Rogers developed these observations of how a client is likely to change during PCT into the concept of the fully functioning person (described in Rogers, 1961 and reprinted in Kirschenbaum and Henderson, 1989). He described this as a process rather than a state of being, characterised by a freedom to be able to move in *any* direction. He lists the key characteristics of this process as: an increasing openness to experience, increasingly existential living (to live fully in each moment) and an increasing trust in their organism.

RESEARCH BASE OF PERSON-CENTRED THERAPY

Rogers' theory of therapy was based on research on what seemed to help clients in therapy. His theory followed his experiences and experimenting with how to help clients over many years. He methodically examined hours and hours of recorded and transcribed therapy sessions to examine what the ingredients of effective therapy were. This was the first time that actual therapist-client interactions in therapy had been opened to the scrutiny of research. Instead of relying on therapists' recollections or interpretations of what therapy was about, he and his researchers looked directly as outside observers at what was said in therapy.

He used the transcripts of therapy sessions to systematically examine what therapists did that was helpful, and what was unhelpful. Initial findings identified that therapy progress was thwarted by therapists being directive, asking probing questions or interpreting. On the contrary, therapist interventions that lead to client insight and deepening or further exploration were those where the therapist 'simply recognises and clarifies the feelings expressed' (Rogers, 1942, reprinted in Kirschenbaum and Henderson, 1989). From these direct observations of therapy, he developed his theory of therapy of the six necessary and sufficient conditions (Rogers, 1959). Later, he used Q-sort methodology to analyse how clients' views of themselves and others changed during therapy (see Rogers and Dymond, 1954).

After the development of his theory of therapy, Rogers and many others spent much time continuing to research the effectiveness of PCT. Since the 1950s and continuing today, there has been much research evidence supporting the efficacy of Person-/Client-Centred Therapy for clients with many different types of difficulties, including psychotic experiences (see Barrett-Lennard, 1998 for review of research). One of the most recent pieces of research in the UK's current climate of 'evidence-based practice' used a randomised controlled trial design to compare three treatments for people with depression or anxiety and depression in primary care. King et al. (2000) compared PCT, Cognitive Behaviour Therapy (CBT) and routine GP care. Unusual for such comparison studies, in this study the therapists providing PCT were qualified at a high level. The study found that both PCT and CBT obtained significantly better results than routine GP care at four months follow-up.

In addition to specific research on the effectiveness of PCT, research to investigate the factors responsible for success in general in therapy have also added to the weight of evidence for PCT. Forty years of psychotherapy research has consistently discovered the importance of the client's resources and the quality of the therapy relationship for effective and good therapy. Lambert (1992 cited in Lambert 2004) estimated that 40% of outcome variance was accounted for by the client's external and internal resources and 30% by the quality of the therapy relationship. Bozarth (1998) discussed the implications of this research, concluding that the type of therapy or technique or training or credentials of the therapist are found to be irrelevant, and the most consistent relationship variables related to effectiveness are empathy, genuineness and unconditional positive regard. The results of this research are consistent with the philosophy and theory of Person-Centred Therapy (PCT), which relies directly on the client's resources and the therapy relationship. This consistency is unsurprising given the research-based way Rogers developed PCT.

FURTHER APPLICATIONS OF PERSON-CENTRED THERAPY

After elaborating his theory of therapy, Rogers suggested that this theory could be applied to all human relationships. Thus, the aims to provide the facilitative conditions could be applied to partnerships, friendships, working relationships and any other relationship. His book *Becoming Partners: Marriage and its Alternatives* applied this theory to partnerships (Rogers, 1972). Rogers also became more interested during his time in California in applying this theory to groups, and along with colleagues, he developed the idea of the encounter group. Again, the aim of the group facilitators was to provide the facilitative conditions to the group, and he wrote about this in his book on encounter groups *Carl Rogers on Encounter Groups* (Rogers, 1970). His first book on education, *Freedom to Learn: A View of What Education Might Become*, crystallised how this approach could be applied to facilitate growth in an education setting (Rogers, 1969). Rogers began to work with larger and larger encounter groups and then used this approach to try and resolve political conflicts internationally by facilitating encounter groups with members of political factions who were in conflict with each other. This peace work is still continued in various parts of the world today and remains a significant influence in many approaches to peace work.

PHILOSOPHY AND ETHICAL PRINCIPLES BEHIND THE PERSON-CENTRED APPROACH

The fundamental ethical principle behind PCT is prioritising the autonomy of the client. In contrast, the ethical principle of beneficence (doing what's judged to be best for the client) is prioritised by many other models of therapy. Gendlin (2002: xi) describes Rogers' beliefs which are embodied in the PCA saying, 'He cared about each person but not about institutions. He did not care about appearances, roles, class, credentials or positions, and he doubted every authority including his own.'

Rogers describes PCT as 'revolutionary' with respect to the political stance and philosophy it upholds: one of his books is entitled *Carl Rogers on Personal Power: Inner Strength and Its Revolutionary Impact* (1978a). In discussing the politics of his approach, he defines politics by saying:

> Politics involves the question of where power is located, who makes the choices and decisions, who carries out or enforces those decisions, and who has the knowledge or data regarding the consequences of those decisions. It involves the strategies involved in the taking of power, the distribution of power, the holding of power, and the sharing or relinquishing of power. (Rogers, 1978b: 1)

PERSON-CENTRED THERAPY AND POWER

I argue (Proctor, 2002) that Carl Rogers was the first theorist to consider issues of power in the therapy relationship. Rogers challenged the power inherent in the role of the therapist in many revolutionary ways. Person-centred theory is based on the principle of respect for each individual and their autonomy. It is a radical theory of therapy and is heretical to psychiatric understanding of mental illness. The theory of psychological distress is based on internalised oppression, and the effect of Person-Centred Therapy is to reduce the power that others have had over clients and thus increase their own sense of personal power, or '*power-from-within*' (see Proctor, 2002). In his later work, Rogers also focused on the structural power in society, and I suggest that to consider all aspects of power fully, the person-centred therapist needs to consider the 'socially positioned individual' (Kearney, 1996). It is not enough to aim to understand each unique individual, without trying to understand how society and the cultural context of that individual impacts on their experiences.

Rogers explicitly set out to change the role of the therapist from that of an expert and to aim for a more egalitarian therapy relationship. This follows from the philosophy underlying Person-Centred Therapy. Rogers contends that the premise of the actualising tendency challenges the need to control people, i.e., challenges:

> The view that the nature of the individual is such that he cannot be trusted—that he must be guided, instructed, rewarded, punished, and controlled by those that are higher in status.' (Rogers, 1978a: 8)

He explains the implications of this philosophy and values:

> The politics of the person-centered approach is a conscious renunciation and avoidance by the therapist of all control over, or decision-making for, the client. It is the facilitation of self-ownership by the client and the strategies by which this can be achieved; the placing of the locus of decision-making and the responsibility for the effects of these decisions. It is politically centered in the client. (Rogers 1978a: 14)

This trust in the client's process leads to the non-directive attitude. The *non-directive attitude* is a way for therapists to express their commitment to avoiding client disempowerment (Brodley, 1997). Rogers (1978a) pointed out the implications of this principle of non-directivity on the part of the therapist by discussing the threat to counsellors from his views: 'I was making it clear that if they agreed with me, it would mean the complete disruption and reversal of their personal control in their counselling relationship' (p. 7). In this sense PCT is a radical disruption of the dynamics of power in therapy. Natiello (2001: 11) explains that 'Such a stand is in radical conflict with the prevailing paradigm of authoritarian power.'

Rogers asserts that opposition to Person-Centred Therapy sprang 'primarily because it struck such an outrageous blow to the therapist's power' (1978a: 16). He challenges the notion of expert knowledge which gives power, and believes in the power of congruence, that:

> In such an individual, functioning in a unified way, we have the best possible base for wise action. It is a process base, not a static authority base. (Rogers, 1978a: 250)

DEMYSTIFICATION OF THERAPY

Another way in which Rogers addressed the imbalance of power in the therapy relationship was to make Person-Centred Therapy transparent and explicit, to demystify therapy. He did this by explaining exactly what the therapist does in therapy and providing much tape-recorded and video-recorded material for public use. He placed great importance on the clarity of the process and the content of therapy including the accountability of the therapists to be able to demonstrate the extent to which they fulfilled the core conditions. He similarly demystified the therapist as a person by stressing the concept of congruence.

CONCLUSION

Despite Rogers' huge impact and significance, his work has also attracted a lot of controversy and disagreement. Kirschenbaum and Henderson (1989: xv) explain that 'Rogers' work has been so controversial, maligned and misunderstood as well as accepted and embraced.' This is hardly surprising given the political implications of his theories. Trusting individuals, letting clients guide their own process, valuing each person and prioritising relationships is a message which runs counter to the priorities of those with political power or money and against the philosophy of global capitalism giving wealth to a few at the expense of many. Similarly, the PCA can strike a blow at the heart of patriarchy, with its clear messages that all people, women and men, are trustworthy and of value.

REFERENCES

Barrett-Lennard, GT (1998) *Carl Rogers Helping System: Journey and substance.* London: Sage.

Barrett-Lennard, GT (2002) Perceptual Variables of the Helping Relationship: A measuring system and its fruits, in G Wyatt and P Sanders (eds) *Rogers' Therapeutic Conditions. Volume 4. Contact and Perception.* Ross-on-Wye: PCCS Books, pp. 25–50.

Bozarth, J (1998) *Person-Centred Therapy: A revolutionary paradigm.* Ross-on-Wye: PCCS Books.

Bozarth, J and Wilkins, P (2002) Introduction to Vol 3: Unconditional Positive Regard in Context, in J Bozarth and P Wilkins (eds) *Rogers' Therapeutic Conditions. Volume 3. Unconditional Positive Regard .* Ross-on-Wye: PCCS Books, pp. vii–ix.

Brodley, BT (1997) The nondirective attitude in client-centered therapy. *Person-Centered Journal* 4(1): 18–30.

Brodley, BT (1999) The actualizing tendency concept in client-centered theory. *Person-Centered Journal, 6*(2): 108–120.

Brodley, BT (2004) 16th May, email personal communication.

Gendlin, E (2002) Foreword, in *Carl Rogers: The quiet revolutionary.* CR Rogers and DE Russell (eds). Roseville, CA, USA: Penmarin Books, pp. xi–xxi.

Goldstein, K (1939) *The Organism.* Boston: Beacon Press.

Kearney, A (1996) *Counselling, Class and Politics: Undeclared influences in therapy.* Ross-on-Wye: PCCS Books.

King, M, Sibbald, B, Ward, E, Bower, P, Lloyd, M, Gabbay, M and Byford, S (2000)

Randomised controlled trial of non-directive counselling, cognitive behaviour therapy and usual general practitioner care in the management of depression as well as mixed anxiety and depression in primary care. *Health Technology Assessment, 4,* 19. Also published in the *British Medical Journal, 321,* (2000), pp. 1383–8.

Kirschenbaum, H and Henderson, VL (1989) (eds) *The Carl Rogers Reader.* Boston: Houghton Mifflin.

Lambert, MJ (ed) (2004) *Handbook of Psychotherapy and Behavioral Change* (5th ed). New York: Wiley.

Mearns, D and Thorne, B (1988) *Person-Centred Counselling in Action.* London: Sage.

Moon, K, Rice, B and Schneider, C (2002) Stanley W Standal and the Need for Positive Regard, in J Bozarth and P Wilkins (eds) *Rogers' Therapeutic Conditions. Volume 3. Unconditional Positive Regard.* Ross-on-Wye: PCCS Books, pp. 19–34.

Natiello, P (2001) *The Person-Centered Approach: A passionate presence.* Ross-on-Wye: PCCS Books.

Proctor, G (2002) *The Dynamics of Power in Therapy: Ethics, politics and practice.* Ross-on-Wye: PCCS Books.

Prouty, G (1994) *Theoretical Evolutions in Person-Centered/Experiential Therapy: Applications to schizophrenic and retarded psychoses.* Greenwood, CT: Praeger.

Prouty, G (2002) Pre-Therapy as a theoretical system, in G Wyatt and P Sanders (eds) *Rogers' Therapeutic Conditions. Volume 4. Contact and Perception.* Ross-on-Wye: PCCS Books, pp. 54–62.

Rogers, CR (1942) The use of electrically recorded interviews in improving psychotherapeutic techniques. *American Journal of Orthopsychiatry 12,* 429–34.

Rogers, CR (1957) The necessary and sufficient conditions of therapeutic personality change. *The Journal of Consulting Psychology 21*(2): 95–103.

Rogers, CR (1959) A Theory of Therapy, Personality, and Interpersonal Relationships, as Developed in the Client-Centered Framework, in S Koch (ed) *Psychology, a Study of a Science. Vol 3. Formulations of the Person and the Social Context.* New York: McGraw Hill, pp. 184–256.

Rogers, CR (1961) *On Becoming a Person.* Boston: Houghton Mifflin.

Rogers, CR (1969) *Freedom to Learn: A view of what education might become.* Constable, OH: Charles E Merrill.

Rogers, CR (1970) *Carl Rogers on Encounter Groups.* New York: Harper and Row.

Rogers, CR (1972) *Becoming Partners: Marriage and its alternatives.* New York: Delacorte Press.

Rogers, CR (1978a) *Carl Rogers on Personal Power: Inner strength and its revolutionary impact.* New York: Delacorte Press.

Rogers, CR (1978b) My Political View. Statement made to the El Escorial Workshop. March 31, unpublished manuscript.

Rogers, CR and Dymond, R (eds) (1954) *Psychotherapy and Personality Change.* Chicago: University Press.

A PERSONAL ODYSSEY—SHAPING POLITICAL AND FEMINIST PRINCIPLES IN THE PERSON-CENTERED APPROACH

GAY (SWENSON) BARFIELD

When I was asked—and committed enthusiastically—to write about my personal experiences in conjoining the Person-Centered Approach (PCA) with feminist values and activities for this significant text, it was also with some trepidation. Writing with passion about ideas and social movements has been relatively easy for me; however, writing about myself within that frame and context is a considerably more daunting challenge.

THE DUBIOUS TRUTHS OF HER/STORY

So I remind the reader that this personal narrative is not hard data, but a private history softened and slanted through the memory, perceptions and perspectives, disappoint-ments and great joys of a now nearly 69-year-old woman who thinks of herself as a 'gatherer' and connector, a social activist and a flawed but committed idealist. This chronicle is also undergirded by the deep conviction that our work in the fields of social change within the feminist and person-centered communities made a difference in some small and larger ways for women, for peace and ultimately for the PCA. It is a privilege for me to be able to link together in this review the guiding principles and philosophies and practices of my life, since each of these philosophical outcroppings had deep roots in my experiences from childhood onward as a female child of both crisis and amazing opportunities.

Since I hold teamwork, inclusion and acknowledgment of others in high value, my one major regret is that space does not allow me to list all of the incredible individual women and men who were involved over the years in *all* that follows. My original version did list hundreds of them, but lists of hundreds do not fit with editorial realities! So I trust that each of you *not* named will know who you are as you read about our long and rich passages through history together, and will consider yourself very present and loved.

39

CLARITY, COMMITMENT AND CONVICTION

Much like the PCA and feminist philosophies themselves—which provide the soil for the personal flowering of so many of us—and deeper than my own possible foreshortenings, prejudices and distortions in this story, something emerges with an unbiased clarity and strong conviction for me as I write this now. It is astonishment at the powerful events that can be created and lived out when women are supported (as was I) and nourished in their visions and their higher callings. What a horrendous loss it has been to centuries of humanity that more women across the globe have not been supported to such a large degree. What is called up for me here is the expression 'Be careful what you ask for—you are likely to get it'. At face value, this is a potentially simplistic positivist cliché, considering that, for billions of women, life does not provide such rich opportunities. However, it can become real and tangible. It *can* happen when our personal visions, commitments and longings *ARE encouraged and enabled* by respect, support and mentoring or '*mentressing*', at opportune moments, and we trust ourselves to risk, described so famously by Goethe:

> Whatever you can do, or dream you can, *begin it*.
> Boldness has Genius, Power and Magic in it.
> *Begin it now.*

I was very fortunate to have both such support and mentoring, and the boldness or effrontery to attempt to realize some of my greatest dreams—something that Goethe encourages in us all.

PERSONAL ROOTS AND PARALLEL REVOLUTIONS—AN OVERVIEW OF NEARLY SEVENTY YEARS

My own personal odyssey nearly perfectly parallels the development of the PCA and feminism as we began to evolve up and out from under a long era of a fundamentally male-dominated consciousness, governing many, if not nearly all, our world cultures. The narrative flow of this chapter emerges from my *own* roots watered in the soil of the 1950s with its traditionalist roles of women, as represented by my home life and high school years. It continues through to the turbulent 60s, the feminist 70s, and the activist grass-roots lay diplomacy efforts in peace and conflict resolution of the 80s. The 1990s once again saw the wars, economic, ecological, racial and gender/preference crises and opportunities of the previous decades increasing in magnitude. My story ends in the present with me as a semi-retired therapist and elder woman still voicing her concerns about these same issues in the new century. As I do this, I witness the appalling religious, ideological and ecological wars being fought over sparse and ever-shrinking resources. These resources are coveted greedily by both the indulged societies and classes on the one hand and the desperately ill, starving and needy nations and groups on the other.

Not a happy place to end, but a powerful place to begin and continue our work for social justice.

Born in 1936, as an infant and child I traveled throughout the United States with my parents and three older siblings in a caravan of musicians 'on the road'. I was the youngest of four children born to a rather famous father, 'big band' leader Buddy Fisher, the 'Chicago Joy Boy', and we traveled until the 1940s when the orchestra disbanded as young musicians went off to war. After that my father became a traveling salesman, struggling now in shame, not fame, to keep his large family out of poverty and his bruised ego intact. Large quantities of alcohol soaked up much of the money he earned to ease his depression and loss. The heavy drinking only released his rage, anger and brutality on us all the more, particularly on my weary and frightened mother, by then going through a harrowing menopause as well.

As a teen in the 1950s, I was enthralled and relieved finally to be settling somewhere, anywhere, in one community (Las Vegas, Nevada!), and living in a real house, not a hotel. So I became the model American young woman in my roles of the virginal 'good girl', high achiever, head cheerleader, prom princess and football queen, along with being the first female senior class president, and class salutatorian and graduation speaker. As an entering freshman in the autumn of 1954 at the University of California, Berkeley, I began to experience intimations of the larger social and political upheavals just ahead. By the time I graduated in 1958 Berkeley students had moved from enjoying fraternity parties and panty raids to protesting and creating the 'free speech movement' on campus. At the same time, but not yet known to me, a man named Carl Rogers and his innovative work were transforming the field of psychology, and powerful feminist voices were emerging in parallel streams to one another, around the country and world.

In the 1960s these feminist voices were being heard more widely through their new magazines (*Ms*) and organizations (National Organization for Women). At the same time, Rogers took his own now renowned, softly rebellious voice and work away from academia to move to the Western Behavioral Sciences Institute (WBSI) in La Jolla, California. He and other colleagues eventually broke away from that group in 1968 to found the Center for Studies of the Person (CSP), an even more revolutionary form of non-organization than the former. There, the themes of experiential knowing, self-discovery, and stretching human potentials far beyond the norms and limitations of my experience in the 1950s, were vividly experienced in encounter groups. Thousands of participants were drawn to CSP through the 'La Jolla Program', the grandfather of encounter groups founded and co-directed by Bruce Meador, Doug Land and Bill Coulson, colleagues of Carl's now at CSP—described in *Carl Rogers On Encounter Groups* (Rogers, 1970).

The 1960s also saw the cataclysmic revolutions in anti-Vietnam war activism, and the racial justice, gender equity and ecological movements that sought to change our entire culture. Living in Berkeley, San Francisco and San Mateo in those years, I was an active part of these experiments and marches, and their democratizing processes. I discovered the amazing liberation and intellectual stimulus that accompanied each of them, and consequently developed my own larger sense of self and meaning. Having discovered Carl Rogers' writing by then, I infused my work as a teacher in an experimental high school in the San Francisco Bay area with his values of 'freedom to learn' and its collaborative teaching and learning modes, all of which led to a sea change in my life soon after.

The early 1970s brought on-going and rapidly accelerating personal evolution for me, including a divorce, a new love, new work, new graduate studies, and new meaning, as I moved in 1973 to La Jolla and to CSP. There I was able to create, with others, the first Women's Center at CSP, along with one of the longest-lived (22 years) programs at the Center, the 'Living Now Summer Institute'. 'Living Now' focused on political and social themes during a 10-day residential retreat held on the University of California San Diego campus. It was held just before the 'La Jolla Program' so that people traveling from other states and countries could attend them both in tandem. The Person-Centered Approach (PCA) remained the bedrock principle and foundation for 'Living Now'. Carl and other leading writers and spokespersons (some 100-plus over the 22 Institutes we convened) were the guest speakers addressing these themes and issues. At first, this proved to be a rather uneasy 'deviation' from basic encounter-only workshops, for some CSP and PCA people to accept.

However, the 1980s saw an increased emphasis on peace and social justice in our CSP programs in California, nationally and certainly internationally. As the cultural wars with communism and its 'Iron Curtain' countries deepened and the fear of nuclear war heightened worldwide, the lay voices of detente and 'citizen diplomacy' groups attempted to change this disastrous direction. The work of Carl, Chuck Devonshire and Valerie Henderson from the USA and others throughout Europe in cross-cultural communications began in the early 1970s with PCA colleagues from many different nations, even some from behind the then 'Iron Curtain' countries, sometimes with great risk to participants there. Carl had already begun important work in similar ways with other colleagues, particularly with Pat Rice, Dick Farson and Bill McGaw in Ireland, and later with Ruth Sanford, who traveled with him to places such as the Soviet Union, Northern Ireland, and South Africa. When all this work was at its zenith, many of us at CSP were also convening numerous other international gatherings and programs throughout the world. Carl initiated and participated in these events, which took on an increasingly political overtone, intent and emphasis.

By 1984, with Carl and myself as co-founders and co-directors—and a dozen or so other CSP staff members as colleagues, and some 50 luminary advisors, many international—we formed the Carl Rogers Institute for Peace (initially called the Institute for Person-Centered Approaches to Peace, and referred to over the years as 'the Peace Project'). The goal was to move PCA work beyond therapy and other important social issues to include high-level international political issues as legitimate arenas for person-centered dialogue and conflict resolution. This was our attempt to help reduce the mounting and deadly tensions between nations and regions besetting the planet. With leading representative politicians and grass-roots peace groups present as participants, often holding disputing perspectives, we hoped that by working together through the person-centered approaches to dialogue, they might then return to their own countries—many of the major 'hot spots' on the planet—to apply these same principles of peaceful dialogue.

With that in mind, the major initial activity of the Peace Project to realize this goal was the meeting on the challenges within Central America held in Rust, Austria, in 1985. It was convened in cooperation with the United Nations University for Peace and its President, the former President of Costa Rica, Don Rodrigo Carazo Odio. He, along with Dr Karl Vak, President of the 'Z' bank in Vienna, Austria, was instrumental in co-creating the meeting with us. It was this particular gathering of diplomats and lay leaders from 17 countries (along with his previous fifty years of renown and revolutionary work) which led to Carl's nomination for the Nobel Peace Prize in 1987—received and read aloud to him as he lay in a coma and dying.[1]

With one very large single donation by Mrs Joan Kroc and the support of hundreds of smaller donors, we went forward with a steadfast determination with our peace work after Carl's death. We held a second meeting of diplomats in Heredia, Costa Rica, in 1973. The conference had the participation and support of attendees from 11 nations and the then sitting president of Costa Rica and Nobel Peace Prize winner for 1987, President Oscar Arias, and once again former President Rodrigo Carazo Odio.

However, after Carl's death in February 1987, the early 1990s saw a diminution in our ability to accomplish our larger visions of global political impact as donations dropped away and anticipated funding from foundations failed to materialize. This was due in large part to three important factors; first, the absence of Carl's leadership, credibility and brilliance; second, the leadership of the Peace Project was left in the hands of people relatively unknown outside of the PCA world, namely our marvelous staff/team and myself (and a woman at that!); and third, a structural design at CSP which, although leading to the independent program creativity mentioned before, did not lend itself to fiduciary confidence by the large foundations we had long been courting. Thus, by 1995 the Peace Project essentially closed down its major efforts and its small bank account.

Before doing so, however, I, by then the sole director, and a small group of us at CSP continued the work as we focused more on local urban diversity issues in the San Diego area. We held 'living room dialogues on diversity' and formed an 'urban diversity council' for the city of San Diego and area leaders. We saw, and helped to encourage, the outgrowth of other PCA diversity groups with Carl's colleagues around the country, particularly those begun by Ruth Sanford, Lewis Gover, Chuck Stewart and their many PCA colleagues on the east coast of the US.

[1.] Several in-depth analyses and critiques of this gathering have been published elsewhere, many in the Journal for Humanistic Psychology. Another will soon appear in the updated version now in process of Carl's biography written by Dr Howard Kirschenbaum and further analysis by this author will appear in a forthcoming text on politics and the Person-Centered Approach.

SPIRITUAL COMPONENTS OF THE WORK

By the late 1990s and early years of the new millennium, these smaller peace and social action efforts within the PCA community had either stabilized or spread through communities. During the same period, many other writers and theoreticians within the PCA were now more overtly including and/or debating the next phase of the development of the PCA—and of psychotherapy in general—namely that of its spiritual dimension, and its legitimacy within our field. These theoretical explorations were particularly catalyzed as a consequence of a rather remarkable paragraph written and published by Carl in 1986. It is nowadays quoted and debated widely, both for its spiritual overtones and for his mention of a potential extra therapeutic condition (beyond his famous 'three necessary and sufficient conditions') which he called 'presence'. The spiritual dimension of our work was especially well captured through the brilliant work of Brian Thorne of Norwich, England, amongst his own prodigious writings on PCA counseling and spirituality. Much of my own work both locally and internationally during that period, and since, has also incorporated, voiced and reflected this aspect of the PCA as a central guiding element of our approach. Feminist understandings were constant companion components reflecting their own sense of spirit and empathy. By this time, for me, the PCA, feminism, politics and spirituality had come to a natural stage of merging, blending and flowing together, while still retaining their integrity as separate bodies of knowledge and ways of knowing and experiencing.

OUR WORK TODAY AND FOR THE FUTURE

I attempted to continue my work both locally, and by traveling widely abroad every two years to train, speak and facilitate. Once again my life changed personally, and happily. In 1990 I married and moved; first to a remote mountain village (Bishop, California), and then five years later with my aspiring (now actual), orchid-grower farmer husband, Glen, to a remote volcanic mountain and seaside village (Mt View and Hilo) on the Big Island of Hawaii. In Hawaii I have offered small PCA training programs and continued to work abroad now and then. I also counsel and train therapists in small ways, speak publicly, and attempt to put my concerns and hopes for the future—and for upcoming generations of young idealists and visionaries—into my 'mentressing' and my writing. The young women cross-cultural co-editors of this book now represent this future. They provide this opportunity for diverse feminist and person-centered voices to collectively resound across age, race and culture, for which I am deeply grateful. Our world offers many daily opportunities for such needed reflections and expressions, not to mention actions by all of us, no matter what our ages or places on this needful planet.

MORE WOMEN/FEMINISTS IN THE PERSON-CENTERED APPROACH

As I look back while writing this, I recall vividly and clearly that the most substantial and heartening changes for me as a woman and PCA feminist over the past 30-plus years, have been the increasing impact and involvement of more women at the Center for Studies of the Person in La Jolla (and in the PCA in general worldwide), and in the peace and gender consciousness-awakening movements internationally. The involvement of increasing numbers of women began with our opening the first Person-Centered Women's Center at CSP in the early 1970s. Other contributors to this book will describe their work in depth in other chapters. The important fact is that the numbers of women working for peace, equality and justice within PCA expanded exponentially over the intervening years, and today extends all across the globe. Many of these CSP/PCA women (e.g., Valerie Henderson, Maureen O'Hara, Marvalene Hughes and Dee Aker) now hold, or have held, positions of leadership, including presidencies, at important educational and peace institutes. I would like to think that for some of them their significant engagement as social change agents today may have, in part, evolved out of their early participation as either organizers or staff members in CSP work. Perhaps in the CSP Women's Center, or from their CSP membership and work with Carl, or from their involvement in the 'Living Now' program, or especially dear to my own heart of course, from their participation as team members and staff with the Carl Rogers Institute for Peace at CSP in the 1980s and early 90s. So I am very grateful to have been instrumental in creating these programs with the support of dozens of other women and men colleagues who believed in, and acted upon, their sense of equity and social justice in its merging with Rogers' approach.

As feminists and person-centered practitioners and philosophers in our troubled world today, we cannot afford to be unconcerned and uninvolved politically, lest all that went before this current generation of young women and men worldwide be lost. We could lose the equality and social justice for which we have worked so hard and long and with such total commitment. We are, each one of us, the products and producers of the values of our eras. We are, willingly or not, participants in great historical movements, as we become either the ardent or reluctant agents of change that make a difference in our times. I can personally acknowledge the hesitation and disinclination to move with the tides of history that hold many of us back, especially as we think with some timidity and embarrassment about our own perceived personal limitations and incongruence. But as Goethe told us in that early quote, 'Boldness has Genius, Power and Magic in it'. Courage is required to create change, no matter what our shortcomings; and using our best talents, resources and strengths is part of such courage.

RELUCTANT FEMINIST

I myself was in fact a reluctant feminist. Yet, as a young woman and doctoral student working on women's self-languaging, I was drawn to and enthralled by Gloria Steinem's brilliance, Betty Friedan's breakthrough work and contentious style, Germaine Greer's intellect, Starhawk's extravagant feminist spirituality, Charlene Spretnaks' work on the politics of women's spirituality, Phyllis Chesler's groundbreaking work on definitions of madness, Ursula LeGuin's linguistic masterpiece on 'the mother tongue', as well as the groundbreaking writings of women such as Riane Eisler, Dinnerstein, Miller, Chodorow, Gilligan and the Stone Center theorists on feminist ethics and psychology, whose works on empathy so resonated with Rogers. Throughout this evolutionary period with its parallel growths and convergences of politics, psychology, feminism and spirituality, I was imbued with the influences and impacts of these early feminists on life and society. Furthermore, I came to see that each of these women was in close alignment with Rogers, and he with them, in each of his and their own unique psychological approaches to personal growth, freedom, equality, justice, and sense of empowerment and community within the human family.

Yet, I still, almost defiantly, resisted accepting for myself the label 'feminist' for a long time. I argued that I did not want to be categorized, slotted, misperceived and seen as a wild-eyed, antagonistic, man-hating, angry, bra-less woman. I was, by then, a committed client/person-centered theorist and practitioner. While I certainly wanted women's voices heard and respected, I wanted even more that Rogers' triad of core conditions of empathy, genuineness and unconditional positive regard be understood as universal human strengths—universal human strengths that rendered each of us stronger as men or women or as social change agents, whether as giver or receiver of these attitudes. I also thought it was brilliant and intuitive of Carl to have fused together what I had considered the very psychological attitudes inherent to women in particular! I still believe much of this strongly, and honor Carl even more in my heart and mind by thinking of him as the first feminist male therapist to help change our cultural values by appreciating and respecting such attitudes as the healthiest configuration of our psyches.

WALKING MY TALK—A HARD AND ROCKY ROAD

Despite my lofty goals, it was difficult for me to 'walk my talk' at times during this period, as I myself went through a painful (to myself and others) period of adamant, vehement, antagonistic (and, according to some, sometimes even intellectually brilliant) castigations of (mostly) those of the male gender who belonged to and ran the larger society, and (certainly) to some of the male staff members of CSP. Faced with injustices and inequities, I often railed and raged and wrote scathing letters and diatribes, well argued in the main, but less hearable because of their haranguing and indignation. I paid dearly for this period of my life by sometimes feeling a sense of isolation and loneliness, sorrow and shame, yet I held on stubbornly to a righteousness about whatever the issue was itself! I later discovered that my own personal reversal from being a 'please everyone' passive prom-princess to being a passionate political polemicist was not an unusual swing of the pendulum for many women at that time. But for a so-called person-centered practitioner and empathic listener … ? It was rather incongruent to say the least! Eventually, I came to rest in the more palatable position of clarity of thought, voiced with some compassion for the other in the process. I think others, and myself for certain, benefitted considerably from this salutary and more congruent change.

MOM, MEN AND MARRIAGE

But even with much incongruence in evidence, I knew then (as I know now) that bringing feminism and the PCA together appealed to me for personal reasons involving my mother, men, and marriage. Because of her model of mothering, with its considerable deficits, due to much suffering in her own marriage and life as a woman, I came to believe that married women could not be emotionally healthy, nor could we have healthy relationships in general with well-balanced and non-harming men. My wonderful brother-in-law, Vic, my older sister's husband, was the one very important exception to the unhappy conclusion about men and women arrived at by a tender pre-adolescent girl. He remained my male model anchor until his too early death from cancer in my early adult years. I shall be forever grateful to him for his tender, tearful, but tough and strong example of the kindness possible in a strong man.

I know that my early childhood decision never to marry, nor to have children, came directly from the terror, helplessness and anger I felt watching my mother's painful experience in her role as an intellectually brilliant woman battered and beaten down as a wife and mother, and her direct message to me not to do the same with my life. My mother's resulting pervasive depression and day-long drinking, only re-enforced that existential decision for me to remain single, sober and self-supporting as long as possible— not all bad decisions as such, but all taken for the wrong reasons. Eventually, I believe this history may well have led—in order to justify my being sexual at all—to my being forced violently into having my first sexual experience (an event we now clearly call rape, but dared not say aloud then), in a German wheat field, awakening as the morning sun shone on the brilliant red poppies in the distant horizon, mirroring the red blood on my khaki skirt.

It was not until I became an educated feminist and a member of CSP, some dozen years later, that I met large numbers of women who were models to me of healthy, productive, well-balanced human beings. It was then that I could begin to more comfortably own the description of myself as a feminist and move actively on those principles. I could finally come to trust, love and respect countless marvelous men as friends and colleagues at CSP and around the world—and even some as lovers. But it was still not always easy between us as women and men at CSP, as we will see in what follows.

THE BEGINNINGS OF (AND RESISTANCES TO) THE WOMEN'S CENTER AT CSP

Early in my involvement at CSP, around 1973 or so, I participated as a member of a small women's group convened by Dr Betty Meador. Betty was one of perhaps only three or four women members of CSP at this time, (a 40-plus member institute), among whom were Maria Villas-Boas Bowen and Orienne Strode Maloney. Other women were at CSP at the time of my arrival there, but in the role of secretary, coordinator, 'significant other', or wife of an 'actual' member. Betty's women's group, and another which many of us formed later from this core group, soon became the seedbed for many of us 'ancillary' associates of CSP to become actual invited members of CSP ourselves, and therefore colleagues and community members of Carl's professional family—it was considered quite an honor for each of us. Year by year thereafter, we began to swell the ranks of women at CSP by inviting other women to join us, sometimes far beyond the readiness of some of the men to accept this inevitable change of the times.

It became a most difficult and challenging moment for CSP when this group of women, in late 1973, decided to move beyond being simply participants in a women's group, or mere auxiliary appendages to CSP, or a token number within the group. We decided instead to open a full-fledged women's center ourselves as a part of CSP, as one of its 'projects'. With at least one or two official women CSP members to legitimize our effort, a group of us rented a small Spanish style house downstairs in front of the CSP offices at 1125 Torrey Pines Road in La Jolla.

Soon we began to offer brochures filled with a variety of events and classes for women. Not all the courses reflected a PCA focus or process, but some were advocating a radical change for women, called 'empowerment' or 'consciousness-raising'—again much to the philosophical chagrin of some male members of CSP. I recall many a Wednesday afternoon CSP staff meeting where the response to our forming the women's center brought sharp reactions from some members. Biting sarcasm, volatile intellectual discussions, and hot debates came from this perturbative change, much as it was doing in society in general. Sometimes we left the weekly afternoon meeting 'in a stew' with one another. More often than not, however, these disputes were beautifully facilitated by one CSP member or another. It was often a man (Will Stillwell, Norman Chambers, Andre Auw and Charlie O'Leary come to mind, and Carl of course), who was able at a crucial moment to hear the deep and sincere concerns of all sides, and thus provide the very bedrock of our world view, the empathic listening for which CSP and Rogers' approach had become world famous.

VARIED PROGRAMS AND ORIENTATIONS AT THE CSP WOMEN'S CENTER

Nevertheless, after much excited planning by about a half dozen of us, and with only one minimally paid 'coordinator' (often self-selected cooperatively from among us 'founders') we opened the Women's Center. Hundreds of women showed up for the meetings held at the Women's Center from 1973 through 1977 to discuss both personal concerns and important issues of the day. So popular were the meetings that we would often spill out of the small rooms onto the patio, For nearly five years we offered courses for the empowerment of women which reflected more of the PCA approach and less of the political energies that the burgeoning activist feminist centers springing up around the country were promoting with great vigor, lucidity and commitment. Concurrently, the first official academic department in the United States in Women's Studies was being born at San Diego State University. There, Maureen O'Hara, newly arrived at CSP herself from the mid-west, was seedbedding the same PCA and feminist values in her original and intellectually soaring women's studies classes. Women's 'liberation' was taking many shapes, and the PCA was adding its own voice to this important social justice movement.

Back at the CSP Women's Center, we offered and facilitated courses—either free or very low cost—in such topics as life planning, values clarification, assertiveness training, communications skills, male/female relationships and biorhythms, as well as individual client-centered counseling, non-structured person-centered community meetings and support groups. Each gathering acted as an avenue to empower women's voices and their sense of entitlement and personal power and confidence. Because the theme of my doctorate was women's self-esteem in the second half of life, and 'creative aging', I also taught classes for women aged 65 to 90 about the many new concepts in gerontology. The purpose of my doctorate was to increase a sense of esteem, respect and prizing, and pride in ourselves as we age, particularly though our use of language— something that I came to call 'languaging' about ourselves—and its powerful connection to health, longevity and psychological well-being in older women. The paradox, of course, was that as I listened to their life-affirming words, I learned much more about positive self-concepts from my elderly students than I taught them in the adult education classes— so much so, that it has infused and become a core of my own work on communications and the power of language ever since. Now at nearly 69, during my own aging process, I try to remember and apply what they taught me back then. Carl was right once again when he told us he learned most of his own theory from listening to the collective voices of his clients, just as we do now, as feminists finally listening to each other as women with shared realities.

By the latter 1970s, more politically militant women, and some lesbian and bisexual women, began to come to the CSP Women's Center. Their presence tested our values about what we hoped the Center represented. It also seemed to frighten many women who were tentatively dipping their feet into the waters of equality and independence, but who were not quite ready for that level of change as they were barely beginning to work it out with their husbands and sons! With many women uneasy with a potentially militant and aligned orientation, the general attendance began to wane and eventually dropped off to a level unsustainable by either staff or participants. In the end, the Women's

Center's vision was not totally realized as an on-going permanent resource. However, I trust it did serve as an important beginning for so many of us 'emerging women', (to use Natalie Rogers' term and title of her book of the same name, Rogers, 1980), and it met a need in the San Diego community for quite a while as a politically non-aligned place for women to gather and grow. It certainly launched numbers of women in the discovery and development of new uncharted aspects of themselves.

A SPRINGBOARD FOR WOMEN'S LEADERSHIP

Many of the women volunteer staff and participants also used the resources at the Women's Center and roles they assumed there as a springboard from which to involve themselves in other important social movements, change their personal lives, continue their education and extend their sense of possibilities professionally. The roles which we assumed collaboratively at the Women's Center became powerful means for developing women's leadership capacities and trained many of us (in classic curriculum vitae terms) as program designers, administrators, professional therapists, facilitators, public speakers, fiscal managers, CEOs and entrepreneurs. In doing so it provided each of us with practical skills in all management and staffing tasks, as well as much new found freedom and independence, more equality in our relationships with the men in our lives, and many opportunities for creativity.

For me the Women's Center was all of this and more, for it actually provided me the internship for my doctorate. Its creation was the integral action aspect of my doctoral program through Union Graduate School, which was based largely on Rogers' approach to learning. We were required to have, as a direct outcome of our PhD studies, a socially relevant action component, then termed a 'Project Demonstrating Excellence'. The founding of the Women's Center by myself and others thus allowed me to live out the principles about which I was writing, as it allowed so many of us to come together to co-create our own personal visions for ourselves and other women.

GLOBAL SISTERHOOD

We were not alone at CSP in doing this work. Person-centered women colleagues and kindred spirits around the country and around the world were making their own way into this large movement, in parallel and sometimes conjoining circles to achieve global sisterhood.

My mind, heart and spirit are brimming with memories of just such world-wide sisterhood (and often brotherhood, lest we forget) which strengthened my own resolve at difficult moments, which took place at amazing gatherings we convened on most of the continents on the planet. Those assemblies, wherever they took place, allowed me to realize some part of my own hopes and visions, along with these women and men. Sadly, space does not permit further elaboration, and to include some and not others would do a disservice to each of their meanings in my life and memory. For me, in sum, feminism and living, breathing feminist women, combined with the PCA philosophy, made possible everything that I have ever done professionally.

And not just the feminism of *women,* but the profound commitment of *feminist men* in the PCA world who also catalyzed and joined with us to build this movement for equity and peace—again, how I wish I could name them all! The role of Carl among these men, however, cannot be understated. He literally totally altered my life on first contact. To recount this meeting and its impact on me, I need to return to a very early time in my first marriage, as a newly reluctantly married woman living in a great Victorian apartment in San Francisco, working her way with her husband through graduate school.

LEAVING AN OLD LIFE BEHIND—ON TO LA JOLLA

I and my first husband were married two years after returning from meeting in Europe in 1960. He from the mid-west and I from Las Vegas, we moved to San Francisco where together we attended graduate school at San Francisco State throughout the early 1960s. We worked part or full-time, and paid $200 a month for a fabulous, tiny, three-room 'railroad' style apartment on Nob Hill in San Francisco, with a pull-down Murphy bed and a spectacular view of the entire San Francisco Bay.

Very early into my marriage I became quite ill with a series of debilitating health issues. These included mononucleosis,[2] severe back problems (that hospitalized and immobilized me in body casts and braces), digestive problems, chest pains, and other manifestations of what I now understand to have been my huge resistance to this essentially unwanted marriage. These illnesses and my depression and rage at the earlier rape in Germany laid me low for weeks at a time and for several years running they kept me safely distant from any satisfying sensual or sexual life with my husband. Instead, what we had in common were our graduate studies, our good intellects, our political and literary interests, and eventually our teaching jobs. Lightened by humor and wit, but all undergirded by our joint sense of guilt and shame, we both covered over our mutual sadness with anger and alcohol for too much of the time and then with reactive extra-marital relationships or flirtations. After seven mutually hurting years, we ultimately used those ways of being as the precipitating events that gave us the permission and courage (that we could not muster on our own) to divorce. This is where Carl came in.

One day in an education class at San Francisco State College, the professor gave us a single-page summary to read written by a man named Dr Carl R. Rogers. It was about *'Three Necessary and Sufficient Conditions'* as they might apply in the classroom. As I read this short paper in the library, a knot appeared in my throat, tears began to well up

---

[2.] In the UK, the term for mononucleosis is glandular fever.

behind my eyeglasses, and then began to pour forth, until I had to go outside to let them flow freely. The sobs and weeping came from the joy of recognition, a realization of what I had been missing all my life—but must have understood at my core—that human beings could treat each other much differently than I had experienced growing up in my violent home, or in my marriage. I saw within these simple but profound ways of being, and listening, and respecting one another described by Carl, that men and women could, in fact, change their relationships together. More than that, *how* they listened and spoke to each other might even change much of the world's suffering in the process.

From that moment forward, I experienced a higher degree of internal incongruence in my marriage than I had ever known before, an incongruence which increased literally day by day, until I could no longer tolerate it without an emotional breakdown—which I began to feel was imminent. What held me together even with all the psychosomatic symptoms and real physical pain, was the fact that after my internship ended, but before divorcing, I obtained my first teaching job as a French and Social Studies teacher in an innovational public high school in San Mateo, a rather well-to-do suburb south of San Francisco. The school was about to change its structure and curriculum from a traditional format to the 'open classroom' experimental design then becoming popular and similar to college schedules. Much of the school's philosophy was based on the Stanford University Palo Alto approach to educational innovations, and on the premises of Carl Rogers' book *Freedom to Learn*, (Rogers, 1969).

So I poured myself into re-organizing my French classes, into the collaborative style—teaching and creating the curriculum conjointly with the students. I described this later in a chapter titled 'Grammar and Growth: The French Connection' which eventually appeared in the second edition of *Freedom to Learn for the '80s* (Rogers, 1983) in the USA. In addition, I was part of our Social Studies team where, we made similar transformations as five of us team-taught together—the students teaching with us. We brought in controversial figures of the era as guest lecturers—peace activists, black movement leaders, political spokespersons, ecologists, etc., to enliven the themes. Back in the French classes we often spoke about these same themes, together developing vocabulary appropriate to the topic at hand and, in that way, merging the two courses.

I began to see that this fresh approach to learning/teaching really worked brilliantly, liberating student creativity more than I had ever hoped or imagined possible. One day after finishing reading *Carl Rogers on Encounter Groups*, (Rogers, 1970) and *Freedom to Learn*, (Rogers, 1969) I impetuously wrote Dr Rogers a letter to tell him of our innovations based on his work. He wrote back to me, inviting me to La Jolla to speak personally with him about this work I was doing in the classroom. After our first phone conversation (me all aflutter, he empathically inviting me to relax, saying that he understood I might be a bit nervous, but that he did truly want to hear what I had to say!), I went home exhilarated and wrote the paper he suggested I write, which later appeared as the chapter mentioned above.

MEETING CARL—THE TURNING POINT

By then separated and divorcing, I returned to La Jolla that summer at the end of the school year, at Carl's invitation, and attended the famous encounter group session called the 'La Jolla Program'. This revolutionary encounter group, with little or no structure as such, was held for three weeks every summer at the University of California San Diego campus, under the auspices of the Center for Studies of the Person. The following summer I returned to the program as an invited staff facilitator, and within the next year I had fallen in love with a CSP member, moved to San Diego to be with him in 1973, began my doctorate in 1974, was elected an 'official' member of CSP in 1975, and as we say, the rest is history.

From this history and many other rich experiences in the years that followed, there are dozens of incidents that I might cite of my experiences working side by side with Carl in numerous contexts and countries around the world. However, I would like to share here only one or two significant ones that are most applicable to this particular book on feminism and the Person-Centered Approach.

WOMEN, FEMINISM AND ROGERS

In relation to the importance of women in helping Carl move in the direction of more explicitly political social actions and gender awareness/consciousness-raising, there were several key women who acted as catalysts to Carl's education in his evolution as a feminist (although he may not have used that term himself). Also important was an uneasy interaction which took place between Carl and me and many others as part of the Peace Project work, and a memo and conversation between us that followed as a result. Similar to his theory of psychological change, as he grew older Carl continued to develop as a person and once again demonstrated his on-going and amazing capacity for growth and change throughout his life, right up to his last days at 85 years old.

RUST, AUSTRIA, PEACE CONFERENCE INCIDENT

Shortly after returning from the Rust, Austria meeting on peace in Central America, held in 1985, and with some time to recover from it all, Carl and I had an important private conversation in my office as a result of a long and unhappy personal memo I had sent to him about an incident that had taken place in Rust at the end of the conference. At that final meeting in Austria, Carl had generously thanked everyone in the various staff groups: facilitation, research, site organization, translation and administration, whether in California, the University for Peace in Costa Rica, or from Austria. He also thanked the courageous political and lay leaders who had joined in this historic event. During Carl's closing remarks, Maria Villas-Boas Bowen, (another anchor on the Peace

Project staff and great sister, feminist and friend to me for years until her sadly too-early death), looked over at me as I was going paler and paler, and then red with astonishment. Carl had failed to mention my name. I was the co-founder and co-director with him of the Peace Project itself, and he had thanked everyone who had worked so hard to bring about this highly risky and revolutionary event, except me.

Suddenly Maria, stunned and angry herself, said aloud to the entire gathering of diplomats and lay leaders present, 'CARL! WHAT ABOUT GAY!' Carl then said, 'Oh, yes and Gay Swenson, of course, for all her hard work as *Coordinator* of the project'. I was crushed, angry, hurt and humiliated, and felt a deep disappointment and sadness. I held back tears with great difficulty. At that moment I felt I had become essentially the project secretary and an after-thought in the eyes of most of the key political and lay attendees present. I feared it would take me weeks and months to undo that role reduction/ perception, and to move forward with many of them in our follow-up efforts to continue the peace work in Central America, not to mention South Africa, the Soviet Union and/ or Israel/Palestine then anticipated as the next venues for similar conferences.

THE MEMO: ITS MEANING FOR ME AND FOR FEMINISTS

Back home in La Jolla, when I could get my head and heart back together enough to be clear, and when Carl recovered fully from the demands of this huge event, (and from the pneumonia he had acquired in Austria), I wrote a long personal memo to him. As I remember (it is now in the Humanistic Archives in UC Santa Barbara along with other CSP files), I wrote about my need to feel empowered as a woman in particular in my daily work with important political and lay leaders. When he either did not acknowledge my role and work as Co-Director when speaking about the project, or redefined or renamed my role to that of a secretarial, coordinator or administrative position, I said that I would not be heard as an equal by these mostly male leaders. Particularly since I was a woman working with many high-level Washington and Latin American male political persons on this project involving Central America, my credibility with them depended a great deal on the attitude Carl conveyed about our working relationship as Co-Directors, regardless of my own clear competence and abilities.

I was particularly concerned about the last community meeting at the Rust conference, where the issue came to a head so obviously for me. I wrote I was more than puzzled—I was hurt deeply as well by what had happened, and I wanted to know what it meant to Carl personally that he forgot to include me in his closing remarks without a reminder from Maria—not coincidentally another woman staff member. Since that gathering in itself was the apex of all our joint work together over many years, and the stepping-off point for future work in other crisis areas of the world, I began to even question in myself whether I could go forward with the work at the same level of intense involvement as before.

I want to be very clear here, and say that there was never *any* question in my or anyone's mind that Carl was *the* essential and primary reason that people responded to this whole peace project. It was based on the huge reservoir of trust and respect created by his life-long body of work, personal congruence and character. However, I was particularly saddened, angry, hurt and confused that Carl himself knew, yet did not acknowledge publicly at that important moment, that I had catalyzed and led the Peace Project's creation with him from the very beginning, and then directed and initiated the many complicated logistics and connections across three continents that led up to the actual peace conference itself. I achieved this with the constant help of our incredible team, of course, and then switched hats once again and co-facilitated one of the four small groups of the diplomats, as did each of us.

I need to say this in order that the reader can understand why the incident stung so deeply, prompting my personal note to Carl and our ensuing private conversation at the Peace Project office at CSP later. What follows is my recollection of our conversation some 20 years later. It is not verbatim, but is rather the essence of our dialogue. Hopefully it conveys the richness of Carl's being, and his ever-present ability to incorporate new information and learn and change from it.

OUR CONVERSATION

Sitting on the couch in the small airy office, Carl immediately apologized very sincerely for forgetting to include me in his many acknowledgments and appreciations at the Rust meeting. He understood how that must have hurt. He could not explain the lapse, he said. Pausing a bit, he seemed very thoughtful for a few moments, very quiet, and then said that he could think of only one thing that might have prompted that lapse— besides his being pretty exhausted and ill with emerging pneumonia at that last meeting. Carl said that he knew he had often noted over the years being uneasy with some of our strong styles when working with, and relating to, highly verbal and assertive women such as me, his daughter Natalie, his wife Helen, Maureen O'Hara and Maria Villas-Boas Bowen, for example. But more importantly, he said, he had also learned so much from each one of us, and maybe didn't say that enough to us, because he did value those strengths deeply in each of us, together with our insights, intelligence and the many contributions we each brought to his family life and our conjoint work together. He said he was very grateful for each of us as colleagues and family and friends, and how much we had each enlightened him and helped him grow personally, particularly regarding feminism, equality and spiritual dimensions of the work. I was touched deeply hearing this from Carl, as he seemed congruently self-aware and self-examining as he explored this as a possible factor in his lapse, without making it an excuse. It was an important moment in our dialogue and our relationship, and very helpful and healing for us both. Yet, I still felt that was not the whole picture somehow for Carl about me in particular, and I said so.

I told him I knew that it was true that I, for one, had often not been so easy to work with on many issues and teams and programs over the years at CSP. I said that while I was admittedly pretty bright and creative, and I knew that he and others appreciated that about me. I also knew, however, that I was often very outspoken and quite righteous about my perspectives when I had some strong objections to issues, people or practices on various teams we designed, developed and worked on locally at CSP and internationally. I realized that that was sometimes very hard on my colleagues. I said all this to Carl to acknowledge my own piece of the puzzle we were trying to understand together. What is important is that this open sharing and genuineness on both our parts that day at the office once again gave me heart about our approach, our values and our effort to live it out together in work that was so meaningful to both of us.

CARL'S CELEBRATED CONGRUENCE

After that conversation in my office, throughout the following year Carl and I met or spoke together nearly daily about the work. We continued to meet weekly (and monthly with the entire Peace Project team) to seek more grants from foundations, make plans to hold other political gatherings and coordinate all the follow-up programs in South Africa, Russia, Central America and perhaps Israel/Palestine, under the aegis of the Peace Project, Carl 'walked his talk' consistently with me as his colleague. He was most diligent in recognizing me verbally in key situations and at all the many public events where we were speaking together about our peace work, during what came to be the final year of his life.

I am deeply grateful for this conscious effort on his part. However, I was even more profoundly grateful for, and awed by, another of his essential qualities—his congruence. It was the fact that after reading his liberating words so many years before, initially idolizing him, and then sharing ideas with him as a colleague, I discovered the happy truth throughout the years, again and again, that, yes, here was a man who in his life actually did what he wrote about. He listened, he truly heard and understood, he respected, he prized, he self-explored, genuinely sharing himself and his own feelings. And then he changed, and by example helped others to change with him in the process. He was this way to the end, always evidencing the capacity for growth and transformation that his theory itself embodied. He was indeed, as in the title of his chapter in *A Way of Being* (Rogers, 1980), 'growing older, older and growing'.

With all my own personal limitations, good gifts and talents blended together, I know that Carl deeply appreciated me for my own congruence, especially as I learned to express it more appropriately! Over many years, we shared lots of fun and light times together and co-created numerous high risk and demanding events with others, as did so many of his colleagues, who may now be reading this. He supported me immeasurably in intangible ways, and encouraged me professionally by his constant participation in the 'Living Now' program and other teams we created at CSP. In a beautiful and lengthy letter of recommendation, to use for wherever I may wish to work in the future, I was touched by his wide-ranging and sincere acknowledgments of my work and person. He was always there for me empathically during grievously sad times of change and loss. He was enormously generous to me in countless other ways over many years as teacher, colleague, friend and family. But these are other stories for other times and places.

In sum, it is clear to me that I found the mentor, male model and surrogate father and grandfather that I did not have, and which a burgeoning feminist needs and deserves to become her better self. Moreover, I like knowing that he believed he had become a more complete and better man, therapist and yes, feminist, from what he had learned from his own birth daughter, his wife of 50 years, and from his many spiritual daughters as well. I am infinitely and ever grateful for being one among many of them.

A FINAL NOTE

And so I end this chapter on a light note, with Carl's own words from a sweet handwritten short letter dated January 18, 1987, just two weeks before his death on February 4th. It was in response to the well-attended beautiful public 85th birthday celebration and Peace Project fundraising event that I and other CSP colleagues organized for him in December, (which was filmed and can be seen in its entirety on video). While this is only one of many notes from him over the years, I offer this one in particular to highlight another form of his generous spirit. My eyes tear up a little reading it again and seeing his familiar handwriting, yet happily so, because I realize once again what an unbelievable, life-changing privilege and blessing it was to have had this amazing man catalyze my life's work, and help me to find my own truer self, my better abilities to love and to contribute something to life while I am still on this blessed and wounded planet.

As Carl did for me, my hope is that by my writing this rather personal historical chapter, and through the brilliant theoretical chapters in this volume written by others of his colleagues and students, more change will come. Together, our voices and values may encourage younger women and men of this, and following generations, in their own search for their 'paths with heart' and their sense of themselves. I also hope very much that they will find en route their own mentors and mentresses in the quest for peace, justice and equality between men and women around the globe.

> Dear Gay, (emphases Carl's)
> I don't feel I have ever properly thanked you for all the work you did to make the 'Celebration' on December 22 such a success.
>
> It was no secret that I was very ambivalent about the event beforehand, but I want to say that I thoroughly enjoyed it, was deeply touched by all the tributes, and am grateful to you for having invested so much of yourself in it. Thanks!
>
> I also appreciate *very* much your continuing dedication to the Peace Project. You have certainly done far more than anyone could have

asked you to do. If we *do* get funds, if we are able to again move ahead into important projects, it will be in large measure due to *you*. I am grateful to you for that.

Only one request—*please* take some of the Celebration money to pay yourself a living wage! If an order from me would help make it official, I'll be delighted to give it.

With much gratitude,

Carl

How whimsical, paradoxical and liberating for us all that the final written words of Carl cited here included an order!

REFERENCES

Rogers, CR (1969) *Freedom to Learn: A view of what education might become.* Constable, OH: Charles E Merrill.

Rogers, CR (1970) *Carl Rogers on Encounter Groups.* New York: Harper and Row.

Rogers, CR (1980) *A Way of Being.* Boston: Houghton Mifflin.

Rogers, CR (1983) *Freedom to Learn for the 80s.* Columbus, OH: Charles E Merrill.

Rogers, CR (1986) The Rust workshop: A personal overview. *Journal of Humanistic Psychology, 26*(3): 23–45 and in H Kirschenbaum and VL Henderson (eds) (1989) *The Carl Rogers Reader.* Boston: Houghton Mifflin, pp. 457–77.

Rogers, N (1980) *Emerging Woman: A decade of midlife transitions.* Point Reyes Station: Personal Press. Reprinted in the UK (1995) Ross-on-Wye: PCCS Books.

AN INTERVIEW WITH DR MAUREEN O'HARA: A PIONEER PERSON-CENTRED THERAPIST AND FEMINIST REFLECTS ON 30 YEARS OF PROCESS AND PROGRESS

MAUREEN O'HARA IS INTERVIEWED BY GILLIAN PROCTOR

Q: Which were you first: feminist or person-centred?

Oh, definitely person-centred but the timing was very close. I was a scientist in the UK before I went to the US, so I wasn't really interested in social sciences at all. I got interested in psychology when I went to the US to accept a teaching job in 1969 and very quickly thereafter got introduced to feminism. I was teaching biology at an American college where there was a very hot group, or cell, of women scholars who were very feminist. I started working with client-centred work in about 1970, using student-centred pedagogy in my classes. Right from the very beginning, I could see how what these feminist women were saying was both related to what I was working with in PCA but also different.

Q: What was it about each of them that attracted you?

With person-centred work, it was actually student-centred education I was interested in, because I was a teacher and I was teaching a course in human sexuality. We wanted a pedagogy that would privilege and honour the specific subjectivity of the people in the class, because at that time there was a tremendous amount of work that had been written about sexuality but always from the objectivist point of view. Peoples' own subjective experiences were not figuring at all in the literature. So when we began our work, our classes, it was very clear to us that the real wisdom about sexuality was to be found in the subjective experience of the people who were struggling to develop their own sexual lives, their own sexual identity. What attracted me about PCA was that here was a psychological position and a pedagogical position that began with the subjective point of view of the client or the student. It was perfect for what we were interested in doing. Beyond that there was the notion that you could trust the inherent human impulse to grow, the impulse to self-liberate, the impulse to self-heal—all of those basic impulses towards health and wholeness that were core to our pedagogy. What seemed so revolutionary was the idea that you didn't have to be making an intervention from the outside; you could work directly from the inside. Very quickly, working in the sexuality arena, we got into the question of women's identity and gay and lesbian identity. So it was a natural transfer of the theory from PCA into working with women and sexual minorities as they were trying to define their identity and define their subjectivity. So I wasn't really interested in person-centred work as a therapy at that time but really interested in it as pedagogy.

Q: And once you'd got into both feminism and PCA, how did they influence your teaching?

Well, the people that were raising questions about gender and questions about sexuality, about relationships and power in relationships, were mostly feminists, people of colour, and sexual minorities—people who were either on the societal margins, or were women and so were treated as if they were on the margin. It was very clear very quickly that my work as a PC practitioner was going to be greatly improved and deepened by a reference to this whole other discourse that was going on in gender studies and in women's studies. So very early I was in dialogue with the feminists on campus. There was much to dialogue about. This was because on the one hand Rogers was being accused by the feminists of being sort of the epitome of the white male individualist position. Feminists pointed out how basic PCA theory and practice was so very much aligned with twentieth century individualism. But on the other hand, because Rogers was such a champion of the subjective, he really did believe that if you created the right conditions to nurture the subjectivity of a person, it really didn't matter whether the person was female or male. He believed that because their unique subjectivity would emerge, whether a male or female, it would emerge in their own voice.

So to begin with I was a bit reluctant to embrace a feminist analysis, because it seemed like Rogers' analysis was already big enough to allow space for a subjectivity that was both essentially human *and* gendered. But the fact of the matter was that that wasn't the conversation that was going on. I could agree with the argument made in opposition to questions coming from feminists as to how there was no barrier to considerations of gender, but there was no conversation going on within PCA circles about feminism at that time.

When I went to La Jolla to work with Carl Rogers in 1973, there was a women's group that was meeting at the Center for Studies of the Person. I joined the group. Many of the men at CSP could not understand why there was any necessity for a women's group. They saw it as hostile, and I suppose it was. I mean there were times when it was really bitter, and part of the bitterness had to do with the absolute denial on the part of the men of the fact that women's situation was any different from theirs. And to this day, there are people in that circle who deny the existence of forces at the group level—societal forces—as being relevant variables, and see everything as explainable in terms of the individual's own capacity to be their own person.

So to begin with, I personally believed, as the men did, that the Person-Centred position was big enough to allow for all the different subjectivities, but I gradually began to see things through a more feminist lens. It gradually became clear to me that in a world where the playing field is not level for men and women, if you treat men and women the same way, then you're actually privileging the white male voice. This is because in a world where many women are silenced not for personal reasons but because of structural forces, mens' are the visible voices, or better still the audible voices. If you don't recognise that in a gendered world, which ours is, women are situated differently and they are historically developing their subjectivity against a context which has denied their subjectivity, if you don't recognise that fundamental dynamic, then you really don't see women's situation at all. It was the feminists in my life that helped me to understand that. Since then I've really made no distinction between feminism and PCA because for me, being a woman and being a PCA practitioner and theoretician *and* being a feminist, my PCA position is a feminist position.

Q: Could you say any more about how your women's group influenced Carl Rogers and PCA at that time?

Well, I have to say that I think Carl was much more open to the ideas that were surfacing from the women's group than many of the men that he was working with at that time. Because Carl *really* did, in a *profound* way, listen to the person he was talking to, and heard more than just the individual speaking. He didn't really have a very good theory for explaining what he was hearing, but he did hear, so when the women started to speak about these issues—and Natalie, his daughter was very influential in this regard too—he began to open up to the idea that there was something missing in the PCA writings that was particularly of concern to women. In particular, he began to see more clearly such social phenomena as racism and sexism, and began to understand that women were speaking out of a position of being disempowered, not *only* as individuals but also as a class of individuals. And he began to get it. It wasn't easy for him because he was so deeply rooted in that individualistic, humanistic existential position. But being the superb listener that he was, it wasn't hard to convince him that if these women who he respected and cared about were bringing something to him, then he'd better pay attention. And he did.

I think he did so more so than the men of the generation right below him, and I think in some ways they had more to lose, because they were still at the stage of their life and careers when women were asking for positions that would push them out. So they were understandably more resistant than Carl was.

Q: So you saw him changing in response to what you were saying?

Oh yes, absolutely. To begin with, learning just simple things such as, if four or five men had spoken in a row in a group, the next person that he would turn to, and look to see if they would say anything, would be a woman. He wouldn't necessarily make an observational comment like 'It looks like four of the last five speakers have been men, so wouldn't it be nice to hear from some of the women.' The women would do that. I certainly would, and Natalie and Maria (Bowen) would, but he did the equivalent, which was to make sure that if a woman was talking she wasn't going to get interrupted. If she did let herself get interrupted, he would go back and would say, 'I see you kind of got shut down there.' That pattern of intervention was clearly influenced by the way in which the women colleagues were pointing out to him the ways in which women in groups were routinely being silenced or weren't speaking up. Natalie was fabulous in that regard because she was constantly on patrol to make sure that if there was a mixed group of men and women, that the men weren't doing all the talking. Carl listened to that and paid attention.

Q: And at that time were there feminists that were influenced by PCA?
Well, it's interesting. I've tried to think about this because much of the feminism that I was reading in the early days I would have called humanistic feminism in the sense that they were arguing from the point of view that everybody struggles. The existential challenge to become authentic and to realise your own possibilities are difficult for all people—to become a person is a struggle for everybody. For women, the struggle is based also on the fact that women have been silenced and marginalised, but essentially the struggle was a human struggle. But sometime in the 1980s in the United States, feminism took on two different voices, which I think took it away from PCA. One of these was a very strong form of social constructivism, or deconstructivist position, that really to a very large degree, eliminated the individual as a conscious agent. This position saw the 'self' or the 'individual' as a construction of the social situation in which they operated. The other thing that happened was a rise in a women's psychology that focused on women as an oppressed group and emphasised 'woman as victim'. There was so much emphasis on victim psychology that again I think the empowering piece of PCA really became a problem for many of the feminist counsellors. For example, there was the PCA notion that you don't help the client, because the client has the resources within themselves to struggle and realise their own way through. For many women's counsellors, that was considered to be a kind of 'withholding'. They argued that because of their victimisation, women needed more active help, active intervention. So I think that those folks really saw the PCA position as sort of wimpy, not fierce enough, not challenging enough of the status quo. This was particularly true with those feminists that had their own agenda for women. That agenda was to mobilise women's rage, you know, to fight back. That didn't go together very well with a PCA position that in a very deep way said to women that it's not the counsellor's business what path you take. The PCA message is: 'What my business as a therapist is, is creating the conditions for you to discover what path you are going to take.' So there was a contradiction between a feminism that was quite activist with an agenda of women having specific new kinds of rights, versus a classical client-centred position which was that the kind of life a client chooses is for them to work out.

Q: So they started out close together and then they diverged?
Absolutely. It started out as more of a generic humanism, and that generic humanist feminist voice still exists by the way, but it was not the most noticeable voice of feminism, in the States anyway, in the eighties and into the nineties. The other thing that happened—and this is my personal piece of the story—is that I began to see that there was something amiss for women in some of the basic notions of the humanistic psychology position. In particular I began to be troubled by the idea that life is a journey from a dependency to independence, and autonomy is a big deal. I came to realise that for women, autonomy defined in that way really isn't all that appealing. Women see their lives much more relationally; they see their lives much more in terms of the people that they're connected to, the groups that they belong to, the families that they belong to, the relationships that they belong to. For many women, identity, authenticity and autonomy are seen from within a relationship context.

I think that is a new idea for PCA and I think it's a better idea. In the mid-eighties, I began to see relational ideas, such as those of the women at the Stone Center for Women's Psychology at Wellesley College, the interpersonal psychology of Harry Stack Sullivan and some of the systems gestalt ideas, as adding something to PCA that I'd always felt it missed. Let me give you an example. In a community group in a Person-Centered Approach workshop, for instance, a women might start to speak up about something that involved a roommate. Typically she'd say something like 'Well, we've been thinking'. Almost routinely, one of the men would jump all over her and say 'No! Would you speak for yourself?' or 'Maybe you could speak for yourself.' Well, she was speaking for herself, but a self that belonged to a relational 'we'. But such a relational concept of self was not part of the orthodoxy of the person-centred or humanistic position. In the humanistic vision (and for that matter of Eurocentric psychology in general) the mature person is one who is completely autonomous—who does not look to others for identity and direction. I think the error here is that to be self-healing doesn't mean that you do it by yourself. It simply means that you are the architect or the author of your healing story, but it doesn't mean that the story is a single person story. So I have really become interested in the incorporation from women's psychology, feminist studies and women's studies in general, of the whole notion that women define themselves and develop their sense of identity—even their sense of reality—largely through their important connections and relationships. For women the voice of the self is reflective of context and relationship.

Q: That's the current challenge for PCA?
Yes, I think so. I think there is still something of a battle. You get into an encounter group and there will be people who really see the story as a 'we' story and who have some awareness of forces and movements that are a product of the relational field. And there will be others who see a group as a collection of 'I's' and see what we refer

63

to as 'we' as nothing more than a kind of virtual emergence at best. But through my work at the social level, and through more feminist, constructivist and relational frames, I'm much more willing to acknowledge that relationships have a reality, that it is not merely the sum of the parts; that the relationship *is* an entity that has its own voice. It has its own effects on its participants, and it has reality status with the rest of the world. So I think that PCA needs an elaboration of some new theory that can allow for a conversation about relationships, about groups and families, and about participation within larger wholes of communities. I think that women have brought that conversation to PCA and I think it's really strengthening it as a psychology as well.

Q: At the time you were teaching, how did each approach influence your work?

I was a university professor in the seventies. As part of my doctoral studies—which Carl was directing, in his non-directive way—I went out to California. At that point, I started working directly with Carl and the Person-Centered Approach team. I left the university and was making a living working as a trainer, and as a writer.

I wasn't doing therapy at that time, although before I went to California, I had received psychotherapy training at the Gestalt Institute of Cleveland and in an internship program in Ohio. I think I started seeing individual clients in psychotherapy in the late seventies. I began doing these large PCA groups with Carl. We started in '74 and for the next decade I was literally doing just that work. I went to Brazil with Carl in '77 and from then on for about another eight years I was literally in Brazil six months of the year and in the United States six months of the year. Almost all the work I did was psychotherapy and group process facilitation training. This work was completely freelance and independent. My early love was Gestalt Therapy, but when I went out to California, I was connecting more with PCA. In reality, though, my work has always really been a combination of the two. My approach has always had the therapist more engaged in the relationship. I think that is probably why I was so interested in the new ideas from the Stone Center, and women's psychology and so on. Gestalt work was much more relational in that sense—I am not speaking about the Fritz Perls type of Gestalt therapy—the kind of therapist-centred work that you see on the Gloria film, for instance, but the Cleveland Gestalt Institute approach. Their style has always been much more relations, systems focused and drew heavily on the work of Kurt Lewin, the Tavistock Institute and the National Training Labs. So I got invited to join a Gestalt institute in San Diego as a faculty member. That was when I realised that I was interested in learning how to be a psychotherapist for individuals. At that point I decided to do a lot more training, both as a client-centred therapist and also as a Gestalt therapist. I was also training other people in Brazil and in Latin America and in the US. I wasn't working in the university at all until, I guess it was about 1984. I decided I didn't want to commute to Brazil anymore because it was beginning to be very draining and was affecting my home life too much. It was then that I got a job at San Diego State University teaching in the Women's Studies Department teaching the psychology of women.

Q: Can I just go back a bit? Did feminism influence your training work at that time?

Oh yes. But it was different in Brazil, because the Brazilian situation was quite different from North America or Europe. Feminism was very much a minority position. In fact, psychology in Brazil at that time was still dominated very heavily by the psychoanalysts. So women still believed that feminism was a protest against femininity and that the feminists were analysed as being neurotic. They were still coming out of that Freudian point of view, so we had to go very carefully with feminism in Brazil. In addition to that, it was a very macho society at that time. There was one occasion when we were doing a women's group in a building in Brasilia where there was one of the women in the group who was a psychiatrist. Her husband had forbidden her to go to the group, because he thought these American feminists were coming to destroy Brazilian family life. She came to the group anyway. When we finished the work one afternoon, we came down in the elevator and he was waiting in the lobby with a revolver. He was pointing the revolver at her and threatening to kill her. And this was when I realised what we were risking. It was pretty obvious by this point that feminism in Brazil was much more threatening than it was in the States by that time.

In our work in Brazil *so much* of the pain that we were seeing in the groups and with clients was related to women's subordination—which was abject in places. Very wealthy women had *zero* power—lots of money, servants, lots of privileges in many ways and *absolutely* no power. No power. Women in Brazil at that time could still be beaten to within an inch of their lives if they refused their husbands sex. Women were having plastic surgery to reconstruct their hymens so they would seem like virgins when they got married. A man was acquitted of the murder of his wife because she had an adulterous affair and the judge had decided that no man should be expected to tolerate such a thing and ruled it was justifiable homicide. So feminism was very hot. We were working during very difficult times in Brazil, but the work was immensely important.

I look back now at the women we worked with at that time and see that many of them are now in leadership positions. Brazilian feminism is real and it's powerful, and it goes all way through the society. So I feel we made a contribution, actually. We made a contribution in a very stealthy way because we weren't speaking about what we were doing as feminism. We were speaking about it in the language of 'finding one's own voice'. The metaphor of voice is very important to Brazilians, largely because of Paulo Freire's work helping illiterate people find their voice. So we used a lot of his work to frame what we were doing, so in answer to your question, feminism was very important for me at that time.

Q: And then you went back to university in '84?

Yes, I began teaching at San Diego State University where I taught Psychology of Women in the Women's Studies Department. That was when I really got deeply into the other versions of feminist psychology, such as the Lacanian, object relations, women's psychoanalytic theory of such writers as Jessica Benjamin, Dorothy Dinnerstein, Carol Gilligan, Mary Belenky, Julia Kristeva and Luce Irigaray and all those brilliant women. I had to teach about them because we had to cover the range of female psychological theorists. We also had to cover the cognitive behavioural models and the existential humanistic and the feminist therapies in general, so I had to completely immerse myself in all the different ways that women's reality was being described and approached. Although I learned a great deal from the works of these women, I never got converted away from the more humanistic position because I still think it brings something more to the conversation. I think it brings a consideration of what men and women have in common. Which I think is very important. To my mind, it's just as bad to leave out what we have in common as it is to leave out what we have that's different. So I've always felt lucky about having both humanistic and feminist perspectives. I can both see women's and men's reality through a gender lens and that brings one set of understandings. Or alternatively I can see it through the humanistic lens that brings another set of understandings. Beyond that you can look through a class lens which brings us something else. So the more lenses you have, the fuller picture you have of what these women's stories are really like.

Q: How do you see gender differences, in terms of being socially constructed or biological?

I don't think that it is useful to think in 'either-or' terms here. If you look at things through the biological lens, there are lots of ways in which men and women are quite the same and there's lots of ways in which men and women are quite different. And I think that realistically we have to take into account the ways in which men and women are different biologically. But the problem is that most of those differences don't seem to account for the societal differences that we have. There are women who can physically match what a goodly proportion of men can actually do and vice versa so the differences that we have in society can't really be explained by biological differences. But of course there are biological differences. We are just beginning to sort through the implications of these biological differences. When I was first involved in feminism, we couldn't even speak about any biological basis for difference. We couldn't even admit that there were biological differences because it was the era when all reality was deemed socially constructed, so to speak about biological differences was regressive or retrograde in terms of theory. I think that level of hard-core social constructivism has passed. I think people are willing to admit now that as the lower boundary conditions we wouldn't expect biology to have no affect at all, but we shouldn't overestimate the effects either. We need to figure out what effects are relevant and what effects are not relevant. It is important to evaluate biological claims in terms of relevant social context. I think it's very relevant to many areas of women's lives that women have children. But not all women have children. So for women who don't have children, it's irrelevant except that insofar as they're going to be evaluated in terms of women who do. But to ignore the reality that for the majority of women their lives are *profoundly* constructed in terms of their capacity to have children and raise children, which we did in the 1970s, well, clearly that's nonsense. It is a relevant variable both in terms of how and why women are oppressed, but also how and why women have capacities that are immensely valuable to society. But I think it's early days for being able to extrapolate from the biological story to the psychological story to the sociological story. I actually think that one of the challenges for all theory in the social sciences right now is developing theory that can handle the multi-levelled holistic picture that neither reduces everything to biology nor ignores biology. We need social theory that doesn't reduce everything to social forces but can hold multiple perspectives in mind and can account for the relationships among levels of organisation.

Q: How do both approaches affect you in your current position as president of a graduate university?

I think that being in a position of relative power, as the President and CEO of Saybrook Graduate School in San Francisco, it's very important for me to keep my feminist eyes open to how easily it is to abuse power. I think if you've been raised to think you're in some historically disempowered class that doesn't have power, whether it's working class, or a woman or whatever, it's sometimes difficult to see that once you have power, the ways you could abuse it. So one of the things my feminist perspective brings is that it has made me work very hard to stay alert to the ways in which power is so easy to abuse. I do that by asking women I trust to keep me honest.

On the other hand though, I do have the power to make sure that Saybrook walks its talk in terms of gender so when I've got a hiring decision to make, I put it in the foreground. I say, 'Well, you know, what kind of a balance do we have here? Do we have the balance we want? Do we have the right voices around this table? Do we have, if we're dealing with an issue such as psychological services for homeless people say, do we have the right voices in the conversation, because if they're all male voices, we don't. If they are only middle class, we don't have breadth either. Or if they're only academics, we don't. So part of my consciousness-raising over the years to the importance of not having one group speak for another and to have each person's subjectivity involved in crafting a solution to a particular challenge, I think that's something I pay attention to every day. I really do.

For me the issue is diversity and balance, and I feel that we have been very successful in this at Saybrook. My desire for diversity and inclusivity extends to making sure that no one is excluded. Because I've been a feminist all these years, and I've done so much work in all of my career in staying aware of sexism, staying aware of gender bias and so on, and taking steps to rectify it, when I see women taking a very 'politically correct' position and stifling male voices, or stifling white voices in the name of feminism, or taking a victim position when they're not actually being victimised and may even have more power than many of the men around, then I won't let that pass either. I'm very sensitive to that too. I think that's what I'm learning from my work as a leader. Power, when you have it, and wherever it comes from, is easy to misuse. And that doesn't change just because you come from a traditionally marginalised class. If you're no longer struggling to come out of marginalisation and you actually have power, then you're just as vulnerable to misusing it as anybody is. So I think part of what I can do, is I can actually hold on to the humanistic balance whilst we also make space around the table for whatever voices need to be there for whatever we're working on. I think this sensitivity actually influences me all the time.

There are ways in which being a woman and being a leader at this point is a new kind of privilege. For instance, I now get invited to participate in things that I wouldn't have been invited to participate in 25 years ago, *because* I'm a woman. More recently, since I became a university president, I often get included in important committees and task forces that make it possible for me to make a real difference at policy levels. That's the space that we've opened up as feminists.

We've opened up spaces for women like me to be at the table with people who make real decisions. But of course, that's an immense responsibility because once you're there, you have to be, I think, super-aware. First of all of how we got there— of all the sacrifices that people have made along the way to open up spaces for women in positions of power. But you also, I think, have to be aware that we have to do it differently. If we just go into those positions of power and do it the same way as before, the way that everybody else has always done it, the only thing that changes is the gender of the players, but the basic unfair game stays the same. So part of what I bring to my work is the realisation that I want to change the game.

I want a game that is not about power, not about hierarchy, not about exploiting one person's life to advance somebody else, but is a game that is about all benefiting. I think this value comes out of that relational notion I spoke of earlier. As I see it, we all have to come along together. It's a different way of being in power. I believe that this is what we must do now that women and minorities are gaining access to the corridors of power. If we just repopulate the same hierarchical system but this time with women, well we really won't see a difference. People will still get disenfranchised, they will still get ripped off, they will still get silenced, only now they're just getting silenced by powerful women instead of powerful men. It doesn't seem like we've gotten very far if that's where we end up.

Q: So everyone has to get to the top together?
I think it's not a top and bottom issue. I think it's more that you have to reconstrue the game or the work of human emancipation to be one about the quality of one's

life rather than about how much money you make or what status you have. Fulfilment has to be more intrinsic, which brings me back to the basic PCA position. I suppose that despite all the influence on me from theory and experience, I do have still that older humanistic 'romantic' position that what really counts is the unique inner subjectivity of each person and that this must be nurtured so that it can flower.

ON BECOMING AN ACTIVIST

ROSEMARY HOPKINS

And the day came when the risk it took to remain tight inside the bud was more painful than the risk it took to blossom.

Anaïs Nin (1903–1977)

For more than 60 years I have travelled literally and figuratively, living in and experiencing the different cultures of South Africa, Canada and Great Britain. My journey in the last 10 years, during which I trained and practised in the Person-Centred Approach, is the focus of this story.

Within a week of completing my counselling diploma, I was sitting in a circle of some 40 people, above Loch Voil, by Balquidder, in the Scottish Highlands. There were flags of rainbow colours flying at our backs, while in front of us blazed a huge fire as we passed the 'talking stick' and 'spoke our truth'. I was part of an Ehama medicine ceremony based on Native American teachings of the Four Shields of Balance,[1] and I was to discover in that weekend what it is to walk in beauty, to honour and be honoured as a woman, to delight in the Magical Child in me, and to celebrate the Warrior in me.

So when a Gestalt-trained therapist friend invited me a few months later to join an all-women programme called *Celebrating Women*, based on the work of Angeles Arrien (1993), I felt ready. Over the course of a year, in places of great beauty, I met in me the archetypes of the Warrior, Visionary, Healer and Teacher. I explored and expressed myself in meditation, aikido, dancing, writing, making sounds, speaking and listening. And celebrate I did too—especially the Warrior Woman in me.

I was more familiar with the Healer and Teacher in me in my work as a

---

[1] See <www.ehama.org/ceremony> and
<www.inknowvate.com/inknowvate/ehama_8_ direction_council_configuration.htm>.

counsellor, and previously as a trainer, and I was certainly more focused on *being* than *doing*. This was what had attracted me to the Person-Centred Approach. To be fully present in a relationship, to empathise, accept and be genuine was my aim, and I believed that this was sufficient for change to occur. Discovering the Warrior in me, a sense of my personal power, a sense of being more fully myself, I exposed more of my potential. And this coincided with meeting and marrying a wonderful man who introduced me to a new culture, and also to new opportunities for personal development, in the United States.

So it was that on the morning of 11 September 2001, I was in the United States in the closing circle of the third session of Araña,[2] a women's leadership programme. I still freeze like a rabbit in the headlights when I remember the moment we were told of the attack on the World Trade Centre. All sense of personal power evaporated and for the next six days, before I could be reunited with my family in Scotland, I saw and heard and felt things beyond my imagination. I was in the wrong place; I was separated from my children and granddaughter by an ocean that had never seemed deeper or wider. Yes, I thought of and spoke with my husband, but somehow the mother in me, the woman in me, had ignited.

As the stories unfolded around me, in Washington where I have family, in New York where I would have been that afternoon on my way home, in Pennsylvania where I have friends, the horror of the attacks was displayed over and over on the television in the Georgia home of the dear friend who took in the Araña internationals. I felt remote in my compassion, numb in my fear, suspended in my reality. When I tried to do a moving meditation I fell over. When we four women went to a vigil at the local college, young women gathered round us, in our silence, asking who we were. Yes, it was weird. It was a strange time. I was in an unknown part of me, a part I was to need time to meet and get to know. I was to discover myself as a different person, carrying all I knew before, with all the pieces there, but scattered, and the whole gradually coming together again arranged differently.

As a counsellor I was accustomed to being with adults who had been sexually abused as children, accustomed to people sharing deep pain, fear, and loss of their organismic self. I trusted the Rogerian principles and theory of personality. I truly believed in a person's ability to reclaim her or his intrinsic self. And I believed that I had the intellectual and emotional capacity to hold all of that in relationship with a person—in fact, with several people in the course of each day. I also believed in my capacity to suspend judgement, to hold others in positive regard, not only in the counselling room, but also elsewhere in my life. I believed that I could differentiate between my own process and that of others, that I could offer empathy to myself, as well as to others.

In the weeks after I got home to Scotland, I discovered I did not have the emotional capacity I thought I had, and became overwhelmed by what I heard

---

[2.] Spanish word meaning the female spider, the web-maker.

from clients, overwhelmed by what I heard and saw in the rest of the world, and most frighteningly, overwhelmed by my unidentified feelings which couldn't find a way out. I was lost inside myself.

I stopped counselling and spent time with my daughter and granddaughter and a few women friends. My husband was bewildered as I went to ground like a she-animal seeking my own kind for protection, solace and understanding. As time went on I knew something wasn't adding up. Deep inside, some part of me, the fuse that had been lit at the instant I felt trapped, was beginning to burn more strongly. I was angry, and I felt my anger before I understood it.

And then the November 2001 issue of New Internationalist arrived with its evocative title: *Twin Terrors*. Inside I read the words of Mark Twain, writing about the French Revolution in *A Connecticut Yankee in King Arthur's Court*, and the floodgate opened inside me. I began to flow again. At a deep level, the horror I was feeling had not made sense, or had made half-sense, and I couldn't grasp the missing half until my rage erupted.

> There are two 'Reigns of Terror', if we could but remember and consider it; the one wrought murder in hot passions, the other in heartless cold blood; the one lasted mere months, the other had lasted a thousand years; the one inflicted death upon a thousand persons, the other upon a hundred million; but our shudders are all for the 'horrors' of the ... momentary Terror, so to speak; whereas, what is the horror of swift death by the axe compared with lifelong death from hunger, cold, insult, cruelty and heartbreak? (New Internationalist, 2001)

The New Internationalist listed the deaths from acts of terrorism alongside deaths from 'Enduring Terrors'. The figures showed what I hadn't dared to think, but I knew and didn't have the capacity to feel, understand and believe until then.

> Number of people who died of hunger on 11 September 2001: 24,000*
> Number of children killed by diarrhoea on 11 September 2001: 6,020*
> (New Internationalist, 2001)
> * Based on reports from UNICEF and reputable NGO campaigns on world hunger, and assuming annual deaths were evenly spread.

And each day before, and each day after ...

There were more statistics showing lack of adequate food, safe drinking water, sanitation and education—basic human rights. Statistics that told of prolonged suffering and dying.

And I knew what my rage was about—inhumanity. Terrorism is not the enemy. Inhumanity is the enemy. And I had discovered the conflict I had been carrying inside me, the overwhelming feelings of guilt, shame and rage, that I am part of all of this. I met the terrorist part of me; I met the inhuman part of me. And I knew that I would not rest until I had found ways of making a difference, and that one person at a time in counselling was not enough. I needed to be *doing* more. I needed to find outlets for my rage. If I was to be outraged, I needed to be effective. And yet, in this cacophony of thoughts, I needed and wanted to stay true to my principles. I knew that I needed to have the capacity to feel compassion for the victims of terrorism as well as the victims of enduring terror.

As a South African living outside the apartheid regime since 1960, I had held myself at a safe enough distance from global inequalities and environmental threats—as a supporter rather than an activist. For many years I had been a supporter of Greenpeace, Friends of the Earth, Oxfam, Shelter and other caring non-governmental organisations. Even my longstanding work with Traidcraft in the Fair Trade Movement felt more like support than activism. In person-centred terms, I had never engaged psychologically with the victims or perpetrators of political and corporate dominance, exploitation and violence. I thought that caring and support, making a difference by raising or giving money was enough until I met my rage and outrage, and knew I had opened myself to another way of being in this world.

I could move from supporting the victims, to being active in effecting change in the world. I could stand up *against* violence and injustice as well as *for* peace and justice. The risk was to show up and demonstrate, to step outside the safety of my community and circle of friends and colleagues—my tribe. The greater risk was to remain in dissonance, incongruence and confusion.

I could and would *do* more. I became active in the Campaign Against Arms Trade, Amnesty International, Campaign for Nuclear Disarmament, and read everything I could to understand what was happening in the post-11 September 'War on Terrorism' and to make sense of a world dominated by one superpower. I needed to know why people hated the United States enough to give and take life.

And that was my second revelation. I became acutely aware that I did not respect or trust the world of political and corporate power dominated by men. The women of Afghanistan, victims of the Taliban, were an excuse in the war on Afghanistan. They had prominence as justification for a war on an already devastated country, and once the war was 'over', women's rights were scarcely relevant (Hawthorne and Winter, 2002). I was beginning to understand the masculinity of global politics.

> Globalisation is not an equal or free system. It is raced, classed and gendered. The dominant groups in the global economy are overwhelmingly male, white and privileged. (Mary Mellor, 2003)

Letter writing is private, petition name gathering is more public, and all of this is safe in the company of fellow thinkers and believers, or people who love you despite what they might perceive as crazy ideas. I suspected that if I spoke out, particularly from a feminist standpoint, that if I was fully present, fully accepting of that Warrior part of me, that if I allowed my rage to be fully felt and expressed nonviolently, I would be open to criticism. But that was better than denying myself.

How often I have thought of Rogers and his potatoes in that dark cellar. How often I have drawn courage from that image, that only when we die do we stop reaching for the light. I was going to live in my fullness, and to do that I needed to risk being honest, to risk being different, to risk losing friends. Susan Sontag (2003) speaks of the risk of being different—different to your usual position, different to the position of those around you, and different to their expectations of you. She draws a vivid picture of what it is to step outside your tribe, daring to be unpopular, even unpatriotic, daring to say that lives in other tribes are as valuable as your own.

I had run into ambiguity and complexity. I have valued complexity and chaos in my therapeutic work and believe that to be person-centred implies a willingness to go with, and stay with, whatever is happening in the process, to go where you know you don't know where you are going, but to value and trust the organic nature of that process. I was discovering that being out of step with my tribe left me feeling isolated, and also free to explore—such is the nature of complexity, the both/and!

In the Ehama ceremonies, in the *Celebrating Women* and Araña programmes, I developed a keen sense of and longing for sisterhood. I believed it would be a safe place for me to express myself fully and freely, to give and receive, and to celebrate being part of something bigger than me. I was learning fast and I was learning wide. This was personal and global journeying, and I was meeting many wonderful people challenging the systems. Ironically, I was letting go of directing my searching, of making things happen, and discovering that women were finding me. Women from CND,[3] curious about the South African beaded AIDS ribbon I was wearing, approached me on the train on 15 February 2003—the day that 30 million people walked for peace and against war in 600 cities across the world. Rather than feeling isolated, as I had at first, there seemed more people out there who shared my values, and many of them were women.

Since then, I have walked for peace under the CND banner, stood vigil outside Cornton Vale Women's Prison on the eve of the trial of an activist, joined the blockade at the Trident nuclear submarine base at Faslane, and remembered Hiroshima and Nagasaki in a Peace Garden with them.

However, sisterhood has not turned out to be what I thought it would be— being a member of a comfortable, intimate group. Sisterhood has been more like the coming together of kindred spirits who share similar values, feel safe together, can laugh and cry together, argue and debate together, and feel enriched by this relationship.

This form of sisterhood appeared unexpectedly in the Big Issue[4] in the spring of 2002—an article on Women in Black,[5] Scotland. Beginning in January 1988, a

---

[3.] Campaign for Nuclear Disarmament, see <www.cnduk.org>.

[4.] The *Big Issue in Scotland* is a magazine sold by homeless, or ex-homeless people as a way of making an income.

[5.] Women in Black in the UK and US, see <www.wibs.org.uk>, <www.womeninblack.org.uk> and <www.womeninblack.net>.

small group of Israeli and Palestinian women dressed in black stood vigil in silence once a week in the same place in Jerusalem holding a sign saying 'Stop the Occupation'. Women in Black, now an international network, was inspired by the Madres de la Plaza de Mayo, mothers and grandmothers holding names and photos of the 'disappeared' in Argentina, and by the Black Sash, women who stood silent vigil against apartheid in South Africa.

Remembering my roots, remembering my Warrior woman who stands for clarity and action, remembering my yearning for sisterhood, I found all of these in the solidarity I experience when I stand with Women in Black in Edinburgh. Each week we stand silent vigil for justice and peace, against war. Women sometimes ask how to join Women in Black. The answer is simple: Show up, wearing black. In fact, it was months before I learned the names of the women I stood beside week after week. This quality of sisterhood has surprised me. It is not the comfortable sense of belonging I had yearned for, and yet I go back week after week to stand in visible silence where I feel so alive and authentic.

Peggy Natiello emphasises the importance of person-centred practitioners incorporating their 'personal style and unique personality traits' (Natiello, 2001). I believe that is what I had been doing in searching for a place for my political activism. I needed to be consistent and congruent, to have my activism match who I am, and I needed to be principled. To act on principle, says Susan Sontag (2003) is not about appeasing your conscience, or even being sure that what you are doing will achieve its aim—to act on principle is to act in solidarity with others of similar heart and mind.

Standing in silence on a busy street corner, I can feel powerfully present, in the presence of others who may choose to engage, or not. I recognise in these moments of being fully present, something of the 'transcendental', the 'intuitive' phenomenon that Carl Rogers referred to towards the end of his life as 'presence' (Thorne, 1992). I have felt physically warmed as I stand, and spiritually moved in compassionate contemplation of victims of wars worldwide. I recognise the experience of Alice Walker (1997) who writes of overcoming fear through collective presence in political, cultural and spiritual activism.

> The ongoing task is ... continued development of our capacity to be wholly and authentically present in the world, to abdicate power and control over others ... to tolerate their pain and struggle, and to grow in the exquisitely respectful attitudes of empathy and positive regard. (Natiello, 2001)

I take responsibility for my feelings and actions, for my *power to*, rather than my *power over*, and to the best of my ability to suspend my judgement of the words and actions of others—not easy! The 'others' include fellow activists, supporters and the supported, those who disagree with or don't care about my principles, as well as those I perceive as the cause of my protest. This is the challenge in becoming an activist using a person-centred approach. To hold protagonists for pre-emptive military action in Iraq, for example, in 'positive regard' is an on-going challenge!

Activism is not just *doing* as in protesting, demonstrating, standing vigil. Activism for me, like the Person-Centred Approach, is essentially about having a deep respect for and valuing of humanity, and listening to the stories people tell. These stories are my inspiration, my source of information, and my connection with people, whether it is listening to my 92-year-old aunt who lives her principles of justice and peace for all; whether it is finding the story of the Iroquois women who prevented war by refusing to make moccasins for the tribe's warriors;[6] whether it is spending time with Yehudit Keshet, an Israeli from Jerusalem who co-founded Machsom (Checkpoint) Watch in the Occupied Territories; whether it is reading Barbara Kingsolver's provocative, wide-visioned collection of essays written following 11 September 2001; whether it is discovering the writings of ecofeminist and anti-globalisation activist, Vandana Shiva; whether it is appreciating the efforts of British politician Mo Mowlem reaching out and listening to the people of Northern Ireland; whether it is hearing the strength and humility of Helen Steven on her retirement from the Scottish Centre for Non-Violence which she founded; whether it is meeting the courageous women of Wola Nani (Xhosa, meaning Embrace), an HIV/AIDS support agency in Cape Town, South Africa; or seeing radiant peace in the face of Ngawang Sangdrol, the 26-year-old Buddhist nun recently released from Drapchi Prison in Tibet after 10 years of brutal incarceration.

I could name so many inspiring women—women of courage, patience and passion. I have them being Warrior women for justice; activists for a better world; listeners, talkers, collaborators, creators. I have them being 'Midwives for Change' (Chopra, 2003).

Inspiration intrigues me. It has a serendipitous synchronistic quality to it, an element of readiness to receive, and a mystery that touches me deeply. Inspiration comes to me each week as I stand in visible silence with Women in Black, in sisterhood with Women in Black around the world, in solidarity for peace and justice.

So that has been my journey so far. There is an irony that in a world where women are silenced, where women are the victims of domestic, corporate and political power, I have chosen to stand in silence to demonstrate against this injustice. For me, to not show up as my authentic self would be to yield to my internalised oppression of self-imposed misogyny and self-censorship. I value the freedom I have to express myself fully, and my journey continues with inspiration from many renewable resources. I travel on with passion, curiosity and imagination.

Passion is my treasure. It fuels me and I live myself more fully in my passion.

[6.] *A Message from the Iroquois Women—Moccasin Makers and War Breakers A Call to Action by the Women of the World*, written by Kahn-Tineta Horn, Mohawk Nation—see www.freepeltier.org/call_to_action.htm.

I am aware that others can feel uncomfortable with my intensity and find my reluctance to proselytise confusing. However, I believe I have found a way of becoming a political activist that is consistent with the 'person-centred approach [that] cannot be practiced without passionate presence. It calls for intense awareness, a genuine renunciation of control, and a sense of wonderment and anticipatory attendance' (Natiello, 2001: 155).

My passion is also a celebration of beauty in its natural forms and human creations, a celebration of humanity, of wonder, and of hope.

Curiosity is my self-fertilizer, stimulating growth of knowledge and expansion of awareness, personally and globally. Feminist writers, academics and analysts like Cynthia Enloe and Diana Bell, and women's organisations like RAWA,[7] WLUML[8] and Bat Shalom,[9] encourage feminist curiosity in a world of militarised and masculine foreign policy (Hawthorne and Winter, 2002). The key question women can ask, whether about armaments or military action, ownership of seed or human genes, trade agreements or human rights, is: Who will benefit? Followed by: And who else? I believe these are the important questions—the awkward questions.

If passion is the fuel, curiosity the catalyst, then imagination is the life force of my organic and evolving self. I continue to rage and to be outraged by violation and violence, outrage that Vandana Shiva says, 'is a necessary complement to being spiritual' (cited in Biggs, 2003). Out of my celebration of women, I have met and expressed the feminist, the Warrior woman part of me. Out of my paralysis, fear, confusion and rage, I have expanded my world and made fertile compassionate connections within that world. Out of my discoveries and my dreams, I will continue to show up, to be silent and to listen, to speak out and to write, to be and to do, and to continue becoming an activist.

[7.] The Revolutionary Association of the Women of Afghanistan, see <www.rawa.org>.

[8.] Women Living Under Moslem Laws, see <www.wluml.org>.

[9.] Bat Shalom is an Israeli national feminist grassroots organization of Jewish and Palestinian Israeli women working together for a peace grounded in a just resolution of the Israel-Palestine conflict, respect for human rights, and an equal voice for Jewish and Arab women within Israeli society, see <www.batshalom.org/english/batshalom/>.

Who are they —
The Women in Black
Standing in silent vigil?

Icy winds tearing
The messages of peace,
Flapping the banners
Saying No to War.

Heads down, eyes averted, some taunting—
The people, they scurry past.
Curious, supportive, some grateful —
The people, they pause in their haste.
Heads bow, hands reach out, eyes fill,
Lips move in heartfull thanks.

Who are they —
The Women in Black
Standing in silent vigil,
Mourning the dead and the living dead,
The *disappeared* in those far off places?

Who are the mothers,
Grandmothers and daughters
Who stand side by side round the world?
Shoulder to shoulder—in solidarity
Shoulder to shoulder—saying No to War
Shoulder to shoulder—saying Yes to Justice.

On Jerusalem's steps they stood up in grief,
Israeli and Palestinian women.
On Jerusalem's steps they showed up for peace
Palestinian and Israeli women.

Around the world
The warrior women
Join in the silent vigil
Around the world
The Women in Black
Stand together in silence for peace.

Rosemary Hopkins
4 March 2003, Scotland, UK

REFERENCES

Arrien, A (1993) *The Fourfold Way.* San Francisco: HarperCollins.

Biggs, BS (2003) *Brave Hearts, Rebel Spirits.* Chichester UK: Anita Roddick Books.

Chopra, A (2003) *Midwives of Change.* Resurgence magazine, 220: 34.

Hawthorne, S and Winter, B (2002) *September 11, 2001: Feminist Perspectives.* Melbourne: Spinifex.

Kingsolver, B (2002) *Small Wonder.* London: Faber & Faber.

Mellor, M (2003) Women & Nature. *Resurgence* (magazine), *216*: 49.

Natiello, P (2001*) The Person-Centred Approach: A passionate presence.* Ross-on-Wye: PCCS Books.

New Internationalist Cooperative, (2001) Twin Terrors. *New Internationalist, 340*: 18–19.

Sontag, S (2003) The Power of Principle. Speech at the presentation of the Rothko Chapel Oscar Romero Award, 30 March 2003. <www.refusersolidarity.net>.

Thorne, B (1992) *Carl Rogers.* London: Sage.

Walker, A (1997) *Anything We Love Can Be Saved.* New York: Ballantine Books.

and many more …

ON BEING A FEMINIST MALE

J WADE HANNON

As I begin writing I am struck with the term 'Feminist Male'. Some females would argue that it is inappropriate for a male to use the term in regard to himself; others would embrace a male doing so. Digby (1998) wrote, 'it's not hard to find explanations for why the very idea of a feminist man is likely to be met with some form of incredulity' (p. 1). 'Some women,' he states, 'are inclined by the manifold ways in which they have found feminism to be empowering to them as women not to see feminism as a sociopolitical stance which could be espoused or rejected by anyone, male or female' (p. 1). Even within the community of males who embrace feminism, some would use the term 'pro-feminist' to describe themselves rather than a 'feminist male' (Bartky, 1998; Brod, 1998; Digby, 1998; Hopkins, 1998).

I have referred to myself as a feminist for many years, decades actually, and do not see any problem with it. Feminism is a set of beliefs, a social theory and, as such, I believe it is very appropriate for males to use the term if they do, indeed, embrace feminist theory in one of its many manifestations. Hopkins (1998) astutely observes, 'feminism, it turns out, is something we all can do' (p. 52).

WHO I AM?

I am a fifty-year-old divorced man of mixed ethnic ancestry (five different European and one Native American nationalities). I have one daughter (age 19) and one son (age 11) who share me as their father and have different mothers.

I grew up in Edna, a small town (approximately 460 people) in southeast Kansas, which is in the center of the main part of the United States of America (US), (excluding Alaska and Hawaii). I was born in 1953 to a waitress mother and construction electrician father (who was an active member of the electrician's union

80

all his work life). I have one brother and one sister, both younger. We were a poor rural working-class family.

Growing up I was fortunate in that I spent much time around my female relations as well as the male ones. I was often in the kitchen watching, learning and helping my mother, aunts and grandmothers. I also spent time doing the same with my father, uncles, and grandfathers, but not in the kitchen. Unfortunately, by the time I was nine, all of my biological grandparents were dead, although my step-paternal grandmother was alive until I was 19.

Growing up in the period that I did exposed me to a number of social and cultural phenomena that influenced how I grew and developed as a person and who I am today.

As a child, McCarthyism was very much alive and well in the United States 'heartland'. The minister at the local fundamentalist Protestant church that my aunt and uncle took my siblings and I to used to go on about 'Communists under every bed', 'Communists under every bush', and the 'evils of Karl Marx and Marxism'. This always perplexed me. His tirades led me to discover a copy of *The Communist Manifesto* by Karl Marx in the school library shelves in my ninth grade year. I remember thinking 'Hmmm … "Communist" and "Marx", very interesting', so I pulled it down and read it. I could not understand what the problem was. His ideas made very good sense to me.

The Civil Rights movement was very important to me in many regards. I recall how many people in my town and the surrounding areas would make many disparaging remarks about people of color, especially African-Americans. This was always hard to understand. There were no people of color in my hometown— although many of us were part Native American. We were just three miles from the state of Oklahoma, where many Native Americans lived, most of them involuntarily moved there in the 1800s. It was known as 'Indian Territory' until 1917 when it became a state. My Cherokee ancestors were among the Native Americans forced to live there. My father was born in Oklahoma, as were his brother and sister and their father and so on. I knew that I was not all 'white' and did not see how one's skin color made her/him 'bad'. I remember seeing Civil Rights marches and rallies on television and hearing Martin Luther King, Jr. His words made a huge impact on me.

The other major currents that shaped me were the student New Left and the Anti-Vietnam War movements. At the time these all blurred together in my mind, although, now, having lived through and studied the period I realize that they were separate with many overlapping characteristics in them. I was also very much involved with what was referred to in the US then as the 'Youth Culture', especially rock-and-roll music, both as a listener and a musician. I played guitar in many local bands from the ages of 11 to 20 (when I 'retired' from being a rock-and-roll musician). The rebelliousness of rock-and-roll music was very attractive, particularly the emphasis on social and political issues.

As a youth I had embraced the Christian religion. The majority of people where I grew up professed to be Christian. For me, though, it was a very serious thing, from age 12 to age 20 I was committed to becoming a minister (although at 20 I realized that Christianity and religion in general made no sense and transformed into an agnostic secular humanist). The commitment to peace and love that I understood of the religion was important to me and led to my embracing the Civil Rights, New Left and Anti-War movements. They all seemed to fit together nicely. By the age of 15 I was a pacifist, anti-racist and an anti-capitalist.

The Women's Movement became a part of my awareness shortly afterward. The basic argument that women were equal to men appealed to my budding sense of justice and equality. I had a very strong and influential female teacher in high school. Imogene North taught vocal music and was a brilliant and compassionate person. She saw in me many things that others did not. I vividly remember her saying to me once, 'Wade, I don't know how a person like you could ever have come from Edna, Kansas.' She clearly viewed me as remarkable. In my 1970–71 high school yearbook she wrote, 'It's quite refreshing to meet a great original thinker, instead of a memorizer. I expect a great new philosophical treatise from [you] … '

When I got to college I met many more women who were strong, vibrant and feminist. One woman in particular exposed me to many of the basic covenants, ideas and writings of the feminist movement. In addition to other political activities I became active in supporting the Equal Rights Amendment (ERA), Pro-Choice legislation, anti-violence (especially anti-domestic violence), childcare initiatives and other feminist efforts. I was a dues-paying member of the National Organization for Women (NOW) for several years in my 20s and 30s. Over the years I have remained engaged and active in all these areas in addition to becoming active in the Labor movement. Coming from a working family with my father, his brother and many other family and friends active in unions, it is no wonder. Being a part of the union movement allows me to bring much of my political work together (although, unfortunately, many in the United States union movement retain their irrational attachments to the so-called 'Democratic' Party).

In general, my view of political activity coalesced around the concept of liberation at an early age and I have maintained that throughout my life. 'Liberation', to me, means the process of struggling to be free and who we truly are as people, individually and collectively. To a large degree that is why I chose to be a counselor and to embrace the Person-Centered/Client-Centered Approach.

A constant struggle for me has been the tension, the dialectic, between working as a counselor and fostering personal change and working as an activist and fostering social change. One synthesis that occurred for me was almost fifteen years ago when I became a professor of counseling. Doing this work has enabled me to work with students who (hopefully) are more socially and culturally aware counselors who will, in at least some small degrees, be more sensitive to and appreciative of diversity and confront the social systems that need to be changed.

Another large part of my life is being a father. Being a feminist impacts the way in which I am as a father. I aim to not replicate the sexist social gender stereotypes. I use non-sexist language and help my children to see how these conventions are unfair (as with the female teachers at my son's school who use the title 'Miss' or 'Mrs' as opposed to 'Ms' I point out that the male teachers are all called 'Mr' and encourage him to use 'Ms'). Being non-violent is an important part of my role as a father. I have never hit or spanked either of my children. That is not to say that I have never been angry with them—I have. But I express my anger with words not violence. I work to share my feelings, both the 'positive' and 'negative' ones (although, in most regards, I tend to view feelings as neither, rather, from a more phenomenological perspective of just being). When I was grieving my father's death ten years ago I cried a lot. I did this in front of my children. In the United States, a male crying is still not a common occurrence, although much more so today than in my youth. I work to not impose heterosexism on my children. I talk about when they are attracted to a male or female, not one or the other. Being an active ally and supporter of the gay/lesbian/bisexual/transgender community also demonstrates to them that I am sincere in this regard. I firmly and strongly believe that fathers should be an equal parent with the mother. Being a divorced father in the United States, this is not an easy feat. In many regards, the divorce and custody system was created to make fathers only responsible for paying child support (if even that) and not to be 'real' parents.

WHAT IS FEMINISM?

To me, feminism simply means that women and men are equal and there should be no barriers to equality. While there are many other dimensions to feminist thought, this is the boiled-down part. For more detailed explorations see Clough (1994), Collins (1998), Davis (1983), hooks (2000), and Smith (1987, 1990) to name a few. Tong's (1998) work is a good overview of feminist thought in it's many variations. Taking feminist theory into practice, Collins (1998) states:

> Globally, a feminist agenda encompasses several major areas. First and foremost, the economic status of women and issues associated with women's poverty, such as educational opportunities for girls, industrial development, employment policies, prostitution, and inheritance laws concerning property, constitute important women's issues globally. Political rights for women, such as the right to vote, to assemble, to travel in public and to hold office, as well as the rights of political prisoners, and basic human rights violations against women, such as rape and torture, constitute a second area of concern. A third area of global attention consists of marital and family issues, such as marriage and divorce laws, child

custody policies, and domestic labor. Women's health and survival issues, such as reproductive rights, pregnancy, sexuality, and AIDS constitute another area of global feminist concern. This broad global feminist agenda finds varying expressions in different regions of the world and among diverse populations. (p. 66)

I find this to be a good 'platform' that fits well with my beliefs about humans. Another component of feminist practice that is important is the valuing of the experiential, subjective spheres of existence. These are, as Smith (1990) asserts, 'central to the feminist challenge to academic discourse' (p. 31). This, of course, is also a key part of the Person-Centered/Client-Centered Approach.

LEARNING FROM FEMINIST THEORY AND PRACTICE

Over the years I have come to see how feminist theory and practice have influenced me and become important to me as a person, counselor and professor. These are:
  • Language—the use of non-sexist language and gender inclusive terminology are very key, such as 'letter carrier' not 'mailman', 'fire fighter' not 'fireman' and looking at phrases that are unsavory such as 'rule of thumb' which used to denote that a husband could beat his wife with a stick no longer than his thumb.
  • Countering male privilege—males are often socialized to expect that they can speak whenever they want, interrupting others (especially women), and to expect to be served first, waited on first, etc. Part of my efforts as a feminist male is to learn to be quiet more often and not do those typical 'male' behaviors. In my classes, I work to facilitate student verbal exchanges that are respectful of all speakers, and I defer from speaking when I can to allow others, especially females, to have more speaking time. I am also very aware of the fact that I am a physically large man and that others, especially women, can see me as intimidating and/or threatening based on this. It is a dynamic that I have to keep tabs on, as my self-concept is not one of being that way, quite to the contrary.
  • Power relationships—this relates somewhat to the previous concept, but it is on a more systems or macro level and includes class and ethnicity (Collins, 1998). I find looking at the many forms of oppression helpful—the ways in which oppression of one group by another take place. For example, US states that severely restrict a woman's right to reproductive health options or the ways that in primarily female workplaces the bosses deny the women workers decent wages and working conditions.
  • Equality and egalitarianism—these concepts are very important to me as a person, a practitioner, a professor and an activist. I actively reject the ways in which people are systematically treated differently based on gender and work to live my life in as much as I can, in concert with the principle of:

• Commitment to non-violence—as I mentioned earlier, this has been a key part of who I am for many years, but my exposure to feminist theory and practice has added urgency to work to counter the excessive violence in US society, which I believe is the most violent in the world and extends into many households in the form of child abuse, partner abuse and physical 'disciplining' of children (which I consider to be child abuse, but is not recognized as such in the United States, unless it is 'excessive').

• Patriarchal hegemony—by this I am referring to the impact of the patriarchal sexist system on consciousness. There are so many factors in our society that impact how we think, feel and act that are related to the means in which the hegemonic structure seems to control us. How we act as 'men', the ways in which the system tells us what is 'manly' and what is not, and how we must work to show 'that what appears as natural is rather socially constructual and therefore political' (Clough, 1994: 30). We must endeavor to develop ways in which to counter these social constructs that seep into our innermost thoughts and feelings!

SOME SUGGESTIONS FOR MALES

There are many ways in which men can change to become less sexist, striving to be a non-sexist male (and hopefully, feminist). Even within Person-Centered meetings I have observed many examples of males behaving in sexist manners (and not just the older males!).

Some suggestions are: (a) males need to talk less and listen more; (b) not assume that females should do certain kinds of activities (such as cooking, cleaning, etc.); (c) not monopolize; (d) behave in ways that are more aware of how women are systematically mistreated, speak out against those injustices, and work for change; (e) increase one's self-awareness in regard to how one's behavior (including verbal behavior) can be seen as intimidating, offensive, etc.; (f) read feminist theory and educate oneself; and, (g) seek to achieve harmony between being respectful toward others without being patriarchal, patronizing or condescending.

ENDING REMARKS

Being a feminist male is not an easy project to adopt, yet I see no other way to exist authentically. The core of Rogers' writing is very consistent with most feminist values. So often in my life, I have felt marginalized, 'the other', 'the weirdo', the deviant. Much of the time I have embraced my 'deviant' self, but at times the upkeep for being me becomes wearisome. Having discovered the Person-Centered Approach and feminist theory while a student at university have both been wellsprings for me. I continue to be nurtured and rejuvenated by both.

REFERENCES

Bartky, S (1998) Foreword, in T Digby (ed) *Men Doing Feminism.* New York: Routledge, pp. xi–xix.

Brod, H (1998) To be a man, or not to be a man—that is the feminist question, in T Digby, (ed) *Men Doing Feminism.* York New: Routledge, pp. 197–212.

Clough, PT (1994) *Feminist Thought: Desire, power, and academic discourse.* Oxford, UK; Cambridge, MA: Blackwell.

Collins, PH (1998) *Fighting Words: Black women and the search for justice.* Minneapolis MN: University of Minnesota Press.

Collins, PH (2000) *Black Feminist Thought: Knowledge, consciousness, and the politics of empowerment.* (10th anniversary ed) New York: Routledge.

Davis, AY (1983) *Women, Race and Class.* New York: Vintage Books.

Digby, T (1998) Introduction, in T Digby (ed) *Men Doing Feminism.* New York: Routledge, pp. 1–16.

hooks, b (2000) *Feminist Theory: From margin to center.* (2nd ed) Cambridge, MA: South End Press.

Hopkins, PD (1998) How feminism made a man out of me: The proper subject of feminism and the problem of men, in T Digby (ed) *Men Doing Feminism.* York New: Routledge pp. 33–56.

Smith, DE (1987) *The Everyday World as Problematic: A feminist sociology.* Boston, MA: Northeastern University Press.

Smith, DE (1990) *The Conceptual Practices of Power: A feminist sociology of knowledge.* Boston, MA: Northeastern University Press.

Tong, RP (1998) *Feminist Thought: A more comprehensive introduction.* (2nd ed) Boulder, CO: Westview Press.

IN OUR HUMANITY IS OUR DIVINITY: INTERCONNECTIONS BETWEEN FEMINIST SPIRITUALITY AND THE PERSON-CENTRED APPROACH

DEB STEELE

Feminist spirituality is a term which allows for a multiplicity of truths; it is a broad church. It could be defined in terms of feminist theology (feminist perspectives on the existing world religions), in terms of the ancient Goddess religions, in terms of witchcraft and shamanism, in terms of the sacred feminine within all religions or in terms of individual women's experiences of the numinous. Feminist spirituality is about an arising from within, connectedness with nature and the planet, spirit as immanence, indwelling, and embracing of the dark as well as the light. It is about embodied experience of the divine. Inherent in this is a deep respect for humanity as a whole, for each individual in particular, and for the primacy of subjective experience. In this way, feminist spirituality shares a common value base and philosophy with the Person-Centred Approach. In this chapter I explore the ways in which I have experienced the coming together of these two worlds in both my personal and professional life.

. . . .

My first encounter with the experience of a reality which transcends that of the material world, and which connected me with what some would call the Goddess came with the birthing of my first child. As I found myself in the grip of a physical process which swept away all illusions of being in control of nature I was lost in awe at what was happening. My body was wracked with pain, I felt frightened, lost and alone and yet simultaneously I knew myself to be in the heart of a wondrous mystery. The chemistry, biology and physics that I knew went nowhere near explaining the miracle in which I was participating, that of giving birth to a new life, of participating in creation.

Having grown up in an atheist, socialist household, I had no religious belief system within which to frame this experience and yet I could only frame it as mystical.

I felt deep in the heart of mystery, and in an altered state of consciousness in which my sense of connection with all of life—animal, vegetable and mineral—was profound. I knew myself as one with all that is, through a physical, intuitive knowing. The emergence of a new perfect life from within my own boundaried body transcended any attempts at a rationalist, materialist explanation; there was nothing in that framework that could begin to speak to me of the utter miracle of this creation.

The miracle of creation had served in the Western world as the basis for twenty thousand years of worship of God as female, as mother, as earth and nature-centred. There are parts of the world where it is still so. This, however, was not a reference point available to me at this stage. The experience which I now understand as mystical and shamanic then became, in the absence of any other conceptual framework—internal or external—one of mental illness. From being in a state of bliss I plunged into a state of despair. Having been diagnosed as having post-partum psychosis, I escaped being hospitalised through sheer terror and determination and through the love and support of my family and my health visitor. Here were sown the first seeds of knowing the profound healing power of being accepted and being heard, in being blessed with a health visitor who had had a similar experience many years previously and who came in day after day to sit with me whilst I poured out what I had come to perceive as my madness. Her capacity to simply listen, to offer me understanding, to trust my ability to still care for my baby, enabled my fear to subside and my return to a more grounded reality.

Thus this personal feminist perspective of spirituality links with feminist perspectives on madness and also with Rogers' theories of personality development. When our lived visceral experiencing and valuing is at odds with our self concept and the social construct of reality that we exist within, then our need to adapt in order to be accepted, to feel belongingness, will lead us to deny the truth of our own internal reality, whether consciously or unconsciously. If we try to claim and to articulate that internal truth we then have to live with our internalised judgements around that experience and are vulnerable to both those and the judgements of those around us.

In the fields of spirituality and mental health, women are made doubly vulnerable. Whilst much has changed in the twenty-eight years since the experience that I am describing it is still the case that people articulating their spiritual experiences are particularly vulnerable within the mental health system. Further, the mental health system is still one that is dominated by a world view which is essentially reductionist, deterministic and androcentric (male-centred, defined in male terms) and where what may be largely a personal value judgement can be reified as diagnosis. It is also the case that the power/knowledge discourse around spirituality is still predominantly that of androcentric religion, whether Western or Eastern. It can be a deeply painful and fearful struggle therefore for women who are attempting to claim their spiritual experiences and to bring them into the public discourse.

• • • • • • • •

A short while ago I was preparing for a workshop that I was offering on spirituality and the Person-Centred Approach at a national conference. I was feeling very anxious at the prospect, to the extent that it was impossible for me to think clearly, so I decided to 'go inside', to just sit quietly as I am used to doing in meditation, and see what happened. What happened was that as I sat, *Client-Centered Therapy* kept going through my head so I got it from the shelf, sat again then opened it at the words:

> It is undoubtedly true that the great majority of our sensory experiences are thus ignored, never raised to the level of conscious symbolization, and exist only as organic sensations, without ever having been related in any way to the organized concept of the self or to the concept of self in relation to the environment. (Rogers, 1951: 504)

This had great meaning for me because this is precisely what I was struggling to do in preparing for the workshop, attempting to articulate (or symbolise) organic sensations and to relate them to my organised concept of self and to my concept of self in relation to the environment. As a woman raised in a patriarchal secular society I have internalised many conditions of worth around my organic experiences of the numinous, the ineffable, that which defies logical explanation. To bring these experiences into conscious awareness, to integrate them into my self concept as part of a process of sharing them with others, was, at some level, terrifying.

Knowing that the above quote was in relation to one of the nineteen propositions I turned to read which one and found that it was number eleven:

> As experiences occur in the life of the individual, they are either, a) symbolised, perceived and organized into some relationship to the self, b) ignored because there is no relationship to the self-structure, c) *denied symbolization or given distorted symbolization because the experience is inconsistent with the structure of the self*. (ibid: 503, my emphasis)

What then came to me was the process that I had found myself in during the previous week in my personal therapy and in supervision where I had been attempting to articulate some of the themes that were with me in relation to spirituality and the Person-Centred Approach. I had repeatedly been asking 'Does this make sense?' saying things like 'It feels as though there are two sets of belief systems in me, two world views that are trying to integrate; it feels potentially transformative yet it also feels like it's a really risky potentially dangerous time. I feel almost like I'm at risk.'

This again links with person-centred personality theory. Earlier in *Client-Centered Therapy* Rogers writes,

> In the case of the radical re-organisation [of self], the client may go through the most racking torment of pain and a complete and

chaotic confusion. This suffering may be associated with rapidly changing configurations of personality, being a new person one day, and sinking back into the old self on the next, only to find that some minor episode puts the new organisation of self again in a position of regnancy. (ibid: 77)

The experience of connection, relatedness with Spirit, the Source, God/dess, whatever name we might give to the Other, can cause such radical re-organisation of self, of the self-structure, if we allow it to be symbolised into awareness. I believe that for many of us, men and women, fear is present when it comes to articulating our most personal spiritual experiences and belief systems, and that there are specific potentials for it to be particularly fearsome for women.

In her book *Silencing the Self,* Dana Crowley Jack researches the experiences of women diagnosed with depression, and investigates the interface between the experiences and the diagnosis. She explores the ways in which women will silence themselves rather than risk having their reality denigrated or denied:

If a woman's authentic self has been devalued in her relationships, in childhood learning, and in impoverished stereotypes of femininity, the authentic self becomes silent to protect the integrity of its own vision.

The origins of these fears are ubiquitous. As female, one inherits an ancestral, collective feeling of vulnerability that is linked with centuries of economic dependence and physical violence against women. (Jack, 1991: 139)

Given that spiritual experience emanates from, or to, the core of our authentic selves and that there have been centuries of physical and emotional violence against women in the name of religion then the fear of speaking our spiritual truths is inevitably going to be great. Particularly when added to the fear of being perceived as mad.

. . . .

When I began the preparatory reading for the training in person-centred counselling that I embarked upon in the mid-eighties, I was actively involved in the women's movement. I had for some while been a member of a women's consciousness-raising group where I experienced the power of deep listening and sharing stories from the heart. I had also been involved in various national actions, including Greenham Common, the central focus of the British women's peace movement. Short visits and stays at Greenham had given me further experiences which I could only frame in terms of the spiritual.

Women from all walks of life and all parts of the United Kingdom were motivated to converge upon this spot to protest their horror at the presence and potential launch of US nuclear weapons. The outer fence, ten, twelve feet high, garlanded with barbed wire, was surrounded by British police, some mounted. Behind that fence were armed US military police, behind them rolls of barbed wire, behind them, the US soldiers and behind them, the bunkers where the Cruise missiles, the weapons of mass destruction, were housed.

The imagery of this amassed power of the two states was stark and very powerful, all the more so given the male presence of the police and soldiers in contrast to the female presence of the protestors. The permanent presence of those women who had left homes, partners, families, jobs, to camp at the gates of Greenham and keep the peace vigil was regularly augmented by hundreds and thousands of women who came for specific actions. Specific actions would take the form of creating a human chain around the base, of weaving photographs, pictures, poems into the wire of the fence, of singing songs, of trying to engage in dialogue with the men guarding the fence. Sometimes word would go round that there was to be an attempt to climb one of the gates or to bring the fence down at such and such a time and that would be where we would all gather. Or we would simply come together in silence, or with noise-makers or with ululation, the sounds rising and dying away through some internal shared rhythm. Such actions would happen with no prior planning, no agenda, no leaders, no hierarchy, no haranguing.

In all of this there was a sense of something *arising*, a power from within which communicated itself as the power of presence, the power of ritual, the power of sound, the power of silence. I had a felt experience of a depth of relatedness and interconnectedness which arose spontaneously from a shared sense of purpose. I had never experienced this before but in later years it came to feel very familiar as a characteristic of being in groups in various settings, but particularly in person-centred groups.

· · · · · · · ·

When reading *Carl Rogers on Personal Power* (Rogers, 1977) and *A Way of Being* (Rogers, 1980) in preparation for my training there was a sense of coming home. The philosophy, values and beliefs which were being expressed felt familiar, known, even whilst they were being read for the first time. Within my training, which was deeply experiential, there was the opportunity to experience these values as prac-tised, to be immersed in the offering and receiving of the core conditions.

During the next two and a half years of the training my walls fell down and I re-entered some of the altered states that I had experienced around the birth of my son, but this time I could know them as visionary rather than as pathological and I could draw healing from them rather than make them into sickness. This was a profound knowing of the transformative power of the Person-Centred Approach.

The year after my training ended my mother died. She chose to stay at home rather than be admitted to hospital and I was with her and my father for the last two weeks of her life. In the early hours of a Friday morning just before Christmas I awoke from a dream where I had been at her funeral. The dream ended with me having a conversation with my mother and my ex-mother-in-law in the aisle of the church where the service had been held. My mother was saying to us that her world had been her home and children and husband, that was her domain; the outer world had been my father's, all the things that went on out there were his realm.

As I awoke from this dream, at 4 am, I knew that my mother's death was imminent and went into the bedroom she was still sharing with my father. She was awake and in some discomfort and asked me to help her to get more comfortable then slipped into a deep sleep from which she left us some five hours later, surrounded by her family.

In my sleep I had still been deeply connected with my mother. Though the symbolism of the dream was mine, the knowledge when I woke that her time was coming arose from the deep connectedness that had grown between us, and from an instinctual, intuitive knowing, not rational, discursive reason. The symbolism of the dream spoke of the feminine and masculine principles, inner and outer, being and doing, the private domain and the public. In terms of my own situation as a single parent it was speaking of my attempts for internal balance, as a feminist it was speaking of my experience of the world, as a daughter it was speaking of my experience of my parents.

The chosen manner of my mother's death, the decision to stay at home, to have her family with her, to have no further medical interventions meant that she had been able to claim her own domain at this crucial stage in her life. It was a womanly way to die.

The experience of living this last two weeks of my mother's dying brought the most tangible, constant knowing of love that I have ever had. Being with her through the time of her leaving her body brought the knowing that what I was partaking in was another form of birthing where, rather than welcoming a soul, I was witnessing its moving on.

· · · · · · · · ·

As a person-centred practitioner I believe that what I am doing is partaking in and witnessing the work of the soul. Rogers says in the preface to *Client-Centered Therapy*:

> It [this book] is about me as I rejoice at the privilege of being a midwife to a new personality—as I stand by with awe at the emergence of a self, a person, as I see a birth process in which I have had an important and facilitating part. It is about both the client and me as we regard with wonder the potent and orderly forces which are evident in this whole experience, forces which seem deeply rooted in the universe as a whole. The book is, I believe, about life, as life vividly reveals itself in the therapeutic process— with its blind power and its tremendous capacity for destruction,

but with its overbalancing thrust toward growth, if the opportunity for growth is provided. (Rogers, 1951: x–xi)

This is a profound statement, which contains within it the very essence of the values of the Person-Centred Approach. I see the birthing that Rogers refers to as a two-way process because my experience is that I am also a recipient of healing in each exchange that I have. And in each experience of healing, another part of me is birthed, is given new life.

Bella was a young woman that I worked with in the context of my being a staff counsellor in a large organisation. During the time that we were meeting we had sometimes worked with visualisation, a phenomenon which arose from the combination of her searching for ways of keeping herself emotionally safe within her work setting and my familiarity with this way of working. Bella was an artist and exploring and working with this realm of the imagination was something that was powerfully effective for her. In terms of our relationship it felt as though we connected at these times at a profound level. It would feel as though we were meeting in a place where there was a mutuality of empathy which brought an interconnectedness where our separate selves were still present yet also somehow transcended.

This was strongly present in our final session, an ending which was brought about by the fact that Bella was leaving her job, a decision that she had come to through the course of the work we had done together.

Towards the end of the session Bella referred to the fact that when she had ended with a previous therapist she had been given some affirmations to work with. She said that these had been helpful for her and asked whether I had anything similar that she could take with her. I said that I didn't but that if we spent some time with it maybe something would emerge. As I was saying this I found a phrase coming into my mind which persisted throughout the ensuing exploration of what it was that Bella was looking for. I was wary of offering the phrase, partly because of not knowing where it had come from, partly because I felt embarrassed by the words that were with me, and partly because of the knots that I can tie myself into in my concerns not to take power in the relationship. However it was so strong and persistent that I finally offered that something had come into my head and I didn't know whether it might mean anything for her but the words were 'I sing my own song and it is beautiful to hear'. At this Bella squealed with glee, grabbed my foot and shook it up and down saying 'That's it! That's exactly it; where's my pen, let me write it down'.

In the moment of saying the words I knew exactly what they meant. They spoke of the essence of so much of our work together; of the way that Bella had come to feel about herself in the world, and her decision to leave work and to go freelance as a manifestation of that. And simultaneously I knew that the phrase was also about me, or rather for me. The words had arisen from the synergy that our relatedness created, a gift of our interconnection and, some would say, a gift of grace.

Another such gift of interconnection came in different circumstances, at a time when I was going through a period of intense change which was creating inner turmoil and triggering a capacity for powerful self-judgement. As I stood one morning at my kitchen sink, the inner judgements reached a point which felt unbearable when suddenly into my mind's eye came the face of one of my clients, Jane, who had been struggling with her own self-judgement. In the moment of seeing her face I was flooded with the unconditional positive regard and compassion which I felt for her. As I felt the truth of that I knew the same acceptance and compassion for myself and all judgements receded, leaving only peace. Although I was not in the physical presence of Jane when this happened, it was the relationship with her which enabled my own inner shift.

This recognition of the gifts that I receive through being in person-centred relationship with others brings me a sense of wonder at the vast inner resources and potential for growth which Carl Rogers affirmed that we all possess as human beings. It reminds me that I am there in the therapeutic relationship as another person who will also be changed by the encounter I am engaged in, in ways that I may not expect. It reminds me that whilst as human beings we are all uniquely different, and in that way separate, we are also deeply interconnected. We are both alone and all one.

• • • • • • • • •

There are many other experiences that I could cite, of times when material reality has been both deeply affirmed and simultaneously transcended. Times when I have been present to my own individual uniqueness and that of the other(s) I was with whilst also experiencing our depth of connectedness. And this is also related to environment, whether human-made or natural. A fundamental of feminist spirituality and the Person-Centred Approach is the awareness of the primacy of relationship and the inclusion of relatedness with the natural world as a part of that. Personal relationship with landscape, with place, is a primary relationship, both explicitly and implicitly. Explicitly, in terms of a conscious awareness of loving or having an aversion to particular places. Implicitly, in terms of place giving an added dimension to what happens between two or more people, an added synergy which happens between people and place. By place I mean buildings, landscape, the planet, and the universe, the cosmos of which we are part. Our perceived, lived-in environment and that which spans beyond.

Matthew Fox, the Dominican priest who was ex-communicated because of his refusal to stop working with the feminist social activist witch Starhawk says 'the universe loves us unconditionally every day the sun rises'. This is the universe as Creator, God, Mother Earth. She from which all arises and to which all shall return, what Rogers called 'the formative tendency', the 'potent forces of the universe'.

I regard Carl Rogers as a spiritual teacher. In identifying the core conditions he identified the core components of love. He explicated a way of being which is the means to facilitate growth and healing, in others and in ourselves. He manifested a respect for the potential of the human being which borders on reverence. He placed all of this in the context of a wider environment; the universe, the cosmos for which he felt wonder and awe. He had a profound concern for social justice, recognised by the nomination for the Nobel Peace Prize which was submitted, unknown to him, just before his death. And he was a spiritual teacher who resisted the role of guru, as he says in *Carl Rogers on Personal Power*:

> Over the years I certainly could have become a guru with the always ready help of loving admirers. But it is a path I have avoided. When people are too worshipful I remind them of the Zen saying 'If you meet the Buddha kill the Buddha.' (Rogers, 1977: 184)

In other words, the source of wisdom, and the rightful focus for loving devotion resides within ourselves. Our subjective experiencing is a potential source of truth and knowledge and a tremendous power for transformation of ourselves and others and the planet. When we can symbolise our experiences, articulate them, have them heard and honoured and understood, we are enabled to go deeper and broader into our humanity. When we are privileged to have others sharing their experiences with us we are similarly taken deeper into our own humanity as well as theirs. And the more that we are able to be all of our full humanity in its wisdom and folly, its brokenness and wholeness, its darkness and light, its measuring by birth and death, the more possible it becomes to glimpse our divinity. The divinity which is the ground of our embodied being and of all beings—animal, vegetable, mineral—the creation which gives us life and which we also know as 'love'.

REFERENCES

Bancroft, A (1989) *Weavers of Wisdom: Women mystics of the 20th century*. London: Penguin.

Christ, CP (1997) *Rebirth of the Goddess: Finding meaning in feminist spirituality*. New York: Routledge.

Clarke, I (ed) (2001) *Psychosis and Spirituality: Exploring the new frontier*. London: Whurr.

Eisler, R (1993) *The Chalice and the Blade*. London: Harper and Row.

Flinders, CL (1998) *At the Root of this Longing: Reconciling a spiritual hunger and a feminist thirst*. New York: Harper Collins.

Fox, M (1991) *Creation Spirituality—Liberating gifts for the peoples of the earth*. New York: HarperCollins

Garcia, G and Maitland, S (1983) *Walking on the Water: Women talk about spirituality*. London: Virago.

Goodison, G (1990) *Moving Heaven and Earth. Sexuality, spirituality and social change*. London: The Women's Press.

Grey, MC (1997) *Prophecy and Mysticism: The heart of the post-modern church*. Edinburgh: T and T Clark.

Harvey, A (1995) *The Return of the Mother*. Berkeley: Frog.

Ingerman, S (2000) *Medicine for the Earth*. New York: Three Rivers Press.

Jack, DC (1991) *Silencing the Self*. New York: HarperCollins.

Jamal, M (1987) *Shape Shifters: Shamen women in contemporary society*. London: Penguin.

Long, AP (1992) *In a Chariot Drawn by Lions: The search for the female in deity*. London: The Women's Press.

Macy, J (1993) *World as Lover, World as Self*. London: Rider.

Miles, R (1988) *The Women's History of the World*. London: Paladin.

Rogers, CR (1951) *Client-Centered Therapy: Its current practice, implications and theory*. London: Constable.

Rogers, CR (1977) *Carl Rogers on Personal Power: Inner strength and its revolutionary impact*. London: Constable.

Rogers, CR (1980) *A Way of Being*. Boston: Houghton Mifflin.

TOWARD CONVERGENCE: CLIENT-CENTERED AND FEMINIST ASSUMPTIONS ABOUT EPISTEMOLOGY AND POWER

CAROL WOLTER-GUSTAFSON

Client-centered theory and feminist theory have each evolved over the past half century as two separate streams running parallel to each other. Each has developed with scant attention or accurate knowledge of the other. Each has written cogent critiques of the dominant psychoanalytic paradigm. Of greater value, however, are the fresh frameworks they offer in several significant areas. These include: restructuring power relationships, reassigning epistemological authority, the centrality of relationality and intersubjectivity, and the historical contextual nature of all knowledge. This radical reconstruction offers a truly inclusive, emancipatory, and egalitarian vision for the practice of psychotherapy and of all human relationships. My intention is to lift some common themes from feminist and client-centered theory to suggest points of convergence. It is my contention that the increased power generated by the convergence of these streams will serve to create the change both envision.

In order to create that possibility, we must increase our mutual understanding of these two theoretical movements, examine the intellectual milieu and historical context in which each developed and carefully consider the existing critiques of each movement.

These models developed independently of each other, separated by several turbulent decades of the twentieth century. What is the legacy of these two powerful attempts to radically re-conceptualize psychotherapy? Theory is always influenced by the conditions which shape it, thus, it is important to ask the following:
• What are the implications of feminist theory emerging in reaction to Freudian psychoanalytic theory?
• What are the implications of client-centered theory emerging from Rogers' early empirical training, and his evolution toward an existential/phenomenological perspective?

What follows is a contribution to answering these questions and building connections between these theoretical viewpoints.

CARL R ROGERS: CLIENT-CENTERED THERAPY

ROGERS' EMPIRICAL ORIGIN

Rogers' approach to theory building was methodological rather than ideological. Practical problem-solving results mattered more to him than any particular pet theory. His introduction to the scientific method came from studying modern agricultural techniques on his family's farm. Rogers' academic lineage must be traced though John Dewey and the Pragmatists, rather than through Sigmund Freud and the Psychoanalysts.[1] The experience-based educational philosophy of Dewey and William Heard Kilpatrick permeated Rogers' education at Columbia Teachers College in New York.

All of Rogers' early experiences taught him to give pragmatic attention to processes and outcomes regardless of belief structures. His training in empirical psychology confirmed for him the fairness of this open-ended scientific attitude. He often said, 'The facts are friendly'.

His preference for discovery and his skepticism of established knowledge was evident from the start of his career in Rochester. In his first twelve years of working with desperate and impoverished children at the Rochester Society for the Prevention of Cruelty to Children, Rogers 'discovered that even some of the most elegant theories he had previously embraced failed to stand up to the test of reality' (Thorne 1992: 9).

When asked how his non-directive, client-centered work came about, he never failed to describe his encounter with one troubled family. The psychologists at the clinic decided in a conference that the problem was the mother's rejection of the boy. When the teenage boy failed to improve despite all Rogers' best efforts with the boy and his mother, Rogers suggested that despite their best efforts, they should acknowledge their lack of progress and terminate the relationship. The mother readily agreed, but before she had gone many steps away, returned and asked Rogers whether or not he ever saw adults. Surprised, he said yes and she sat down with him and began pouring out her deepest problems with her husband and her desire for help. It was nothing like the neat history he had previously taken. What Rogers did was to listen, 'instead of trying to nudge her toward a diagnostic understanding I had already reached' (Rogers, 1980: 37). Over the next months the boy showed the improvements in his behavior that had led the family to seek help. Rogers describes himself entering into a 'more personal relationship' which continued occasionally even after the boy had gone to college. Rogers trusted the power of his own experience with clients over the prevailing mandate that 'psychiatrists know best'.

Rogers' experienced-based practice was supported through a seemingly unlikely

---

[1] There was, however, one related link. Jessie Taft who Rogers admired, was a student of Freud's former colleague, Otto Rank. Taft's influence on Rogers is discussed shortly.

source. Rogers had some interest in Freud's former colleague Otto Rank.[2] Nat Raskin, Chicago Counseling Center author of 'The development of non-directive therapy', noted that Rogers was 'quite fascinated' with Rank's description of his approach in which the client had 'creative powers of his own', and in which the person becomes the 'central figure in the therapeutic situation' (Raskin, cited in Kirschenbaum, 1979: 91).

But it was Rank's student Jessie Taft that had the greatest influence on the early development of Rogers' theory. He called her book 'a small masterpiece of writing and thinking' (Rogers, cited in Kirschenbaum 1979: 92)[3] Rogers' own experience had led him to 'distrust therapist interpretation of past *or* present events'. Taft went beyond Rank when she chose to 'abandon interpretation altogether' (*ibid.*: 92). For Taft, the therapeutic relationship itself was a microcosm of a person's relationship to all of life. What Jessie Taft called 'relationship therapy' resonated with Carl Rogers' growing edge of 'non-directive therapy'.

Rogers' early academic track of empathic listening instead of expert diagnosis was synchronistic with the anti-authoritarianism of the historical moment. He had already learned from his clients the futility of the expert/dominance, power-over stance.[4] Lessons from the rise of Nazism and Fascism reaffirmed for him the importance of strengthening the individual voice and collective resistance in the face of strong social forces.[5]

In their exploration of voices of cynicism and hope, Arnett and Arneson offer this summary:

> Rogers' work became conceptual at the conclusion of the Nuremburg trials, where individual conscience was called as the alternative to blind institutional commitment. Working in an historical moment of increasing distrust toward institutions, it is not surprising that Carl Rogers' practice would lead him to look for alternative ways to support and guide lives ... Questioning narrative guidelines of institutions, culture, and religion lead him to trust in the self.
> (Arnett and Arneson 1999: 85)

[2.] The split between Freud and Rank came after the publication in 1925 of Otto Rank's book, *The Trauma of Birth*.

[3.] The book, *The Dynamics of Therapy in a Controlled Relationship* was published in 1933. I remember hearing her poetic prose read to me with tenderness and excitement, by Rogers' colleague Jules Seeman, some fifty years later.

[4.] Humanistic psychotherapist and author Rollo May's intriguing book *Power and Innocence: A search for the source of violence* (1972) investigates the meaning of power and names five kinds of power: exploitive, manipulative, competitive, nutrient, and integrative. Integrative power is power with another person.

[5.] Colleagues Drs Reinhard and Anne-Marie Taush, David Aspy and Flora Roebuck dedicated their professional careers to humanizing the way children were raised at home and at school. See Rogers, 1983: 197–224.

Rogers' study of 'the self' was never about an isolated individual seeking 'his' own needs. It was always about how that self was created, sustained, and sometimes damaged by its relationships with others. He always saw the self as a self-in-relation. As a result, he studied the therapy relationship itself by audio taping actual client sessions in order to gather data. By studying these recordings Rogers discovered that the more precisely he followed, as opposed to directing, his clients' communication, the more he observed significant change in their lives. From that time on, he centered his formal empirical studies on that interaction and its role in constructive change.

What is the nature of the relationship in which constructive change towards well-being occurs?

Rogers now had significant data and direct clinical experience in which to create a tentative hypothesis for empirical investigation. He asked whether or not the relationship, in which the core conditions of empathy, unconditional positive regard, and congruence were provided by the therapist and perceived by the client, was sufficient for change to occur (Rogers, 1957).[6] This hypothesis precipitated over three decades of research on these core conditions and yielded overall support for Rogers' proposition. The American Psychological Association awarded its first Distinguished Scientific Contribution Award to Rogers in recognition of his academic rigor.

Everything in his life led Rogers to this point of clarity: it is through relationships in which respect, empathy, unconditionality, and congruence are alive and embodied, that constructive change will occur. This hypothesis was confirmed by successful application of the theory in larger systems. The possibility of affecting larger systems intrigued Rogers increasingly throughout his life and led to his nomination for the Nobel Peace Prize in 1987.[7]

Rogers' attention to the power in relationships, and of intrapsychic and interpersonal processes, continued throughout his life. His keen observation of processes and their role in change convinced him to refuse any fixed dogmatic thesis. Instead, he turned to cutting-edge scholarship to inform his theory.

ROGERS' EPISTEMOLOGICAL POSITION: EXISTENTIAL/PHENOMENOLOGICAL EXPANSION

Rogers' fascination with students in every field in the knowledge revolution led him to become conversant with existential philosophers, Eastern religion, phenomenological methods, quantum mechanics, and more. No longer could he

---

[6.] See J Bozarth's 'Empathy from the Framework of Client-Centered Theory and the Rogerian Hypothesis' in Bohart and Greenberg (1997).

[7.] This included working for change in the public school system of Louisville, Kentucky, where 71% of students were below the national average, and the conflicts in Northern Ireland, South Africa, Latin and Central America, Hungary and Russia. The Nobel Prize nomination was the result of his work in Central America sponsored by the Peace Project he created with Gay (Swenson) Barfield.

base his work on either so-called objective science, or on speculative explanations of behavior. His own experience and research had always led him to pay faithful attention to what phenomenologists call 'lived-experience'.

For postmodernists, the universally agreed upon cultural story that has defined our historical moment, the meta-narrative, is shattering. Arnett and Arneson note that Rogers' insights did not come from postmodernists Michel Foucault, Jacques Derrida, or Jean-Francois Lyotard. Instead he 'discovered what we term "narrative decline" in the practice of therapy with his clients ... concerns of patients moved him intuitively to conclusions about the loss of meta-narratives'. They conclude, 'The healthy nature of his patients' personal values emerged when the self, not meta-narratives became the focus' (Arnett and Arneson, 1999: 85).

Rogers' affinity toward postmodern skepticism is evident throughout his writing. In his 1967 book *Person to Person: the Problem of Being Human*, Rogers writes:

> Instead of universal values 'out there' or a universal value system imposed by some group—philosophers, rulers or priests—we have the possibility of universal human value directions emerging from the experiencing of the human organism. Evidence from therapy indicates that both personal and social values emerge as natural, and experienced, when the individual is close to his [or her] own organismic valuing process. (Rogers, 1967: 27)

Rogers' experience led him to a world-view at odds with the status quo regarding epistemological authority, conceptions of power, and social visions. Epistemological authority and power are inseparable for Rogers. Like phenomenologist Herbert Spiegelberg, Rogers acknowledges prejudice throughout all academia, and its tendency to silence less powerful voices.

He often used his professional credibility to draw attention to social issues of conflict and oppression. In 1977 he published *On Personal Power: Inner Strength and its Revolutionary Impact* admitting that he had only recently grasped the political nature of his work. He quickly adopts the 'new use' of the term, as in 'politics of the family' or 'sexual politics' and concludes that all of our institutions take the view that the person cannot and must not be trusted, that he/she 'must be guided, instructed, rewarded, punished, and controlled by those who are wiser or higher in status ... [with] lip service to a democratic philosophy in which all power is vested in the people' (Rogers 1977: 8–9). He acknowledges that to describe 'the fundamental premise of Client-Centered Therapy is to make a challenging political statement' (*ibid.*: 9). This was accomplished through his insistence that authenticity was an inextricable element of the core conditions.[8]

---

8. Authenticity, or congruence, is an essential element of the core conditions. Any understanding of CCT that includes empathy and unconditional positive regard, but omits congruence is incomplete, and thus, inaccurate.

While Rogers began in empirical research, he did not remain entrenched in logical positivism and scientism. Rogers maintained a radical doubt of given narratives without slipping into a value-free moral relativism.

Like Einstein, Rogers found the quest for understanding reality enormous, but Rogers held out for the possibility of discovering a unifying human theory. He relied on empirical data when appropriate as in medical research, but held no meta-narrative sacred with a claim of capital 'T' truth (Rogers, 1964). Rogers describes our Universe as filled with multiple realities where consciousness is shifting.

For Rogers, authentic knowledge must come when narratives, 'stock of knowledge at hand', stereotypes and biases are not accepted as fact, but rather are acknowledged and bracketed. Rogers' resonance with Lao-tse is evident in the following quote cited by Rogers: 'It is as though he listened and such listening as his enfolds us in a silence in which at last we begin to hear what we are meant to be' (Rogers, 1980: 41). This mode of listening is infused with the open and acceptant valuing and respectful 'letting-be' characteristic of unconditional positive regard.

All phenomena presenting themselves must be received and regarded unconditionally in Rogers' theory. This feature is of great importance in phenomenology, 'that we consider all the data, real or unreal or doubtful, as having equal rights, and investigate them without fear or favor. This ... will help us to do justice to all of them, especially to those which are under the handicap of initial suspicion as to their existential claim' (Spiegelberg, 1969: 692). This state of alert letting-be confers epistemological authority[9] to marginal voices and thus provides a bridge to feminist and other non-dominant groups.

FEMINIST THEORY

ACADEMIC ROOTS IN THE UNITED STATES POST WORLD WAR II

Feminism is a multifaceted phenomenon. Feminists may identify themselves/ourselves as Postmodern, Green, Radical, Spiritual, Socialist, Marxist, and Humanist, among other descriptors. Among feminist therapists, primary orientations include: Psychoanalytic, Humanistic, Behavioral, Assertiveness Training, and Jungian, and even those may be divided further.

For example, I identify myself as primarily a client-centered practitioner and a feminist, closely aligned with postmodern/social constructivist and some humanistic strands, who is at home with some features of socialist/spiritual ... I will stop here! It is clearly only going to become more messy. In the process of categorizing and

---

[9.] In a previous paper, Wolter-Gustafson, (1999), I have traced how Rogers' embodiment of unconditional positive regard and empathic understanding is a way of bracketing the natural attitude, loosening our habitual ties with the world.

subcategorizing, the inherent trouble of labeling is revealed. I will come back to this point after I have set some feminist theory into a highly selective historical context.

Being a white woman from the East Coast of the United States born after World War II, I choose to start this academic linage with Naomi Weisstein. I had just started graduate studies in the Department of Humanistic and Behavioral Studies, when I was given an article to read titled, 'Psychology Constructs the Female or The Fantasy Life of the Male Psychologist (with some attention to the fantasies of his friends, the male biologist and the male anthropologist)' (Weisstein, 1972: 178–97). I read that she already held a PhD in psychology from Harvard, had completed her NSF (whatever that meant) postdoctoral fellowship in mathematical biology at the University of Chicago and played in a 'women's liberation rock band'. She had earned my full attention as she chronicled the pervasive rule of 'theory without evidence' throughout psychology, the poor use of science, 'jumping from hard data to ideological speculation' in biologically-based theories and the total disregard for the social context in which these 'findings' are seen as inevitable. Her original question was what a 'true' liberation of women would mean. She concluded by saying that until we provide respect for both men and women and until social expectations for both are equal, our answers will 'simply reflect our prejudices'. I have learned that this essay is characterized as having started the discipline of the psychology of women, and has been reprinted over 42 times in six different languages.

Jean Baker Miller's work developed in the feminist academic milieu of Boston University and Harvard in the late 1970s, in a climate challenging the misogyny embedded in every academic field and in society in general. In contrast to the upstart fiery graduate students launching their feminist critiques in the social sciences, Miller's legitimacy was already established. She was a medical doctor, had already edited *Psychoanalysis and Women* in 1973, and held a position as Clinical Professor of Psychiatry at Boston University School of Medicine.

In 1976, Boston's Beacon Press published a bright pink volume entitled *Toward a New Psychology of Women* by Jean Baker Miller, MD. This book quickly became a classic and standard-bearer for the growing feminist critique of traditional academia.

Jean Baker Miller saw the big picture. Her images of psychological and societal health are founded on values of respect and equality. She writes, 'humanity has been held to a limited and distorted view of its self—from interpretation of the most intimate of personal emotions to its grandest vision of human possibilities—precisely by virtue of its subordination of women' (Miller, 1976: 1).

She observed and displayed the details of women's and men's lives and their complex relationship to each other and to society. It was Miller who illustrated how the schemas 'given' to explain gender roles were not in fact given, but were rather a product of the marriage of patriarchy and hierarchy, supported by psychoanalysis and existent economic structures. 'Women have played a specific role in male-led society in ways no other suppressed groups have done. They have been entwined with men in intimate and intense relationships, creating the milieu—the family—

in which the human mind as we know it has been formed. Thus women's situation is a crucial key to understanding the psychological order' (*ibid.*: 1).

It is no wonder that the feminist community latched onto this book. In light of the traditional psychodynamic dogma that exalted the separate self and autonomy as the measure of psychological health, Miller and her colleagues provided the appropriate social corrective by emphasizing relational empathy and mutual empowerment.

Steeped in her psychoanalytic roots, she recognizes the need to develop a relationally mutual, interpersonally empowering psychology.[10] We knew that 'the Personal is Political' and Jean Baker Miller showed us how this is true. What Miller provided was a complete conceptual whole into which others could contribute parts. She pioneered and became devoted to the development of the Stone Center for Research on Women, the nation's largest women's research center.

FEMINIST EPISTEMOLOGICAL POSITIONS

In order to gain an understanding of the feminist epistemological landscape, I have turned to Philosophy Professor Sandra Harding's 1986 work on *The Science Question in Feminism* as discussed by Mary Gergen (2000). Harding delineates three distinct feminist epistemologies which correspond to the more general categories within the social sciences.

The first is called the 'feminist empiricist position' and has its origin in the Enlightenment. It is readily recognizable to anyone who learned that the modern empirical revolution freed us from earlier more primitive reliance on understanding reality through superstition, or whatever the Deity of the time might reveal to those He ordained, primarily His priests and learned scholars. Observable, measurable experimental data would produce objectivity and replace mere beliefs or 'soft' subjective ways of knowing. It is this split between hard and soft knowledge, with one subordinate to the other, that feminist scholars challenged. Genevieve Lloyd (1993), Mary Briody Mahowald (1994) and others examined philosophical writing from Plato to Descartes to Simone de Beauvoir and beyond. They revealed the embedded coupling of rationality with maleness. Their work played one part in the creation of the second position.

This is the 'feminist standpoint position', which moves away from objectivity and gender-neutral assumptions in which masculine traditions are replicated de facto. The 'standpoint position' moves toward a more woman-centered value base. Mary Gergen sees the publication of Carol Gilligan's ground-breaking book *In a*

[10.] Her colleagues included Freudians and Neo-Freudians including early Feminists such as Nancy Chodorow and Frieda Fromme-Reichmann. It also included sex-role stereotype researchers such as the Brovermans and Harriett Lerner, and sociologists Jessie Bernard, David McClelland, and Elizabeth Janeway.

Different Voice as lending a 'new authority' for women's viewpoints and values in which the ethic of care and the importance of connection are seen as characteristic of women's moral reasoning.

The third wave is called either the 'feminist postmodern' or 'postmodern feminism'. It incorporates assumptions from the social constructionists' frame of reference. Gergen describes its epistemological core as 'Knowledge is situated, local, contingent and temporary, inextricably intertwined with a situated nature of the community of knowledge makers' (Gergen, 2000: 21). She sees this postmodern frame as an emancipatory one and writes 'With the constant shuffling and re-stacking of the decks of the Real, options for synthesis and change, for new configurations of power, and for new potentials are created' (*ibid.*: 1). In this sphere, the scholar, therapist or researcher puts her/himself into the picture.

Julia Kristeva, radical scholar and innovator, also posits three waves of feminism. The first wave attempted to join patriarchy. A second wave in the late 1960s attempted to withdraw from patriarchal culture 'to give a language to the intra-subjective and corporeal experiences left mute by the culture in the past' (Ermarth, 1989: 43). Instead of identification with the symbolic and patriarchal functions, attention and honor were placed in the semiotic and maternal functions. The third wave moves beyond the duality implied in both preceding positions. They argue that these pseudo-alternatives merely served to preserve 'the same dichotomy between gendered functions. Thus the association of particular values with gender prevents feminist theory from reaching the premises it seeks' (*ibid.*: 38). The third wave seeks to mix patriarchy, associated with linear time and projects, with matriarchy, associated with being outside of linear time and projects. This most promising step, to go beyond structure to process, may be the most difficult.

In a study of the politics of women's caregiving, 'Feeding Egos and Tending Wounds: Deference and Disaffection in Women's Emotional Labor', Bartky goes beyond, or perhaps, underneath ideological party lines, while remaining lucid about power and our habitual relation to it. She writes:

> In order to develop an effective politics of everyday life, we need to understand better than we do now not only the processes of personality development, but the 'micropolitics' of our most ordinary transactions, the ways in which we inscribe and reinscribe our subjection in the fabric of the ordinary. (Bartky, 1990: 118–19)

This detailed attention to process and meaning is the norm in client-centered work and is consistently evident in Bartky's work. In her diligence and faithfulness to the facts, and her attention to the specificity of the smallest moments, the greater pattern is inexorably revealed. She shows us that the way out is through. Put simply, the most personal is the most universal.

I am in fundamental agreement with Mary Gergen's and Julia Kristeva's work within the social constructionist postmodern field. Writing about our 'turbulent

Transmodern era', client-centered author and Saybrook Institute President Maureen O'Hara suggests that 'The postmodern discourse offers contemporary psychology the potential for reconciling and surpassing the limits of both objectivism and subjectivism' (O'Hara, 1997: 12–13). This third feminist perspective, which is also shared by client-centered clinicians, is the place from which we may finally break free of our dualistic traditions.

REGARDING EPISTEMOLOGY AND POWER

In the introduction to their book *Feminist Epistemologies*, Linda Alcoff and Elizabeth Potter acknowledge that in the recent past, feminist epistemology was an oxymoron. They acknowledge that their use of the term represents an uneasy alliance between feminism and philosophy. Since classic feminist analysis insists on an historic particularity in the context of theory, many doubt the possibility of anything resembling a universal account of the nature of knowledge. The contributing writers vary widely in their perspectives. But it was Alcoff and Potter themselves who interested me most. They suggest that feminist investigations of political relationships that are implicated in theories of knowledge have led scholars to the conclusion that gender hierarchies are hardly alone in influencing the production of knowledge. Rather race, class, sexuality, culture and age determine cognitive authority as well.

Further, they state that recent developments in feminist theory demonstrate that 'gender as a category of analysis cannot be abstracted from a particular context while other factors are held stable' (Alcoff and Potter, 1993: 3). This reasoning replicated Heisenberg's uncertainty principle that it is impossible to measure both the position and momentum of a particle with precision. Rogers notes the limitation to the 'frozen moment' that such objective research yields as opposed to the 'understanding of the ongoing movement' research which he saw as preferable, albeit, more difficult to conduct (Rogers, 1961: 127).

Alcoff and Potter report a strong consensus among feminists that the project of feminism be more inclusive. They write, 'The ontological status of women ... has shifted for academic feminists in light of the influential arguments showing that women, per se, do not exist. There exist upper-caste Indian little girls; older, heterosexual Latinas; and white, working class lesbians' (Alcoff and Potter, 1993: 4).

This point represents the clearest path toward convergence for feminist and client-centered scholars. While ever mindful of each individual's particular contextual reality, that 'reality' is always mediated by the idiosyncratic meaning structure within any particular person. To understand humans, listen long and with great care to the unique, irreducible, irreplaceable person. Rogers writes, 'I believe that this way of knowing is limited only by the limits of our capacity for empathy, and to the degree of our ingenuity in getting at the internal frame of reference of the organism' (Rogers, 1964: 116).

The tendency to project our own meaning out beyond our own perception and call it Reality is not compatible with the Rogers framework. In an interview with Richard Evans, Rogers says, 'The human organism immediately attaches a meaning to whatever is perceived ... For me, perception is reality as far as the individual is concerned. I don't even know whether there is an objective reality. Probably there is, but none of us will really know that' (Evans, 1975: 9). This causes Rogers to say again and again that he has no interest in labels, 'I'd rather [they] observe the phenomena themselves' (*ibid.*: 8). And again, we hear the need to suspend the natural attitude, evident in our own internal frame of reference, with an unconditional regard and empathic understanding of whatever presents itself as reality.

My client-centered belief in the creative persistence of the developing person suggests that although gendered binarism is deeply encoded and habituated in us, it is not the final word on who we may become.[11]

In the development of both feminist and client-centered thought, we see the tendency to continue to explore and be open to the growing and fluid nature of scholarship. Serious errors in our understanding of both theories can be made when we consider outdated theoretical formulations to be current, and fail to attend to more recent scholarship. This requires careful attention to the assumptions we make.

FEMINIST CRITIQUES OF HUMANISTIC THERAPY AND A CLIENT-CENTERED RESPONSE

Critiques are based on assumptions that may, or may not be accurately attributed. However, even in cases where the assumption can be challenged or corrected, there still may be a concern worthy of more careful attention. I believe such is the case regarding the most fundamental critique of humanistic therapy, with some attention to Client-Centered Therapy in particular.

1. It's not all in your head

This most frequently raised critique of Humanistic therapists is that humanistic psychology in essence blames the victim. They tell a client that she is responsible for her own oppression. Miriam Greenspan, in 'The Unsuccessful Marriage of Humanist Therapy and Feminism' (Greenspan, 1993), acknowledges that Rogers went against the prevailing emphasis on correct diagnosis and interpretation as the key feature in therapy, and writes 'Rogers insisted that it was the therapeutic *relationship* itself that was crucial. In contrast to the medical stress on individual pathology and its cure, Rogers introduced the idea of personal growth through therapy' (*ibid.*: 122). But the core conditions can 'only go so far if they do not take place in the context of a therapy that is based on a political understanding of women's problems' (*ibid.*: 135).

[11.] Martine Rothblatt, author of *The Apartheid of Sex* and attorney for the Human Genome Project, suggests that we will eventually move beyond being *Homo sapiens*, literally the wise man, and will become *Persona creatas*, the creative person.

She continues, 'But because the humanistic approach to therapy fails to see the relationship between the personal psychic lives of clients and the social values and institutions which shape these lives, it ends up severely hampered in its use of the very skills proposed by Rogers' (*ibid.*: 135).

From a client-centered perspective, the problem is that there *is* something in all our heads about gender, power, and epistemological authority that does hold many people back. There are also economic, structural and legal realities that daily destroy women's lives throughout the world. It is here that we need our post-dualistic understanding of reality most of all.

As Maxine Hong Kingston declares at the end of her play *The Warrior Woman*, 'We must make room for Paradox'. Great minds have made room for this encompassing embrace of reality throughout the ages. As an example, Albert Einstein's encompassing mind reconciled the apparent paradox of his time regarding the interactions of light and matter. The development of his theory on the 'photoelectric effect' showed that the argument was moot, as light, being comprised of photons could have properties of both a particle and a wave, thus revealing the paradox to be non-existent.

While I make no claims for Einstein's level of clarity, I believe the apparent paradox of the individual person versus the social realities to be similarly non-existent as these concepts are distinct pieces of the larger phenomenon of 'being-in-the-world'.[12]

What feminists often call 'internalized oppression' clearly exists. Feminist philosopher Sandra Lee Bartky describes the phenomenon in her article 'On Psychological Oppression' (Bartky, 1990: 22–32). Carl Rogers describes this phenomenon in his theory of personality as 'internalized conditions of worth'. Parents (or primary caregivers) often supply conditional positive regard to children. The child is only 'lovable' when he/she adopts the behaviors and attitudes consistent with those accepted by those adults and/or the dominant culture. In order to achieve positive regard, the child introjects the desired values, making them his/her own, and acquires *conditions* of worth (Rogers, 1989). The developing child loses her/his authentic self in order to gain that positive regard. The self-concept then becomes based on these standards of value rather than on organismic evaluation. When a child receives unconditional positive regard, they are free to honor their own voice and experiencing as a source of epistemological authority.

My response to this critique includes a discussion of the central role of unconditional positive regard (UPR) in both judgment of the client and respect for the 'up to something-ness' of the client. The role of empathic understanding carries with it the implicit assumption that the organism is acting as a unified whole. The person's 'whole organism' includes de facto their situatedness in historic, economic and social reality.

[12.] My use of Heidegger's phrase 'being-in-the-world' does not connote my carte blanche acceptance of his philosophical system.

One of the core conditions of Client-Centered Therapy is unconditional positive regard, in which the therapist creates a relationship free from the imposition of the therapist's, or society's, conditions of worth. For the client to be prized unconditionally by the therapist, she must feel that she is the sole author determining what is right for her and what is not. As Carol Gilligan describes in the first phases of women's moral reasoning that in choosing whether or not to terminate her pregnancy, she is often conflicted between hurting her parents or the fetus or others. Seeing her own self as a person of care and worthy of not being hurt is an achievement. It is this process of reclamation of herself as a source of knowledge, as worthy and legitimate in her own right, that is at the heart of client-centered theory and practice.

Rogers is his radical respect for the client as the author of her own story. Without the principle of non-directivity, the respect for the client sought in feminist theory may be rendered weak. In *Feminist Counselling in Action*, Jocelyn Chaplin writes that the 'Client-Centered Approach fits well with feminist approaches to counseling' (Chaplin, 1999: 18) because the powers of empathy and warmth are more developed in women than in men. However, she sees the fundamental non-directivity of CCT as relevant only in the first stage of therapy. Chaplin sees non-directivity as just a strategy for understanding 'inner hierarchies', which she can then use to explain the world to her client. In so doing, the feminist counselor becomes one more person from whom the client needs to learn. Client-centered scholar Barbara Brodley states that non-directivity will 'preclude the therapist from experiencing the mental set of using means to achieve ends while doing therapy' (Brodley, 2000: 1).

Non-directivity is essential in every interaction with a client, in order to express unconditional positive regard. Unless the therapist has a radical respect for the directionality of the client and trusts the client to name her own reality, the conditions of worth that have been used to undermine her epistemological authority in the past will once again be replicated by the therapist. For the client-centered therapist, the client's epistemological authority is affirmed.

Empathy is another core condition of Client-Centered Therapy. Greenspan writes that it is 'not enough' to mirror the clients feelings as Rogerians do. That is precisely Rogers' point as well. Goff Barrett-Lennard writes that empathic understanding requires

> ... an active process of desiring to know the full, present and changing awareness of another person, of reaching out to receive his/her communication and meaning, and of translating his/her words and signs into experienced meaning that matches at least those aspects of ... awareness that are most important ... at the moment. (Barrett-Lennard, cited in Rogers, 1980: 143–4)

Dave Mearns echoes this need for working in relational depth (Mearns, 1996). Clearly, it is not enough to skim the surface of the client's narrative wave.

Since the initial development of Client-Centered Therapy, empathy has required taking the whole person into account. The socio-economic and political realities of the client's life are always received by the client-centered therapist as core elements in their empathic understanding of the client. Starting with Rogers' work with World War II veterans, the geo-political, physical, and cultural conditions were empathically received by the therapist, whether or not the client expressly named those influences on his/her present condition. Carl Rogers and the colleagues who have carried on his work have consistently sought out places and people suffering under oppressive or socially perilous conditions.[13]

2. Rogers is too individualistic, we need relational power

In the fall of 1988, reading the Boston Globe Magazine, I was excited to see the title 'A Theory of Empathy' featured on the cover. I expected to see an article tracing Rogers' half-century of work. Instead, I found an article about the Stone Center for Research on Women at Wellesley College. What I didn't expect to read was that psychology had ignored empathy until its theoretical articulation by the Stone Center. I came to understand that these researchers believed that Rogers promoted the standard Western view of the self as being highly individuated, and that shared power was absent from the psychological literature.

One element in this critique is that Rogers did not see a need for mutuality in relationships and shared power. Stone Center scholars Judith Jordan and Janet Surrey write,

> An alternative concept of personal power as inner strength and self-determination has appeared throughout the psychological literature (e.g., Rogers, 1975; Maslow, 1954), but this concept still evokes the image of the highly individuated self-actualizer ... We have needed a different concept to suggest power with others, that is, power in connection or relational power. Thus we have talked about mutual empowerment (each person is empowered) through relational empowerment (the relationship is empowered). (Surrey, 1991: 163)

This critique is accurate in describing the dominant psychological paradigm. However, humanistic psychology and the existential-phenomenological strand often stand in opposition to that paradigm. Client-Centered Therapy has a unique voice, even within the humanist world. Carl Rogers warns, 'We in the West seem to have made a fetish out of complete individual self-sufficiency, of not needing help, of

---

13. To 'understand' a woman in South Africa, you have to know whether she is black or white. Rogers had refused invitations to lecture in South Africa under Apartheid until an invitation came in 1982. He agreed to go to Johannesburg under the condition that he would be able to work with men and women from the traditional black communities. He also met with professionals regarding Afro-Centrism at a black university in Soweto.

110

being completely private except in a very few selected relationships … But we pay a price' (Rogers, 1980: 198–9).

Another element of the Stone Center's critique is rooted in a misunderstanding of how Rogers' theory of development came into being. The focus on the individuated self modeled after the autonomous male self has, in fact, dominated developmental and clinical psychology. Judith Jordan and Janet Surrey assert that Rogers' focus on the 'self' represents adherence to the developmentally gender-bound lineage of Erikson.

Rogers had never stepped into the developmental theory of personality originating with Freud's psycho-sexual stages, with subsequent modifications made by Erikson, Horney, and Chodorow. Nor did it originate with Piaget's developmental schemas for cognition and morality further developed by Kohlberg. Rather, Rogers' theory of personality evolved secondarily after his significant contribution to the theory of psychotherapy. This was made explicit in his most scholarly work (Rogers, 1959). Rogers writes that a theory of the development of personality followed from their attempt to order their perceptions of the client as s/he appeared in therapy.

The very first heading in this theory reads 'Postulated Characteristics of the Human Infant'. He writes of the 'goal-directed attempt of the organism to satisfy the experience needs for *actualization* in the reality as *perceived*' (*ibid.*: 222, original italics). A portion of the infant 'individual's experience becomes differentiated and *symbolized* in an *awareness* of functioning' (*ibid.*: 223, original italics). Rogers says that as this awareness of self emerges, so does the *need for positive regard*. He writes, 'This need is universal in human beings, and in the individual is pervasive and persistent' (*ibid.*: 223, original italics). Note that Rogers is not constructing a separate developmental track for the male infant in contrast with the female infant. 'The healthy development of the new human depends on a relationship with caretakers in which particular qualities in relation are essential. These qualities include understanding, respecting and trusting the phenomenological frame of reference of that new human' (Wolter-Gustafson, 1999: 210). This relational emphasis echoes Rogers' earliest writing, *Client-Centered Therapy*. The index to this book shows eight separate references for 'Self-in-relationship'.

RELATIONALITY AND SHARED POWER

The primary research the Stone Center supports is of great value. Their explicit language and the publications their scholars generate shed a strong beam of light on the relationship. I believe that the same emphasis exists and has been described in person-centered literature for several decades, but it has not been available in the public domain, nor has it been featured with such strength and clarity. Two exceptions can be seen in the published work of Peggy Natiello and Jules Seeman.

Since the early 1970s, person-centered and feminist scholar Peggy Natiello has concentrated her work and writing on these issues. Chapter titles in her book *The*

Person-Centred Approach: A passionate presence include 'For a Quality Relationship, Include Equality', and 'Collaborative Power and Social Change', and 'The Relationship that Heals'.

In 'The Relationship that Heals', Natiello writes that decades of research document the tie between a positive outcome in therapy and the quality of connection between client and therapist.[14] So it is not a question of treatment strategies and techniques. Rather, we need new questions about:

> Our ability to enter into an intimate, authentic, trustworthy relationship with another ... It is really about who we are—the spiritual, emotion, attitudinal characteristics that we embody as persons, our ability to make a deep connection, to tolerate intimacy, and to offer a climate of safety. A relationship-oriented approach to therapy requires us to step down from the throne of expertness and collaborate with our client rather than 'cure' him, or even tell him *how to cure himself.* (Natiello, 2001: 25–6, original italics)

Jules Seeman recently explained that his entire career, from the early days of the Chicago Counseling Center to his recent study in psycho-immunology, has been devoted to understanding the depth of our human connectedness and communication. For Seeman, the latest research reaffirms what he and Rogers always knew: the organism always operates as a whole and is busy at any given moment separating the 'me' from the 'not me'. He notes that 'Although the early emphasis in humanistic theory was tilted toward the development of the self as an entity, an emerging emphasis has been the increasing focus on the intersubjective and relational aspects of psychotherapy' (Seeman, 2002: 621).

In keeping with Rogers' insistence on lived-experience as the source of his work, he and his colleagues created a series of residential, often cross-cultural workshops, to see how we can deal with power in a large group setting. I was a participant in a 12-day residential experiment called 'Releasing Personal and Community Power through the Person-Centered Approach', with Rogers and a staff of person-centered therapists in 1978. Our aim was to find an alternative to 'the traditional way of dealing with problems', i.e., 'to attempt to control the other person or people'.

Here is Rogers' description of the process in his own words. In 1980, he described the power sharing model for decision making in this way:

> When one observes this process at work, its awesome power becomes increasingly apparent ... Slowly, beautifully, painstakingly, a decision is crafted to take care of each person ... The process seems slow, and participants complain about 'the time we are wasting'. But the larger wisdom of the group recognizes the value of the

---

14. See also Bohart and Greenberg (1997).

process, since it is continually knitting together a community in which every soft voice, every subtle feeling has its respected place. (Rogers, 1980: 196)

Finally, Rogers quotes a participant's description of the experience:

> I felt the oneness of spirit in community ... We breathed together, felt together, even spoke for one another ... without the usual barricades of 'me-ness' or 'you-ness'—it was like a meditative experience when I feel myself as a center of consciousness, very much a part of the broader, universal consciousness. And yet with that extraordinary sense of oneness, the separateness of each person present has never been more clearly preserved. (*ibid.*: 196–7)

TOWARD CONVERGENCE

I believe that we can work to create sustainable bridges between client-centered and feminist streams of theory and practice. While we are quite sophisticated in our understanding of the core conditions of empathy, congruence, and unconditional positive regard, it is rare that we apply them with academically diverse kindred spirits. We have worked to communicate across cultures, but not enough across disciplines. Too often, traditional conference formats stifle spontaneity and take on an 'us-versus-them' tone. The prevalence and danger of that tendency is quite visible in today's political climate. I am proposing creation of a sustainable bridge between the client-centered and feminist worlds.

Ours are distinct voices that need to be heard. Our shared commitment to empathic relationships and shared power fundamentally challenges the dominant paradigm. We struggle against marginalization. Divergent streams become more powerful when they flow into the same river.

REFERENCES

Alcoff, L and Potter, E (eds) (1993) Introduction: When feminists intersect epistemology, in *Feminist Epistemologies*. New York: Routledge, pp. 1–14.

Arnett, RC and Arneson, P (1999) *Dialogic Civility in a Cynical Age: Community, hope, and interpersonal relationships*. Albany, NY: State University of New York Press.

Bartky, S (1990) *Femininity and Domination, Studies in the phenomenology of oppression*. New York: Routledge.

Bohart, A and Greenberg, L (1997) *Empathy Reconsidered: New directions in psychotherapy*. Washington, DC: American Psychological Association.

Brodley, BT (2000) *Client-Centered: An expressive therapy*. Chicago: Illinois School of

Professional Psychology.

Chaplin, J (1999) *Feminist Counselling in Action*. Thousand Oaks, CA: Sage Publications.

Ermath, ED (1989) The solitude of women and social time, in FJ Forman (ed) *Taking Our Time: Feminist perspectives on temporality*. New York: Pergamon Press, pp. 37–46.

Evans, R (1975) *Carl Rogers, The Man and His Ideas*. New York: EP Dutton & Co.

Forman, F (1989) *Taking Our Time: Feminist perspectives on temporality*. New York: Pergamon Press.

Fox-Genovese, E (1991) *Feminism Without Illusions, A critique of individualism*. Chapel Hill, NC: University of North Carolina Press.

Gergen, M (2000) The emergence of feminist postmodern psychology. *Feminist Reconstructions in Psychology: Narrative, gender, and performance*. Thousand Oaks, CA: Sage Publications.

Gilligan C (1982) *In a Different Voice: Psychological theory and women's development*. Cambridge: Harvard University Press.

Greenspan, M (1993) *A New Approach to Women and Therapy*. (2nd ed) Blue Ridge Summit, PA: McGraw Hill.

Kirschenbaum, H (1979) *On Becoming Carl Rogers*. New York: Delacorte Press.

Lloyd, G (1993) *The Man of Reason: 'male' and 'female' in western philosophy*. (2nd ed) Minneapolis, MN: University of Minnesota Press.

Mahowald, MB (ed) (1994) *Philosophy of Woman: An anthology of classic to current concepts*. (3rd ed) Indianapolis, IN: Hackett Publishing Company.

Maslow, A (1954) *Motivation and Personality*. New York: Harper.

May, R (1972) *Power and Innocence: A search for the source of violence*. New York: Norton and Company.

Mearns, D (1996) Working at Relational Depth with Clients in Person-Centred Therapy. *Counselling, 7*(4): 306–11.

Miller, JB (1973) *Psychoanalysis and Women*. Baltimore: Penguin Books.

Miller, JB (1976) *Toward a New Psychology of Women*. (2nd ed) Boston: Beacon Press.

Natiello, P (2001) *The Person-Centred Approach: A passionate presence*. Ross-on-Wye: PCCS Books.

Nicholson LJ (ed) (1990) *Feminism/Postmodernism*. New York: Routledge.

O'Hara, M (1997) Emancipatory therapeutic practice in a turbulent transmodern era: a work of retrieval. *Journal of Humanistic Psychology, 37*(3): 7–33.

Rogers, CR (1957) The necessary and sufficient conditions of therapeutic personality change. *Journal of Consulting Psychology, 21*(2): 95–103.

Rogers, CR (1959) A theory of therapy, personality and interpersonal relationships, as developed in the client-centered framework, in S Koch (ed) *Psychology: A Study of a Science. Vol 3. Formulation of the person and the social context*. New York: McGraw-Hill.

Rogers, CR (1961) *On Becoming a Person: A therapist's view of psychotherapy*. Boston: Houghton Mifflin.

Rogers, CR (1964) Toward a science of the person, in T Wann (ed) *Behaviorism and Phenomenology, Contrasting bases for modern psychology*. Chicago: University of Chicago

Press, pp. 109–40.

Rogers, CR (1967). Toward a modern approach to values: The valuing process in the mature person, in C Rogers and B Stevens (eds) *Person to Person: The problem of being human.* Lafayette, CA: Real People Press, pp. 13–28.

Rogers, CR (1968) Some thoughts regarding the current presuppositions of the behavioral sciences, in WR Coulson and C Rogers (eds) *Man and the Science of Man.* Columbus, OH: Charles E Merrill Publishing, pp. 55–83.

Rogers, CR (1975) Empathic: An unappreciated way of being. *The Counseling Psychologist,* 5(2): 2–10.

Rogers, CR (1977) *On Personal Power: Inner strength and its revolutionary impact.* New York: Delacorte Press.

Rogers, CR (1980) *A Way of Being.* Boston: Houghton Mifflin.

Rogers, CR (1983) *Freedom to Learn for the 80s.* Columbus, OH: Charles E Merrill Publishing.

Rogers, CR (1989). A theory of therapy, personality, and interpersonal relationships, as developed in the client-centered framework, in H Kirschenbaum and VL Henderson (eds) *The Carl Rogers Reader.* Boston: Houghton Mifflin, pp. 236–57.

Rothblatt, M (1995) *The Apartheid of Sex, A manifesto on the freedom of gender.* New York: Crown Publishers.

Seeman, J (2002) in D Cain and J Seeman (2002) *Humanistic Psychotherapies: Handbook of research and practice.* Washington, DC: American Psychological Association.

Spiegelberg, H (1969) *The Phenomenological Movement: An historical introduction.* The Hague: Martinus Nijoff.

Surrey, J (1991) Relationship and empowerment, in JV Jordan, AG Kaplan, JB Miller, IP Stiver and JL Surrey (eds) *Women's Growth in Connection: Writings from the Stone Center.* New York: The Guilford Press, pp. 162–80.

Thorne, B (1992) *Carl Rogers.* London: Sage Publications.

Weisstein, N (1972) *Psychology Constructs the Female.* Revised and expanded version of: (1968) *Kinder, Kuche, Kirche as Scientific Law: Psychology constructs the female.* Boston: New England Free Press.

Wolter-Gustafson, C (1999) Power of the premise: Reconstructing gender and human development with Rogers' theory, in I Fairhurst (ed) *Women Writing in the Person-Centred Approach.* Ross-on-Wye: PCCS Books, pp. 199–214.

TRUSTING OUR CLIENTS:
THE STONE CENTER MODEL OF
THERAPY ENCOUNTERS A
NON-DIRECTIVE ATTITUDE

Mary Beth Napier

Feminist therapy has many different 'faces' and there are many theorists who have advanced our understanding and notions of what feminist therapy is. A prominent group of feminist theorists in the United States are the clinicians and professors at the Stone Center of Wellesley College. The Stone Center group have developed a model of feminist therapy they call 'the relational-cultural model of therapy'. In this chapter I will attempt to demonstrate how incorporating a client-centered non-directive attitude into the Stone Center's model of therapy will transform the therapy into a phenomenological model to make it more congruent with feminist principles of client self-determination and empowerment.

The Stone Center's model of relational-cultural therapy (also called relational therapy) rests on the belief that therapy has to provide the client with a new relational experience and that the particular quality of the therapist-client relationship is the key to healing (Miller and Stiver, 1997). According to Stone Center theorists a healing therapeutic relationship is one in which the therapist is with a client in ways that promote a growing sense of mutuality between them. It is this connection between the client and the therapist that produces psychological healing for the client. I propose that a key way for the therapist to stay connected to the client is by adopting a client-centered non-directive attitude. An attitude of non-directivity rests on the values of respect and trust in the client's process to heal and grow when given an environment that is free of judgments and conditions of worth, and when the therapist avoids behaviors and attitudes that disempower the client (Brodley, 1997). I propose if these changes are made to the Stone Center model, therapists using this model will maintain a better and more consistent connection with the client, thus promoting the client's natural inclination towards connection and growth fostering relationships.

KEY CONCEPTS OF THE STONE CENTER'S MODEL OF THERAPY[1]

According to Stone Center theorists, starting at a very young age, we all form internal images or schemas of what relationships are about. They are called relational images (Miller, 1988; Miller and Stiver, 1995; Miller and Stiver, 1997). These images are formed as we interact with others around us. The images, along with the meanings we attach to them, continue to evolve throughout our lives, and we continue to add new ones as we have different kinds of encounters with those with whom we interact. Whether these images are positive and empowering or whether these images are restricting and self-condemning depends upon the amount and quality of connections and disconnections characteristic of the significant relationships in a person's life. In addition to the images themselves, we also construct, at the same time, a set of beliefs about *why* our relationships are the way they are. These constructions determine our beliefs about others and ourselves in all areas of our lives.

Relational images and meanings, formed in the context of a relationship characterized mainly by connections, have certain characteristics. A *connection* is an interaction that is mutually empowering and one in which each person creates something new together through their interaction. Relationships that are characterized by connections are *growth fostering relationships* in which both people are enlarged and grow from the experience. As a result, the relational images we create from these interactions are characterized by relationships that are mutually empathic and mutually empowering; that is, they give us the means and motivation to act, lead us to more self-knowledge, allow us to feel more worthwhile and leave us yearning for more connections with others. The meanings we construct for why relationships are this way include a belief that we are valuable, worthwhile, knowledgeable and active people.

Relational images and meanings formed in the context of a relationship that is mainly characterized by disconnections have certain characteristics also. A *disconnection* happens when an adult or child is prevented from participating in mutually empathic and mutually enhancing or empowering relationships. It does not mean leaving or ending a relationship. Rather, it means a break in the psychological connection accompanied by a sense of being emotionally cut off from the other person. Disconnections occur when an adult or child is grossly abused or attacked but can also occur when the people in the person's relational world are unresponsive to the adult or child's expression of his or her experience. Hence, the degree of disconnection can vary from a very minor feeling of being out of touch with a significant other to a major trauma and violation.

[1.] The information in this section primarily has been taken from Miller, 1988 and Miller and Stiver, 1997.

From disconnections, we form very different relational images than we do from connections. These images of relationships include not being heard, or understood in a mutually empathic way. The meanings that a person attaches to relational images like these are that her relationships are the way they are because she is ineffective, deficient, defective or blameworthy. Because the most important people in her life do not seem to care about or value her experience, she comes to believe that she is an undesirable person.[2]

In order to avoid further and complete isolation, the person will devise strategies for remaining in connection while keeping large parts of herself out of the relationship. These strategies are called strategies of disconnection. People use these strategies to limit their sense of vulnerability, and in extreme cases, they use these strategies for survival (Jordan and Dooley, 2000). Strategies of disconnection do not permit the full range of experiences, thoughts or emotions. The strategies begin as the form through which psychological problems are expressed. As soon as people create strategies for staying out of relationships, they are contributing to the disconnections that cause psychological distress and lead to inauthentic relationships. Stone Center theoreticians believe that people can learn to be in authentic relationships and give up the protection of extreme strategies of disconnection by being in a 'growth fostering relationship'. Any relationship has the potential of being a growth fostering relationship including a therapy relationship.

THE THERAPY RELATIONSHIP

A good therapeutic relationship will create a new relational image for the client that is based on mutual empowerment. This relationship will help to counteract the damaging effects of relational images and meanings that are based on past disconnections characterized by nonmutual, destructive patterns of relating. The therapist is committed to trying to understand the client's experience through emotional resonance (Jordan, 1997). The therapist conveys to the client that what was unbearable to the client alone can become bearable when they deal with it together. As they are engaged in this kind of emotional resonance, both client and therapist come to understand and appreciate the meaning systems that have grown around the pain, and how it has shaped the person's life, giving meaning to the relational images that the person holds.

[2.] The model of relational cultural therapy grew out of the Stone Center's clinicians experiencing and honoring women's psychological experience. Over time, Stone Center theorists realized that the concepts they presented also held truth for men's psychological growth and development (Miller and Stiver, 1997). The original Stone Center group was comprised of women discussing and writing about women. To honor these beginnings, when the text reflects the gender of the therapist or client, they are referred to as female.

It is the therapist's job to monitor the level of connection and disconnections that happen and to actively engage with the client to bring their relationship to a stronger reconnection after a disconnection. In fact, Stone Center theoreticians believe that this is where the real work of therapy happens, in navigating and transforming the inevitable disconnections (Miller et al., 1999).

In addition to monitoring the times of connections and disconnection between them, the therapist's job is also to work with the client's strategies of disconnection. She does this by 'honoring both sides' of the client's strategy. Miller and Stiver (1994) explained, 'It is not only a question of "understanding" the strategies but also a question of the therapist really being able to "get with" the feeling of them' (p. 4), not just in an intellectual way but emotionally as well by understanding the reason for these strategies through the client's eyes. In order to be able to honor a client's strategies of disconnection, the therapist must be authentic in her relationship with the client. As the therapist does this, the client will experience a decrease in her need to use strategies that keep parts of herself out of the connection with the therapist.

In addition to these tasks, the therapist must also engage in mutual empathy with the client, and she must be perceived by the client as authentic. In terms of mutual empathy Jordan (1991) explains:

> Mutual empathy occurs when two people relate to each other in a context of interest in the other, emotional availability and responsiveness, cognitive appreciation of the wholeness of the other; the intent is to understand ... It is not simply a static mirroring process but an expansive growth process for both. In the excitement of exploration, getting to know one another—who are you? who am I? who are we?—there is the opportunity for new self-definition; new aspects of self are expressed and each provides that opportunity for the other. (p. 89)

It is experiencing and seeing a situation through the eyes of the other. Mutuality in therapy rests on the assumption that real growth of an individual can only occur in the context of a real, mutually responsive relationship (Jordan, 1997). In the Stone Center's model, the capacity to engage in mutual relationships is the goal of psychological development, and the growth of mutuality and enlarged connection in the therapy relationship is the core of therapy (Surrey, 1997).

According to Jordan (1993), mutuality in therapy also implies a responsiveness to the client rather than control of the client on the part of the therapist. When the therapist is empathic to the client she is being present, vulnerable, open, responsive and concerned. The therapist must be open to the client so that she can be emotionally impacted by the client and open to growth herself as a result this impact. When the therapy relationship is working well, both client and therapist have a shared sense of working together, a shared commitment and emotional investment in the relationship, an openness to change because of the relationship (Surrey, 1997). When the therapist can be this in tune with the client, the client can begin to explore shameful and frightening affect, bringing those feelings into connection and finding that someone can be with her as she does this. This allows the client to explore her capacity to move and influence another person as she explores her own inner reality. A stance of power and control on behalf of the therapist will impede this effort, but a spirit of respect and empathy will allow this exploration to unfold.

Authenticity refers to a quality of emotional presence and responsiveness that one person shows to another. It is the person's ongoing ability to represent herself more genuinely in relationships (Miller et al., 1999). Authenticity is ever evolving and grows and changes over time as the relationship between the therapist and client grows. A therapist's authenticity leads to growth of mutual empathy in the therapy relationship.

When the therapist can remain authentic, in tune to the moment-to-moment interactions between herself and her client through empathic attunement, she can respond to the client in a way that allows the client to freely explore her inner world. This exploration does not depend upon the client's ability to verbalize her experience in a clear, understandable way. The therapist shares the responsibility for achieving clarity, thus, diminishing the sense of shame the client experiences when she cannot easily articulate her experience (Jordan, 1997). It is each moment-to-moment interaction with a client that either allows her to grow or diminishes her sense of worth and feelings of competence in the world. Therefore, it is essential that the therapist provide the client with a relationship in which the moment-to-moment interactions are characterized by mutual empathy and authenticity. This is the most crucial way the therapist establishes and maintains a connection to the client (Jordan, 1992, 1995, 1999; Jordan and Dooley, 2000; Miller and Stiver, 1997).

A PARADIGM SHIFT

The Stone Center's model of relational therapy emphasizes the nature of the relationship between the client and the therapist as the key to psychological healing. In this respect, the relational model of therapy comes out of an entirely different therapeutic approach than does a traditional psychodynamic model (Miller et al., 1999). It is not a model that places the therapist in a position of authority over the client as an all-knowing expert who acts on a sick person. Instead, both the therapist and client try to counter the destructive effects that a patriarchal, power-over society has on the life of the clinician as well as the client. In order to counter these destructive elements, the therapist needs to have and be able to learn certain abilities, responsibilities and knowledge, the most important of which is for the therapist to learn how to participate in the therapy relationship in a way that allows her to facilitate 'movement in relationship.'

Miller and Stiver (1997) explained:

> Most traditional approaches to therapy focus on increased independence, greater self-knowledge or insight, or a stronger sense of self as endpoints of therapy. In contrast, we see the greater capacity for engaging in mutually empathic and mutually empowering connections as the goal. Out of this increased connection, the person becomes a fuller, stronger person as she simultaneously becomes more connected to her experience. (pp. 121–2)

EXPERT AND TRUST ELEMENTS IN THE STONE CENTER'S MODEL

There appear to be contradictory elements in the Stone Center theory regarding how the goals of relational therapy are achieved and the therapist's role in achieving them. The Stone Center theorists suggest that the therapist's job is to create a growth fostering relationship with the client. To do this:

- The therapist is a real and genuine person in the relationship. She engages in mutual empathy with the client rather than serving in an expert role.
- She monitors and works with connections and disconnections in the moment-to-moment relationship.
- She helps the client to identify and then work with strategies of disconnection and old relational images that are based on disconnections.

There are elements in the theory that I have termed *trust elements* and elements that I have termed *expert elements*. The trust elements are concerned with allowing the client to feel empowered through her relationship with the therapist. The therapist is not seeking to impose meanings on the client's experience. Rather, she attempts to set aside her own internal frame of reference in order to experience the client's internal frame of reference as deeply and accurately as possible (Jordan, 1991).

I suggest that these elements are based on the following assumptions:

- If the therapist provides a relationship for the client that is characterized by mutual empathy, the client's own need and desire for connection can be trusted to move the client towards deeper connection with her therapist, which then has the benefit of changing relational images based on disconnections.
- The client can be trusted to move towards connection when she is provided an environment in which her internal experience is heard and respected, not judged, interpreted or changed.
- Healing does not occur through therapist intervention but when a therapist can deeply understand the need for strategies of disconnection and can respect the times when the client needs connection and disconnection. The client can be

trusted *to give up* her strategies of disconnection when she continues to experience high and consistent levels of mutual empathy by a therapist who is genuine.
• The client, not the therapist, is the expert on the client's experience.

I suggest that the goal of all of the trust elements is for the therapist to *deeply understand the client's experience through the client's internal frame of reference* rather than to serve as an expert on her experience. The therapist then communicates her understanding to the client and also shows the client that the client's experiences, thoughts and feelings do affect her.

The other elements, I refer to as *expert elements*. These elements rely on the therapist's expertise in the relational-cultural model and place her in the role of being responsible for moving the relationship between herself and the client in a specific direction. The therapist's responsibilities or expert elements are as follows:
• The therapist is responsible for moving the relationship with the client in a particular direction: towards mutual empowerment, and to increase the client's ability to engage in mutual empathy.
• The therapist is responsible for understanding and recognizing strategies of disconnection in her client. This means that the therapist uses her expertise to view the client's experience through the relational-cultural lens and looks for behaviors, thoughts and feelings in the client that match the concepts of this model.
• The therapist is responsible for highlighting, for the client, specific events that happen in the client's experience within and outside of therapy in order to emphasize connections, disconnections, and strategies of disconnection.
• The therapist is responsible for providing tentative interpretations for the client about her experiences to assist the client in making connections in her own experiences, especially to uncover old relational images and their meanings that are preventing the client from participating in growth fostering relationships.
• The therapist is responsible for recognizing when and how to present an interpretation or challenge to a client to maximize the receptivity of the client to the therapist's intervention.

The kinds of attitudes, thinking and assumptions of the two types of elements cause the therapist to engage in behaviors that can be contradictory. If the therapist is focused on the expert elements, she cannot also be focused on trying to understand the client's internal frame of reference and respond to the client through mutual empathy. Consequently, when the therapist is engaged in an expert task she is responding to the client through her own internal frame of reference and not the client's. The therapist is seeing the client's experience through her own filter that predisposes her to look for *specific* things in the client's experience and to disregard other aspects. In fact, when the therapist is operating from her own frame of reference, it drastically affects what the therapist looks for, what she points out to the client, and how and when she responds to the client.[3] The process (and often times content) between them becomes controlled by the therapist's goals.

In order for the therapist to be successful in moving the relationship, she must focus on her own inner thoughts and feelings, then study the client's communication to see where and how it fits with the theory of psychological health and pathology. This kind of mental activity on the part of the therapist is the exact opposite of the therapist attempting to see the client's experience through the client's inner world.

When the therapist is engaged in mutual empathy with the client, she is attempting to get out of her frame of reference and to experience the client's frame of reference as deeply as possible. However, if the therapist is using mutual empathy to gain enough knowledge about the client to use her expertise to guide the client's process, then the goal of mutual empathy is not to provide the client with a different kind of relational environment; instead it becomes a tool used in the service of other expert elements. The client may begin to feel like the therapist is *up to something* because the therapist is using her understanding of the client's experience to assist her in *doing something* to the client. In this case the *doing something* is moving their relationship by highlighting times of connections, disconnections and strategies of disconnection; and looking for and *working with* old relational images.

There are problems with the Stone Center's emphasis on the therapist's expert ability to move the relationship (and, therefore, the client) in a certain direction. Even if this direction seems like a desirable one (towards mutual empowerment), it still assumes the following:
• The therapist knows that this is the best direction for every client because it is assumed that every client should be assisted towards the same goals.
• The therapist is responsible for moving the relationship because the client is incapable of doing so (this is especially true at the beginning of therapy).
• The success of the therapy rests on the ability of the therapist to correctly identify certain elements of a client's experience (connections, disconnections, strategies of disconnection and relational images) and to use her expertise about these concepts to foster a particular type of change in the client (change in relational images, growth in client's relational awareness and competence).

When I speak of expert elements, I am not referring to the 'power-over' concept of power delineated in the Stone Center's work (Miller and Stiver, 1997). I am not suggesting that the Stone Center's model of relational-cultural therapy aims to perpetuate dominance of one group over others, or that it suggests that therapists have the right to define the reality of their clients. On the contrary, their work is in the service of working against such oppression and forms of power. However, I am suggesting that expert elements do place the therapist in a position of power because

---

[3.] In social psychology this is referred to as confirmation bias (Aronson, 1995, Chapter 5).

inherent in these elements is the assumption that the therapist's role is to facilitate 'movement' within the relationship—and this movement is in a particular direction— *the direction that the therapist believes is in the best interest of the client.* This is a paternalistic way to view the relationship and is contrary to the idea that the client has the ability to be self-directed, responsible and autonomous in selecting desirable goals for herself. When a therapist acts out of the expert elements of this theory, she may create many more disconnections between herself and her client because she is focused on her own internal frame of reference rather than on the client's internal frame of reference. This prevents her from staying more connected to and understanding the client's experience through the client's eyes.

It is my contention that although it is extremely important for a therapist to address disconnections in a way that builds mutual empowerment and relational awareness and competency, the attitudes and behaviors that stem from expert elements of the Stone Center's theory create disconnections between the therapist and client that could be avoided. Consequently, I do not believe that working through disconnections between the therapist and the client has to be a major way for the client to build relational competence or awareness because I do not believe that there are necessarily many times of disconnection between the therapist and the client.

Instead, I suggest that there is a way for a therapist to maintain almost constant connection with her client throughout the therapy process—that is, by operating almost exclusively within the trust elements of this theory. Additionally, I propose that if the Stone Center incorporates what is called a 'non-directive attitude' from client-centered therapy into its theory, that its theory will be more internally consistent and that therapist behavior will be more congruent with the Stone Center's beliefs and values about what constitutes good therapy. That is, it is *mutual empathy* that leads to mutual empowerment and relationships that are characterized by connections. Consequently, the therapist's attempt to engage in mutual empathy and remain connected to the client's frame of reference is what provides an environment that is conducive to change and growth in the client, not the therapist *working with* any particular part of the client's experience or attempting to move the client in any particular direction.

Mutual empathy and therapist authenticity are trust elements in the Stone Center theory because they are what allow the therapist to provide an environment for the client to grow. I suggest that if one believes a person's basic motivation is to seek connections with others, it follows that if the right conditions are provided by the therapist (a growth fostering relationship), then the person's own drive towards connection will move the person toward mutual empowerment and relational competency in her relationship with the therapist. No other planned therapist intervention is needed. The therapist must be an expert in providing the right relationship that facilitates the client's own movement towards connection. The therapist does not have to be an expert on the client's inner world or on knowing how to move the client in a particular direction.

It appears that the expert elements of the relational-cultural model are remnants from psychodynamic models that work against mutuality and connection between the therapist and client. I suggest a further paradigm shift from psychodynamic models and concepts to a phenomenological approach to therapy that places the client's experience, rather than adherence to particular theories, at the center of the therapeutic enterprise. The therapist must be able to join the client in her world without imposing outside standards onto the client's experience, which also serve to distance the therapist from the client.

Jordan (1997) addressed this kind of relationship between client and therapist:

> Therapy cannot be a mechanistic enterprise but must take the therapist as well as the client to deep places of vulnerability ... Unlike many professions that count on definable skills or taking particular roles, psychotherapy calls upon the presence of the whole person of the therapist. How we *do* therapy is a lot about who we *are* as people. Therapy is importantly about *being*. It does not depend on a clear and easily mastered set of skills. We, too, must struggle to stay in connection in the face of vulnerability. (p. 152)

Jordan (1997) also made the following plea to anyone writing about therapy: 'Please say what is actually happening in the therapy relationship, not what theory prescribes or what sounds smart or clever or theoretically formed' (p. 152). Client-Centered Therapy, with its backbone of the non-directive attitude, is based on research about what actually happens in the therapeutic relationship and is informed by over 60 years of clinical experience with clients presenting many kinds of concerns. It is a therapy concerned about the quality of the relationship between therapist and client as well as the whole being of the therapist. It is about the therapist *being with* the client through a deep sense of connection to the client's experience and being *authentic*. It is in this spirit that I suggest that a client-centered attitude of non-directivity can allow the therapist to establish and maintain a growth fostering relationship with the client, a relationship that can consistently provide the client with a relational experience rich in mutual empathy and empowerment.

HOW CAN THIS BE ACCOMPLISHED?[4]

I am not suggesting that the relational-cultural model become another version of client-centered theory and practice. The Stone Center's theory of human development and model of therapy represent unique contributions to the fields of psychological and human development. Their model has evolved from an analysis

---

[4.] For a more thorough explanation of how to incorporate a non-directive attitude into the Stone Center's model, see Napier, 2001.

of gender and places its emphasis on the importance of relationship and connection as the means to psychological health or pathology. It also emphasizes the role culture plays on an individual's psychological development, health and distress.

Both client-centered and Stone Center theoreticians propose that the way to shift a person's relational images or to dissolve conditions of worth that the person has internalized is through a particular kind of relationship. In client-centered work that kind of relationship is provided to a person in therapy by a clinician who can provide consistent levels of the facilitative attitudes along with a non-directive attitude (Rogers, 1959, 1986).

In the Stone Center's work that kind of relationship is provided through mutual empathy by a therapist who is perceived by the client to be genuine and authentic. Mutuality is not defined as sameness or equality, rather it is a way of relating, a shared activity in which each (or all) of the people involved are participating as fully as possible. They explain that it is not a matter of equal reciprocity—I give to you and then you give to me—but it describes a quality of relationality, a movement or dynamic of the relationship. They stress that, 'The capacity to participate in mutually empathic relationships can replace the concept of the *need for or need to provide* empathy' (Miller and Stiver, 1997: 43). This statement suggests to me that perhaps the Stone Center theoreticians have picked up on the instrumental attitudes of most other therapies when they refer to empathy as a tool used by the therapist on the client rather than empathy as a characteristic of the relationship itself.

The ramifications of incorporating the non-directive attitude into the relational model is that the actual practice of the therapist would be transformed from an instrumental therapy to an expressive therapy.[5] To incorporate the non-directive attitude into the relational model, the therapist would have to believe in the client's basic motivation towards connection, and trust that a therapeutic relationship that is characterized by consistently high levels of mutual empathy will provide an environment where mutual empowerment can grow. The therapist would have to believe that her only goal is for herself—to understand the client's internal frame of reference as deeply as possible and then to communicate that acceptance and understanding to the client. The therapist would have to believe that she is not an expert of the client's experience and hold a deep respect for the client's phenomenology.

I believe that the Stone Center's theoretical positions are already very close and at times already embody these beliefs. I suggest that by incorporating a non-directive attitude into the model, the therapist will be able to form a deeper, richer and more consistent connection with the client. And, ultimately as Stone Center theoreticians suggest, it is the quality of the relationship and connection—the experience of the client seeing that she has an effect on the therapist and vice versa—that is the key to healing and growth.

[5] See Brodley (2000) for more information about expressive versus instrumental therapy.

REFERENCES

Aronson, E (1995) *The Social Animal.* (7th ed) New York: WH Freeman and Company.

Brodley, BT (1997) The non-directive attitude in client-centered therapy. *The Person-Centered Journal,* 4(1), 18–30.

Brodley, BT (2000) Client-centered: An expressive therapy, in J Marques-Teixeira and S Antunes (eds) *Client-Centered and Experiential Psychotherapy.* Linda a Velhas, Portugal: Vale & Vale, pp.133–47.

Jordan, JV (1991) The meaning of mutuality, in JV Jordan, AG Kaplan, JB Miller, IP Stiver and JL Surrey (eds) *Women's Growth in Connection.* New York: The Guilford Press, pp. 81–96.

Jordan, JV (1992) Relational resilience (Work in Progress No 57). Wellesley, MA: Wellesley College, The Stone Center.

Jordan, J (1993) Challenges to connection (Work in Progress No 60). Wellesley, MA: Wellesley College, The Stone Center.

Jordan, JV (1995) Relational awareness: Transforming disconnection (Work in Progress No 76). Wellesley, MA: Wellesley College, The Stone Center.

Jordan, JV (1997) Relational development: Therapeutic implications of empathy and shame, in JV Jordan (ed) *Women's Growth in Diversity: More writings from the Stone Center.* New York: The Guilford Press, pp. 138–61.

Jordan, J (1999) Toward connection and competence (Work in Progress No 83). Wellesley, MA: Wellesley College, The Stone Center.

Jordan, JV, and Dooley, C (2000) *Relational Practice in Action: A group manual.* Wellesley, MA: Wellesley College, The Stone Center.

Miller, JB (1988) Connections, disconnections and violations (Work in Progress No 33). Wellesley, MA: Wellesley College, The Stone Center.

Miller, JB and Stiver, IP (1994) Movement in therapy: Honoring the 'strategies of disconnection' (Work in Progress No 65). Wellesley, MA: Wellesley College, The Stone Center.

Miller, JB and Stiver, IP (1995) Relational images and their meanings in psychotherapy (Work in Progress No 74). Wellesley, MA: Wellesley College, The Stone Center.

Miller, JB and Stiver, IP (1997) *The Healing Connection: How women form relationships in therapy and life.* Boston: Beacon Press.

Miller, JB, Jordan, JV, Stiver, IP, Walker, M, Surrey, JL and Eldridge, NS (1999) Therapist's authenticity (Work in Progress No 82). Wellesley, MA: Wellesley College, The Stone Center.

Napier, MB (2001) Staying Connected: Incorporating a nondirective attitude into the Stone Center's Model of Relational-Cultural Therapy. Unpublished dissertation.

Rogers, CR (1959) A theory of therapy, personality, and interpersonal relationships as developed in the client-centered framework, in S Koch (ed) *Psychology: A study of a science: Vol. 3. Formulations of the person and the social context.* New York: McGraw Hill, pp. 184–256.

Rogers, CR (1986) Client-centered therapy, in IL Kutash and A Wolf (eds) *Psychotherapist's Casebook*. San Francisco: Jossey-Bass, pp. 194–208.

Surrey, JL (1997) What do we mean by mutuality in therapy? in JV Jordan (ed) *Women's Growth in Diversity: More writings from the Stone Center*. New York: The Guilford Press. pp. 42–9.

WHAT CAN PERSON-CENTRED THERAPY LEARN FROM FEMINISM?

GILLIAN PROCTOR

In this chapter, I argue that person-centred therapists (PCTs) could benefit from an understanding of feminism in their therapy practice. I do not argue that therapists should educate their clients about feminism or aim to direct their clients in any way as a result of learning about feminism. Instead, I argue that this understanding will affect the therapist's ability to understand their clients, and understand their explorations and difficulties both from a unique phenomenological perspective, and also from a societal understanding of gender roles, sexism and other oppressions. In addition, an appreciation of feminist theory would help person-centred therapists in their understanding of the dynamics of power in the therapy relationship and also help therapists to understand clients not just as individual, autonomous selves but as people constantly in relation.

POWER

Feminist theory helps us to understand different aspects of power and how relations of power affect psychological distress and therapy. Feminist theory is the most developed body of theory concerning structural inequalities. Feminism reminds us of our own and our clients' structural embodied positions reflecting inequalities in society. This may help us not by assuming how particular positions or identities affect any one individual, but to learn about how oppression works and *can* affect people. This awareness may also help us to learn about our own assumptions and prejudices that prevent us from understanding or accepting particular others.

Most feminist theories of power[1] are based on a structural model of power

---

[1.] See Proctor (2002) for detailed discussion of structural and post-structural power and feminist theory.

(assuming power is a possession held by a person or group over others in a negative way). Feminism concentrates on the power given to men over women in a patriarchal society, although it also theorises class, 'race', age, sexuality and other oppressions. However some feminist theorists have extended the notion of power from a purely structural notion to a more post-structural (relational and dynamic) notion of power. For French (1985), power is an interaction not a substance. She distinguishes between 'power-to' and 'power-over'. Power-to refers to ability, capacity, a sense of strength of the individual and is achieved by communities supporting the individual. Power-over is domination, coercive authority. However, 'power-over' is still relational—power is not possessed but granted to the dominator by others and this is not unretractable. She suggests the reappropriation of pleasure, the core of which is mutuality and freedom as the basis of a new morality beyond power.

Similarly Starhawk (1987) distinguishes three types of power: 'power-over', 'power-from-within' and 'power-with'. Again, power-over refers to domination. Power-from-within comes from the root of the word power (pouvoir in French) meaning to be able—an inner strength from the sense of one's own ability and innate value and from a sense of connection with other humans and the environment. Power-with is the power of an individual in a group of equals to suggest and be listened to; this is only possible if all in the group recognise they are equal. The distinctions between the concepts of power-over and power-from-within are represented in the German language by two distinct words—*Macht* and *Kraft*. *Kraft* often refers more to inner physical and mental strength, similar to the concept of power-from-within. *Macht* often refers more to power-over.

I argue that there are three aspects to power in the therapy relationship: *role power, historical power* and *societal power* (Proctor, 2002). *Role power* is the power inherent in the roles of therapist and client resulting from the authority given to the therapist to define the client's problem and the power the therapist has in the organisation and institutions of their work. Various micro-environments also affect how much role power a counsellor/therapist has in any one situation or work environment. This aspect of power is also dynamic and relational; each individual that the counsellor/therapist interacts with will have different views about this role power. *Historical power* is the power resulting from the personal histories of the therapist and client and their experiences of power and powerlessness. The personal histories and experiences will affect, and to some extent determine, how individuals are in relationships and how they think, feel and sometimes behave with respect to the power in the relationship. *Societal power* is the power arising from the structural positions in society of the therapist and client, with respect to aspects of identities associated with power including gender, age, (dis)ability, sexuality, etc.

ROLE POWER

There is a clear political agenda in Person-Centred Therapy (PCT) to eliminate the therapist's power-over the client and it is revolutionary in the extent to which it manages to do this.[2] But however the therapist behaves as an equal person in the therapy relationship, therapy is still an institution and the role of 'therapist' still has power attached to it in society. However transparent, therapy is still institutionalised within a particular mode of practice (Lowe, 1999).

Feminist authors also help us to understand the power in the institution of therapy. Chesler (1972) reminds us that the therapeutic encounter needs to be understood as an institution beyond how individual therapists are with individual clients and how this *institution* re-enacts the relationship of girls to their father figure in a patriarchal society. Although individual PC therapists challenge this hierarchical expert-based idea of therapy, therapy itself as an institution remains unnoticed, which is likely to be a major factor in clients not perceiving the therapy relationship as equal however the therapist behaves. There is a clear inequality in the roles of therapist and client which is not removed by any kind of therapist behaviour as a person.

Buber and Rogers had a debate about this very point discussed by Bozarth (1998). Bozarth (1998: 21) quotes Rogers saying 'There is something immediate, equal, a meeting of two persons on an equal basis, even though in the world of I-It, it could be seen as a very unequal relationship.' Bozarth suggests and I agree that this disagreement represents different definitions of power used by Rogers and Buber. Whereas Buber seems to be referring to the concept of power-over in the institution of the roles of therapist and client, Rogers definition refers to being all one is capable of being (the German *Kraft*). This is like Starhawk's power-from-within, power as a positive force incorporating respect for others and their own power-from-within. Natiello (2001: 11) describes this as Rogers' concept of 'personal power'—' the ability to act effectively under one's own volition rather than external control … where individuals are acutely aware of and can act upon their own feelings, needs and values'. The difference in paradigms of power is the effect of the therapist's power in each case. The more power-over exerted by the therapist, the less power the client has. However the more 'personal power' or power-from-within felt by the therapist, the more a client is enabled to feel their personal power.

The ethics of the PC approach are to resist power-over as much as possible. However there are still dangers in ignoring the power of the therapist's role. If Person-Centred therapists ignore the power in the role of therapist, we risk missing the opportunity to help clients from our positions of power. We may also fail to give clients information that we have access to from our position of power. We may risk underestimating or misunderstanding the effects of structural power on the lives of our clients. Finally we are in danger of misunderstanding the client's perception of our attitudes, assuming they see the relationship as equal because of how we behave as people but the client is still well aware of the power in the role of therapist.

[2.] See Proctor (2002) for a detailed discussion of power in person-centred therapy.

HISTORICAL POWER

I argue that historical power can be theorised in PCT by the internalisation of the conditions of worth (Proctor, 2002). However, feminist theory can add to our understanding of conditions of worth by reminding us how there are also societal conditions of worth that are gendered. I argue that gender role socialisation can be understood to be part of conditions of worth, arising not just idiosyncratically from individual parenting but also structurally on each child from interactions with wider society such as the media, books and other adults. The inscription of gender roles is one way of ascribing conditions of worth to girls and boys, but this process needs to be understood as a societal and structural process, affecting individuals.

The awareness of gender role socialisation can help a therapist to understand their own conditions of worth in a social and political context and how their current behaviour and ways of relating are likely to be influenced by gender role expectations. Also this awareness may help us as therapists to be aware of how we may affect clients in concordance with our gender roles. For example, a male therapist who explains to a client that they feel annoyed or let down by a late payment for therapy may have a different impact on the client than a female therapist saying the same thing. I am not saying that the differing impacts can be predicted or generalised. However, gender (as with other aspects of our structural identities) has a big impact on who we are and how we relate to people. Understanding society's messages about gender and how these are internalised (although responded to differently) by everyone may help us to understand an individual more accurately as situated within their cultural context. As society's messages about gender expectations are for the most part implicit and often denied, it is likely to be difficult for clients to be able to explain their impact on their way of viewing the world and themselves. If these messages are not understood as part of the implicit context in each of our lives, we run the risk of taking for granted gender socialisation as an unquestioned part of our culture.

SOCIETAL POWER

Rogers focused much of his later work on structural inequalities and oppression. Feminist theory can educate us about the effects of oppression (particularly concerning gender) and help us to understand the self-in-social-context. There are huge variations in the prevalence of psychological distress dependent on structural positions. Kearney (1996) suggests that PCT can and should include awareness of the social constraints on people's lives to understand the socially positioned individual. If we are unaware of our own internalised ideologies, we will neither be congruent nor accurately able to understand the way others see themselves.

PSYCHOLOGICAL DISTRESS AND THE DEFINITION OF MADNESS

Rogers' personality theory theorises that psychological distress arises from conditions of worth. This analysis can be usefully supplemented by an analysis that looks at society and what society deems 'mad' or 'dysfunctional'. Rogers' theory assumes an internal individualised basis for the decision about whether one is psychologically distressed or in need of therapy, which seems to be a rather naïve position, assuming we are unaffected by society's ideologies of 'normality' or acceptability. To understand the societal ideology of madness and who is defined 'mad', we need a sociological understanding of the construction of psychological distress to supplement Rogers' individualistic conditions of worth theory.

Feminist theory can provide this analysis. Phyllis Chesler (1972) exposed the gendered nature of who is defined mad in our society and how this is related to gender conformity. Her thesis was that 'What we consider "madness", whether it appears in women or in men, is either the acting out of the devalued female role or the total or partial rejection or one's sex-role stereotype' (Chesler, 1972: 93). She argues that psychiatry perpetuates the 'normality' of sex-role stereotypes. 'Mental health' is described by clinicians as characteristics which are associated with 'masculinity', and most theories of madness or mental health are based on biological essentialism. Women are pathologised for extreme conformity or non-conformity with gender roles, particularly concerning caring for others, being emotional, mothering and being sexually passive.

She further argues that the treatment of women in asylums paralleled women's experiences in the patriarchal family, being treated as helpless, dependent, sexless and unreasonable. She suggests that 'crazy' women may be looking for the nurture they never received as female children as they were encouraged to take on the role of nurturing others from a young age. She asserts that men have a wider range of 'acceptable' behaviour than women. Although women seeking help are tolerated more than men, they are still treated (Chesler, 1972: 78) 'with disbelief and pity, emotional distance, physical brutality, economic and sexual deprivation, drugs, shock therapy and long term psychiatric confinement.' She considers Szasz' idea about 'slave psychology' and suggests that (Chesler, 1972: 80) 'women's psychological identity consists in exhibiting signs and "symptoms" of slavery'. Similarly (Chesler, 1972: 288) 'Modern female psychology reflects a powerless and deprived condition'.

Hysteria—described by Showalter (1985: 128) as 'the essence of the "feminine"'—occupies a central position in the history of women's madness. Long used to indicate behaviours which are disapproved of, and specifically employed as a male term of abuse for 'difficult' female behaviour, it has, more recently, been theorised as a response to powerlessness; a reaction to expectations of passivity and an attempt to establish self-identity (Showalter, 1985). These analyses establish hysteria as a diagnosis which is centrally implicated in the pathologisation of women's responses to oppression. Shaw and Proctor (2004) argue that the diagnosis of Borderline Personality Disorder is the latest manifestation of this historical attempt to explain away the strategies which some women use to survive and resist the oppression and abuse they experience, by describing these strategies as symptomatic of a disturbed personality/pathology.

These feminist analyses are also backed up by other critiques of psychiatry. Szasz (1972) traces the history of the modern concept of madness to the pre-modern discourse of witchcraft. He describes how this discourse positioned as 'witch' and 'outsider' the woman whose deviant behaviour threatened social norms. As he described, a woman positioned in this way could be contained and punished for her deviancy, and the threat that she posed to social norms could be controlled and neutralised. In tracing the movement from this pre-modern, religious worldview to the current scientific, rational paradigm of modernism, Foucault (1967) describes the emergence of a scientifically determined and controlled concept of insanity. This is reflected in the shift from 'witchcraft' as the primary discourse applied to women's deviancy—as described by Szasz—to the emergence of the concept of 'hysteria' in the nineteenth century.

The system of mental health and psychiatry and society's ideology of 'mental health' perpetuates our existence as therapists and our clients' willingness to define themselves as mentally unhealthy. Therefore, we need to expand Rogers' idea of mental distress caused by conditions of worth to include a societal notion of who and why individuals are diagnosed as 'mad' (by others or by themselves).

VIOLENCE AGAINST WOMEN

Sexual violence against women is a key focus for feminist analysis as one of the results of a patriarchal society. However, sexual violence has also been co-opted by the industry of psychiatry and called 'madness', both in survivors and perpetrators. This pathologising focus on individual perpetrators and survivors of abuse prevents an understanding of abuse as causally and consequentially related to inequalities of power, particularly in respect to gender. Statistics which show that one in four women have experienced rape or attempted rape (Painter, 1991), and that one in two girls have been subjected to some form of unwanted sexual experience before they are eighteen (Kelly, Regan and Burton, 1991) suggest that male sexual violence against women does not represent a deviation from the norm. Female survivors have not experienced an anomalous event, but rather a violent example of gender relations within society. The effects of this violence on women are often pathologised and diagnosed as mental illness.

The sexual abuse of women and girls is centrally implicated in gender inequalities. 'Feminist practice begins from the recognition that most women are survivors of sexual violence, that all women are potential targets for abusive men, and that coping with the threat and reality of men's violence is an everyday reality for women' (Kelly, 1988/9: 15–16). It is this recognition of the extent and impact of sexual abuse of women and girls, and the central position that potential and/or actual sexual violence, abuse and harassment occupies within our culture, which is effectively obscured by the psychiatric labelling of perpetrators and survivors.

The history of societal responses to childhood sexual abuse is a history of denial and distortion. Masson (1985) documents the role that Freud plays within this. Freud took a particular interest in women with the diagnosis of hysteria, and tried to understand their experiences through the process of analysis, during which many women disclosed experiences of sexual abuse as children. Freud chose to conceal these revelations by presenting them as memories of fantasies, rather than memories of actual experiences. Whilst this explanation was no doubt more acceptable to Victorian society, the result was that the extent and impact of childhood sexual abuse was again obscured for nearly a century.

When the endemic prevalence of childhood sexual abuse began tentatively to re-enter the public consciousness in the 1970s and 1980s, it met with a similarly distorting response in the form of the concept of 'false memory syndrome': a term constructed by the founders of the False Memory Syndrome Foundation in the USA in 1992 to refer to 'memories of sexual abuse they believe are not real and which have been planted by a therapist or which have been "borrowed" by the person hearing accounts of sexual abuse' (Follini, 1995: 12). This syndrome gained considerable media attention within a relatively short space of time, and doing so graphically illustrated the backlash against any recognition of the extent and the impact of the sexual abuse of women and children. Our own analysis echoes Herman (1997) in recognising the similarity between the strategies of distortion and denial which characterise Freud's theory and the 'false memory syndrome': strategies which were in both cases sanctioned and encouraged by the political climate of the time.

Having examined the historical tendency towards the denial of the extent and impact of childhood sexual abuse, Shaw and Proctor (2004) argue that the diagnosis of Borderline Personality Disorder (BPD) is a powerful new manifestation of this tendency. Briere (2002), for example, describes how the 'symptoms' which define BPD can be better understood as memories, thoughts and feelings associated with early relational traumas and activities that survivors have used to cope with these experiences. The decontextualisation of the distress and coping strategies associated with abuse has been reflected in their experiences within services. Whereas in the early 90s there was a focus in psychiatry in the UK on Post Traumatic Stress Disorder (PTSD), services for survivors of abuse, and calls for training for all mental health professionals about issues of trauma and abuse, this has been replaced by a focus on BPD or Personality Disorder, (PD), and calls for training by mental health professionals on how to deal with people with this diagnosis. Whereas the diagnosis of PTSD or complex PTSD (Herman, 1997) certainly individualised and pathologised survivors, at least in its acknowledgement of the aetiological importance of trauma, there was a degree of recognition of context. In contrast, BPD completely decontextualises distress from its social causes, locating all distress within the individual. This shift from the recognition of the extent and impact of sexual violence—limited as it was in extent and by the constraints of an individualising and pathologising medical model of mental distress—serves to conceal sexual abuse and instead blame and 'treat' the survivors.

This shift has been paralleled by the move from the category of 'paedophile' to the diagnosis of 'antisocial PD'. More recently, the UK government's diagnosis of 'Dangerous and Severe PD' (Home Office/Department of Health, 1999) is still being considered despite most professional bodies (such as the Royal College of Psychiatrists and the British Psychological Society) questioning its validity and meaning. This produces a situation in which a perpetrator of sexual abuse may have his behaviours and motivations explained by the diagnosis of antisocial PD; whilst a survivor of abuse may find that their strategies of survival, coping and resistance attract a diagnosis of BPD.

Clearly, feminist analyses of violence against women can supplement Rogers' hypotheses of the causes of psychological distress. The impact of sexual violence could be theorised as a particular extreme example of conditions of worth, but this analysis would be reductionist and ignore the place of gender relations in society. A feminist analysis can improve a therapist's understanding of the potential impact on clients of sexual violence as well as increase their understanding of the dynamics of power relationships involved in such experiences.

THE RELATIONAL PERSPECTIVE

PC theory has been accused of being focused on the individual autonomous 'self' as opposed to a 'self-in-relation'. Schmid (1998b, 2003) argues that PC theory encompasses both these aspects of what being a person means. Feminist theory has long focused on the relational perspective and can add to our understanding of this aspect of being a person. This is relevant to both PC theory, in terms of the notion of the 'self', and practice, in terms of therapy and PC groups.

THE ESSENTIAL 'SELF'

The idea of the essential individual self is challenged by post-structural feminists. An early example of this was Gilligan's challenge to Erikson's ideas of moral development being about progress towards autonomy, by suggesting this idea was steeped in male ideas of morality and suggesting that women's moral development prioritised relationship. Feminism has challenged the male notion of 'being myself' as a pure idea of self separate from the social context. Within the post-structural/post-modern challenge to the notion of an essential self, post-structural feminism challenges the notion of an 'essential self' that is not context- and relationship-dependent (e.g., see Tong, 1997).

This has implications for PC theory and therapy. Even our feelings that we strive to be aware of, to be congruent, in PCT are not pure experiences but originate from our socio-political context and how our social experiences have taught us to evaluate the world. As we strive to be more and more aware of our inner experiencing (congruence), there is a danger in assuming these 'organismic experiences' are a pure expression of an inner self unaffected by the context. For example, this stance could lead to us taking for granted feelings based on prejudice or stereotypes. Even though the notion of the actualising tendency includes for humans a prosocial tendency (Brodley, 1999), i.e., it acknowledges the self-in-relation, I contend that Rogers' (1959) notion of the organismic self is less acknowledging of how even perceptions and feelings are at least partially socially constructed.

THERAPY

Chesler (1972) suggests that both psychotherapy and white or middle-class marriage isolate women from each other, both emphasising individual rather than collective solutions to women's unhappiness. Both are based on a woman's helplessness and dependence on a stronger male authority figure; both may, in fact, be viewed as a re-enactment of a little girl's relation to her father in a patriarchal society. Both control and oppress women similarly, yet at the same time are the two safest (most approved and familiar) havens for middle-class women in a society that offers them few, if any, alternatives. She suggests that the institutions of therapy and marriage support each other and encourage talk and defusing emotions rather than action. Even in radical psychiatry or therapy, she suggests there is a danger in 'viewing humans' basic needs for security and communication as "therapy" rather than as normal human needs and rights' (Chesler, 1972: 143).

Given the negative potential of the power relations involved in therapy, it would seem sensible for PC therapists to consider how working in groups, or in more overtly political ways, could alleviate some of the negative power implications, whilst at the same time, maximising the chances of the positive power of collectivity or 'power-with'. Indeed, Schmid (1996, 1998a) suggests that the radical implications of PC theory are of 'social therapy', i.e., groupwork where all learn from each other.

GENDER ROLES IN GROUPS

I have come across in person-centred groups what seems to me to be a misunderstanding of Unconditional Positive Regard in gendered ways. Power and ways of relating in groups result partly from gender role socialisation. For me, the full implications of UPR are about being in relation. I have often experienced UPR

137

being misused to imply passive acceptance in PC groups with a loss of the warmth and prizing aspect that Rogers talked about. For example, when a group member has been upset or offended by something another group member has said, the member who said something which caused offence has 'accepted' how the offended group member feels, but without seeming to care about their distress. It has been said explicitly 'I accept other peoples' feelings and reactions and want my behaviour or expressions to be similarly accepted.' This seems to be the use of the concept of UPR to justify prioritising being oneself and being accepted however we express ourselves, above thinking about and caring about how we affect others. I am not comfortable with people in a PC group abdicating responsibility from considering how they affect others, by a plea for acceptance of their individuality. This leaves unexamined two different ways of relating in groups, one traditionally masculine (I am me and you should accept how I am being) and one feminine (I'd like to be me but am worried how that will affect other people and I don't want to hurt people). The traditionally masculine view represents the focus on the autonomous individual, whilst the feminine represents the focus on the relational. Feminist theory and practice reminds us to challenge traditional gender roles and to not neglect the relational aspects of this personhood.

SUMMARY AND CONCLUSION

In this chapter, I have identified many reasons why PC therapists would benefit from an understanding of feminist theory. Without it, therapists are in danger of perpetuating unthinkingly the power relations in a patriarchal society, and continuing the sex role expectations which disempower women. With a feminist understanding of how women and men are labelled mad, and how women suffer from the effects of patriarchy and in particular sexual violence, PC therapists will be better equipped to provide help for clients suffering from a patriarchal society in ways which are most likely to empower people to change society. At the same time, PC therapists would do well to consider ways of working outside therapy where there is less danger of perpetuating the patriarchal power relations institutionalised in individual therapy.

Many thanks to Bill Wood for helpful discussion about an earlier draft of this chapter.

REFERENCES

Briere, J (2002) Treating adult survivors of severe childhood abuse and neglect: Further development of an integrative model, in JEB Myers, L Berliner, J Briere, CT Hendrix, T Reid and C Jenny (eds) *The APSAC Handbook on Child Maltreatment* (2nd ed). Newbury Park, CA: Sage Publications.

Brodley, BT (1999) The actualizing tendency concept in client-centered theory. *Person-Centered Journal, 6*(2), 108–20.

Bozarth, J (1998) *Person-Centered Therapy: A revolutionary paradigm.* Ross-on-Wye: PCCS Books.

Chesler, P (1972) *Women and Madness.* New York: Doubleday.

Follini, B (1995) 'FMS: Fraudulent, Misogynist and Sinister', *Trouble and Strife,* 31: 12–14.

Foucault, M (1967) *Madness and Civilisation—A history of insanity in the age of reason.* London: Tavistock.

French, M (1985) *Beyond Power: On women, men and morals.* London: Jonathan Cape.

Herman, JL (1997) *Trauma and Recovery.* US: Basic Books.

Home Office/Dept of Health (1999) *Managing Dangerous People with Severe Personality Disorder: Proposals for Policy Development.* UK Government.

Kearney, A (1996) *Counselling, Class and Politics: Undeclared influences in therapy.* Ross-on-Wye: PCCS Books.

Kelly, L (1988/9) From politics to pathology: the medicalisation of the impact of rape and childhood sexual abuse, *Radical Community Medicine* 14–18.

Kelly, L, Regan and Burton (1991) *An Exploratory Study of the Prevalence of Sexual Abuse in a Sample of 1244 16–21 year-olds,* Final Report to the Economic and Social Research Council.

Lowe, R (1999) Between the 'No longer' and the 'Not yet': Postmodernism as a context for critical therapeutic work, in I Parker (ed) *Deconstructing Psychotherapy.* London: Sage, pp. 71–85.

Masson, J (1985) *The Assault on Truth: Freud's suppression of the seduction theory.* UK: Penguin.

Natiello, P (2001) *The Person-Centred Approach: A passionate presence.* Ross-on-Wye: PCCS Books.

Painter, K (1991) *Wife Rape, Marriage and Law: Survey report, key findings and recommendations.* Manchester: Manchester University Department of Social Policy and Social Work.

Proctor, G (2002) *The Dynamics of Power in Counselling and Psychotherapy: Ethics, politics and practice.* Ross-on-Wye: PCCS Books.

Rogers, CR (1959) A theory of therapy, personality and interpersonal relationships as developed in the client-centered framework, in S Koch (ed) *Psychology: A study of a science, Vol. III: Formulations of the Person and the Social Context.* New York and London: McGraw-Hill, pp. 184–256.

Schmid, P (1996) Probably the most potent social invention of the century: Person-Centered Therapy is fundamentally group therapy, in R Hutterer, G Pawlowsky, PF Schmid, and R Stipsits (eds) *Client-Centered and Experiential Psychotherapy. A paradigm in motion.* Frankfurt/M: Peter Lang, pp. 611–25.

Schmid, P (1998a) 'Face to face': The art of encounter, in B Thorne and E Lambers (eds) *Person-Centred Therapy. A European perspective.* London: Sage, pp. 74–90.

Schmid, P (1998b) A person-centred understanding of the person, in B Thorne, and E Lambers (eds) *Person-Centred Therapy, A European perspective.* London: Sage, pp. 38–52.

Schmid, P (2003) Keynote speech at PCE conference, Egmond-und-Zee (www.pca-online.net).

Shaw, C and Proctor, G (2004) Women at the Margins. *Asylum,* *4*(3): 8–10.

Showalter, E (1985) *The Female Malady: Women, madness and English culture, 1830–1890.* London: Virago.

Starhawk (1987) *Truth or Dare: Encounters with power, authority, and mystery.* San Francisco: Harper & Row.

Szasz, T (1972) *The Myth of Mental Illness.* London: Paladin.

Tong, R (1997) *Feminist thought—A comprehensive introduction.* London: Routledge.

SEXUAL ABUSE: THE PSYCHIATRIC RESPONSE AND THE CONSTRUCTION OF BETTER ALTERNATIVES

CLARE SHAW

INTRODUCTION

Feminist research and activism has repeatedly shown the value of working with women survivors of sexual abuse in an empowering and validating way, constructing a response which prioritises the expertise of the survivor and which understands her distress in the context of her life circumstances. Given this, the psychiatric response of pathologising and labeling women does not seem particularly helpful, grounded as it is upon an unproved assumption of physiological illness as the root of the distress; and focusing as it therefore does upon a medical response of hospitalisation and medication. The call therefore must be for therapists and other professionals to avoid the pathologisation, individualisation and depoliticisation of abuse which characterises the psychiatric response. I will draw from my own experience of sexual abuse and the psychiatric response, to construct an understanding of how Person-Centred Therapy (PCT) may—or may not—form part of an empowering, healing response to sexual abuse.

Throughout this chapter, I use the term 'sexual abuse' to refer to all acts of abuse which have a covert or overt sexual element. I propose to limit my focus to the sexual abuse of women by men, as I will be approaching sexual abuse as a political process which is centrally located in the oppression of women, by men. It should not need to be stated that I am aware that men and boys also—to a lesser extent—experience sexual abuse by men, and less commonly, by women: however, I don't accept that this fact undermines my conviction that the actual and potential sexual abuse of women by men plays a major factor in women's lives and in the collective life of our society. I am drawing here from a major strand of feminist theory (e.g., MacKinnon, 1983; Dworkin, 1974) which argues that sexual abuse is both a cause and a consequence of the gendered inequalities which characterise this society. This theory points out that the primary dynamic of rape and sexual abuse is

141

power, rather than sexual gratification. The prevalence of male sexual violence against women reflects the fact that men hold disproportionate economic, legal, political, coercive and other forms of power in this society. Male sexual violence against women works to confirm and perpetuate this imbalance of power: as Monica Hill points out in Chapter 18 in this book, 'Rape and the fear of rape affect the way every woman lives her life and the choices she makes' so that 'as well as being a devastating attack on an individual woman, sexual violence is a means by which all women are socially controlled'. It is because I am drawing from this specific political argument that I am focusing solely on the abuse of women and girls by men.

FEMINISM AND SOCIAL CONSTRUCTIONISM

It should come as no surprise then that I approach this issue from a feminist perspective, and from the belief that this society is characterised by gendered inequalities of power, money, status, safety and other important resources. It might also be useful for me to clarify that I write from an explicitly social constructionist perspective, and to explain what this means.

Social constructionist approaches have one or more of these assumptions at their foundation (Burr, 1995):
• A critical stance towards taken-for-granted ways of understanding and explaining the world and ourselves
• Anti-essentialism (the theory that people, and hence the social world, are shaped by social processes rather than having pre-determined natures/essences)
• Historical and cultural specificity (ways of understanding and explaining the world are specific to, and products of, time and place)
• A belief that social knowledge is inseparable from social action

Social constructionist approaches have underlaid many of the important theoretical and practical developments of feminism—many of which have depended on challenging and deconstructing previously taken-for-granted aspects of the gendering of our society. Feminists have attempted to deconstruct 'taken-for-granted' assumptions about gender, e.g., that a woman's rightful place is in the home. They have exposed the historical and cultural specificity of such assumptions, pointing out how other eras and cultures have centred around very different understandings of the role of gender. They have critiqued how such assumptions are backed up by social processes and structures, such as unequal pay and insufficient childcare. Finally, they have shown how changing our awareness of a situation is inseparable from changing that situation. So, once women (and men) began to recognise that women are not predestined for a life of homemaking and childrearing, society began to slowly change, almost as if that knowledge was social action in itself.

Social constructionist approaches have also characterised many of the feminist analyses of mainstream understandings of women's distress. These analyses suggest that the unequal gender relations of wider society are firmly implicated in our experience and understanding of distress. Women's experiences of distress and madness are framed as responses to gendered oppression—'Women's position in society may be particularly conducive to madness' (Busfield, 1996: 5), and diagnostic categories are understood as gendered responses to women's ways of surviving and coping in an oppressive context, rather than as objective scientific statements about the existence of a 'mental illness' or 'personality disorder'.

Like the anti/post-psychiatry argument, feminist challenges to psychiatry have pointed out that, despite psychiatry's claims to scientific validity, there in fact exists no direct evidence of the existence of a physiological basis for mental illness/disorder/distress. Readers may be interested in the recent hunger strike held in North America, in which hunger-striking survivors of the psychiatric system challenged the American Psychiatric Association to provide evidence of a single study which proved the physiological-basis argument which is so central to the psychiatric response. The APA responded but failed to provide evidence, leading the Scientific Panel of the strikers to conclude 'There is not a single study that provides valid and reliable evidence for the "biological basis of mental illness"' (see Shaw, 2003). Feminists and other critics have argued therefore that, far from being grounded upon an objective, scientific basis, the dominant medical model of psychiatry is, in fact, a culturally and historically specific approach to mental distress; one which has some very negative consequences for women and other oppressed groups whose perspectives, behaviours and opinions are subjected to psychiatric diagnosis.

Having briefly outlined the feminist/social constructionist challenge to the psychiatric model of mental distress, I will move to consider how this approach can be applied specifically to the issue of sexual abuse.

FEMINISM AND SEXUAL ABUSE

One of the major achievements of feminism was to bring about a recognition of the extent and impact of sexual abuse. Most research confirms that a significant proportion of women will experience some form of sexual abuse at some point in their lives. The Women's Support Project (1990), for example, found that two out of every five women have survived rape or sexual assault and that this experience can have dramatic implications for a woman's emotional wellbeing.

As well as exposing the prevalence of sexual abuse, feminists sought to deconstruct some of the ideas which surrounded it. For example, most readers will be familiar with the feminist rallying call of 'The Personal is Political' which challenged the previously taken-for-granted division between public and private life; a division which had allowed men to beat and abuse their partners and children with impunity in the privacy of their own homes. Women fought and continue to fight to have sexual abuse and violence recognised as a crime and as a significant political issue, rather than as an individual event which takes place in the apolitical sphere of human relationships.

These recognitions lie behind the feminist response to sexual abuse, which is most clearly defined in the Rape Crisis movement which is explored in more depth by Monica Hill in this volume in Chapter 18. Drawing from a feminist analysis of rape and abuse, 'the goal was to create feminist institutions in which women could work collectively to help one another' (Koss and Harvey, 1991: 123). Given that the loss of control of your own body and self is a defining aspect of the experience of abuse, empowerment through resumed control and through informed choice is a central aspect of the feminist response, and a direct inversion of the dynamic of abuse. Rape Crisis and other feminist services exist as alternatives to rigidly hierarchical mainstream responses such as psychiatry, which I will now go on to describe.

THE PSYCHIATRIC MODEL

As I described earlier in this chapter, the current psychiatric system is characterised by a medical model approach. 'The phrase "medical model" implies primary concern for the health status of *individual patients*, and the credentiated practitioner's expert application of medical arts and skills. Foremost amongst those arts are *diagnosis, prognosis and treatment*'. (Koss and Harvey, 1991: 248). When applied to the impact of abuse, this approach translates in practice into the expectation of, for example, 'greater severity of overall symptomatology amongst women with a history of childhood abuse, more severe and psychotic-like symptomatology, more diagnoses of borderline personality disorder, and a greater likelihood of pharmacological treatment' (Surrey et al., 1990: 412).

When I approached the psychiatric system as a severely distressed woman of twenty years old, I was diagnosed with clinical depression and told that I would improve if I took my medication. For the next ten years, the psychiatric response followed the same pattern, though with different diagnoses, prognoses and treatments. I spent considerable lengths of time in hospital as a 'voluntary' patient, sometimes being threatened with the loss of my voluntary status if I tried to leave. As my primary diagnosis is now Borderline Personality Disorder, my prognosis is bleak, and I am considered to be untreatable—although it's hoped that I may 'grow out of it' or develop 'a more stable personality disorder' if I reach middle age! (See Finley-Belgrad and Davies, 2004.)

THE PERSON-CENTRED APPROACH

Although Rogers fails to specifically address the issue of sexual abuse, the Person-Centred Approach, with its emphasis on empathy and non-judgemental positive regard, offers a marked alternative to the psychiatric response.

When I was abused within my family, the message that was given to me by this abuser was 'You are only valued and loved because you meet my sexual needs'. When no-one challenged this behaviour, this condition was confirmed. When I was violently attacked outside of the family, it was confirmed further. When no-one talked to me afterwards, I learnt to be silent about my distress and to deny it to myself and other people. Throughout my childhood and adolescence, I learned that I was valuable as a sex object. I learned not to say no. This stood me in good stead for some pretty abusive relationships in adulthood, and so on. In person-centred terms, by the age of twenty I was living in a state of excruciatingly painful denial and distortion. 'Breakdown' came at the point where I could no longer maintain the illusion that life was bearable. Things needed to change. How would a person-centred therapist have responded to me at that point in my life?

A classically trained person-centred therapist would not be aiming to formulate my condition in terms of the conditions of worth whilst being with me, although they may be using Rogers' personality theory to help them understand my situation. However, the aim during therapy would be to be with me in my experiences of myself and life at that time, to aim to understand my experiences as well as possible from my perspective (empathy), in the context of not judging me or any aspects of my experience, and prizing me as a unique person (unconditional positive regard). At the same time, the person-centred therapist would be aiming to be aware of their own feelings and experiences in their relationship with me (congruence) and to be a person in that relationship, without a professional façade or distance. From Rogers' theory of personality, this relationship is theorised to help me because whilst experiencing the therapist's attitudes of empathy, UPR and congruence, I would, in reciprocity, develop more positive self-regard, more self-understanding and more confidence to be myself. Thus I would begin to value myself as a unique, valuable person in my own right, as opposed to being there to fulfill the needs of others. I would be able to reclaim my feelings at the time and as a result of my experiences of abuse, and to stop denying these experiences, in the context of a relationship where these experiences were not judged, and where I and my therapist could increasingly understand my life and the impact of my experiences on me.

EVALUATING THE RESPONSES

Having outlined how a response to sexual abuse might be constructed within psychiatric and PCT principles, I will now evaluate these two different responses, with reference to what women say that they want from the services to which they turn in times of distress.

The medicalised approach of the psychiatric response can be critiqued on a number of grounds. From the outset, through the act of diagnosis, attention is focused onto the individual response of the individual survivor with the consequence that 'damage and dysfunction' is located 'not within the system that produces it but within the individual who experiences it' (Penfold and Walker, 1983: 31). Thus the survivor becomes the 'emotional scapegoat' (Ussher, 1991: 142) whilst a social system of endemic sexual abuse goes unexamined and uncriticised.

The survivor also experiences a profound loss of control over her own life as power—including the power to define the survivor's distress and how it should be responded to—is assumed by the psychiatric professional (Johnstone, 1995). This loss of control can be heavily critiqued on the basis of theories and accounts about how important it is for survivors to feel a sense of regaining power and control following the experience of sexual abuse, theories which are at the centre of the feminist response to sexual abuse (Kelly, 1988). Indeed, it can sometimes mean the psychiatric interventions are experienced as abusive in and of themselves (Breggin, 1991), especially practices such as control and restraint, forced medication, ECT and hospitalisation. In short, psychiatric responses can actually worsen the impact of abuse by 'denying to victims the healing experience of informed consent. They reinforce her status as victim, ignore her capacity for survival, and undermine her recovery' (Koss and Harvey, 1991: 133).

The development of the Rape Crisis network described earlier in this chapter grew out of a feminist critique of mainstream responses to sexual abuse. 'Feminists articulated the emotional and physical trauma of rape and the extent to which this was ignored and exacerbated by medical, mental health and criminal justice institutions' (Koss and Harvey, 1991: 123) developing instead a model of response which is based upon principles of empowerment, mutual support and politicisation. Qualitative research has illustrated how such models meet with what women say that they want—to be listened to, accepted and supported, and to have practical issues dealt with appropriately. In the Bristol Crisis Service Survey (Arnold, 1995) women identified those services which criticised, dismissed and controlled as being amongst the most unhelpful service responses. Treatment approaches failed to address underlying issues and focused just on 'symptoms' such as self injury. On the contrary, the main point of a helpful intervention was being heard and supported. Service could make a huge difference 'simply by being accepting and supportive, listening and taking seriously the person's experience and needs' (Arnold 1995: 21) and responding appropriately to each individual, providing practical help, crisis support, and ongoing, regular contact where it was needed.

To an extent, these principles are evident in the PC approach to women who have survived sexual abuse. The response is characterised by listening and acceptance. All feelings are given room. A woman is offered the space to interpret her own experience and control her own response. PCT empowers through the concept of empathy: the value is placed upon the internal frame of reference of the woman, rather than on 'professional' sources of knowledge.

It would feel comfortable at this point to congratulate the PCT model for its success in constructing an empowering and healing response to sexual abuse: a powerful alternative to that offered by mainstream psychiatry. Yet this would be to ignore some serious flaws. I am going to go on to explore how much PCT has yet to learn from feminism in constructing a truly helpful response to the issue of sexual abuse.

CRITIQUING THE PCT RESPONSE

INDIVIDUALISATION

Within the PC approach, sexual abuse would probably be theorised in terms of the conditions of worth and how these impact upon the individual personality. This means that the focus of the therapy is kept at the individual level, looking at how the abuse affected the individual woman rather then acknowledging how expectations and conditions are constructed and enacted at a societal level.

I would argue that conditions of worth must also be understood at this wider societal level. The sexual abuse which I experienced should not be understood as an individual event which happened to have an impact upon my personality—it should be understood as something which happened as part of a society which is deeply influenced by the belief that women exist to service the needs of others, primarily men. If women's distress is explained away as an isolated set of experiences, or as an individual woman's failure to cope, we deny her the opportunity to locate her own experiences amongst those of countless women. Importantly, we once again depoliticise the issue of abuse, in much the same way as psychiatry has historically hidden the effects of abuse through the diagnoses of hysteria, and more recently, BPD (Shaw and Proctor, 2004).

DE/CONSTRUCTING DISTRESS

As Proctor (Chapter 11 in this volume) points out, 'Rogers' theory assumes an internal individualised basis for the decision about whether one is psychologically distressed or in need of therapy, which seems to be a rather naïve position, assuming we are unaffected by society's ideologies of "normality" or acceptability.' Her argument that PCT needs to be supplemented with a sociological analysis of how psychological normality and abnormality are understood is applicable to the issue of how PCT responds to sexual abuse.

Feminist theory has documented how women who have survived abuse and violence are subject to many social judgements about how they should and should not behave. Women are often defined as 'mad' for behaving in ways which could be understood as entirely appropriate to their situation (e.g., Chesler, 1972; Busfield, 1996; Ussher, 1991). For the purpose of this discussion I will use anger as an example.

Historically, it has not been deemed appropriate for women to express anger, as this clashes with expectations of feminine passivity. Angry women have been punished throughout the centuries with methods ranging from the scold's bridle, to cliterodectomy, ECT, imprisonment and hospitalisation. Women who act angrily are still likely to be judged and labelled (Proctor, 2004). A powerful contemporary example is the BPD diagnostic criteria of 'inappropriate intense anger' (APA: DSM IV, 1994)—a judgement which is predominantly made by male psychiatrists against female patients.

However, women who turn their anger against themselves—in the form of self harming behaviours, for example—are also likely to be judged. When given the opportunity to voice their experiences, women explain how self injury acts as a valuable coping mechanism which has enabled them to survive overwhelmingly painful feelings, often connected with the experience of abuse (Arnold, 1995). Yet self injury is a highly stigmatised form of behaviour: women who self injure are likely to encounter responses of shock and disgust; and can be subjected to highly controlling service responses. This acts as a powerful illustration of Chesler's 'double bind' (1972) by which women are condemned for living up to expectations of femininity; and are also condemned for failing to meet these expectations—if women direct their anger at themselves through self injury, they are likely to be highly stigmatised both within services and wider society; yet if women direct their anger externally, they are also subjected to judgemental, stigmatising attitudes and labels. This is an example of how judgements about who is in need of therapy are made on the basis of social judgements about what is and is not socially acceptable.

Women often internalise these social judgements about their 'inappropriate behaviours'. When I first started to self injure, I was sure I was one of the only people engaging in such an insane and shocking behaviour. I was disgusted and ashamed of my actions and spent years trying to hide my injuries. Luckily I was able to meet with other people who self injured and understood this as a coping mechanism. One woman I interviewed, whose self injury was very much connected with her experiences of abuse (Shaw, 1999) described how her first encounter with a person-centred counselor who had no knowledge or experience of self injury left her feeling more isolated and self-loathing than ever before. I encountered similar attitudes at a university (person-centred) counseling service which refused to display posters advertising our self-help group, on the grounds that self-help encouraged competition—'who could inflict the worst injuries'. We asked one of the counsellors on what evidence she based her approach, and she told us how she had met a member of our group who was wearing short sleeves and flaunting her 'terrible scars'. That was me. I had attended that university that day as a visiting lecturer. Like nearly everyone else in the city that day, I was wearing short sleeves as it was hot and sunny. To me, these are not simply two isolated examples of PC therapists failing to show unconditional positive regard. Rather, these two incidents show what happens when even the most well-intentioned therapist fails to deconstruct dominant discourses about which behaviours are acceptable and unacceptable.

Discourses about what is 'unacceptable' work to exclude people in some very profound ways. Equally, unchallenged discourses can act as some of the most powerful forces for oppression and privilege. Rogers' assumption about the individual, internal basis for decisions about whether a person is in need of therapy fails to recognise that our understandings of feelings and behaviour are socially constructed, profoundly shaped by societal conventions of what is normal and abnormal. Given the power of these conventions, when therapists fail to recognise that their understandings—and their clients' understandings—are socially constructed, they can unwittingly find themselves upholding structures of oppression and exclusion. And when therapists fail to question their attitudes to their own and other people's behaviour, the result can sometimes be that women who have survived sexual abuse are yet again pathologised, stigmatised and excluded.

If the counsellor that I described above had been aware of some of the feminist theories of society and of mental distress which I outlined earlier in this chapter, I expect that she would have understood my behaviour very differently. Because she did not have access to—and did not inform her actions with—these theories, she added to the stigmatisation and exclusion of women who self injure. As person-centred theory does not include feminist analysis of society or of distress, it is therefore possible for therapists to end up being part of the problem faced by people in distress.

POWER

Gillian Proctor, (in Chapter 11 this volume and 2002) addresses many of the issues of power and power imbalance within PC therapy. I am going to add to this by examining the assumptions around mental health which are at the basis of the PCT approach to sexual abuse.

My experience of a person-centred therapy relationship in which I was located as 'the client' was one of relative powerlessness. I was present in that relationship as 'the participant with the problem'. This contrasted strongly with my experience of self-help and mutual support groups, in which everyone was at once the helper and the helped. In these groups, there was no automatic assumption that any participant was more able to help than any other. Instead, groups were based on the belief that having shared the experience of having survived sexual abuse, we were all in a position to learn from and support each other. This seemed to be based on a profound valuing of our strengths and expertise.

In contrast, PCT is based upon the assumption that the client is more vulnerable, anxious and incongruent than the counsellor. This sets up an immediate power relationship, and a judgement about the mind states of both participants which in some ways mirrors those which characterise the psychiatric relationship (critiqued by feminist writers such as Burstow (1987). Proctor (Chapter 11 this volume) points out how the PCT industry gains from dominant, psychiatric discourses of mental health and illness according to which the client is located as the mad, and the counselor as the sane. As we have already acknowledged, that experience of being judged and disempowered is particularly unhelpful for women who have survived abuse. For some theorists, this leads to the conclusion that individual therapy relationships are inherently disempowering (Masson, 1997; Smail, 1987; Chamberlin, 1988). Instead, they argue for a group/self-help model of response: given 'the humiliating and disempowering nature of rape, the sense of powerlessness that rape trauma entails and the empowering potential of rape survivor groups ... the need for group treatment models which, by virtue of their egalitarian structure and respectful, supportive progress, counter a disempowering socialization of women' (Koss and Harvey, 1991: 212).

What can the person-centred therapist who does not yet wish to abandon the individual therapy model learn from this argument? Most simply, to make an awareness of power dynamics within the therapy relationship a priority; and above all, not to set themselves up as experts who can offer help to poor damaged survivors of abuse; but rather to recognise the expertise and strength of the women that they have the privilege to work with and learn from.

PCT AND POLITICS

By approaching sexual abuse in terms of its individual psychological impact, PCT fails to locate the issue in its wider social context, and so fails to understand sexual abuse as a hugely significant political issue. In doing so, PCT fails to locate itself within the emancipatory framework of theoretical and activist movements such as feminism. It also fails the individual client by offering her a limited, individualised understanding of abuse, and not offering her the opportunity to locate her experiences within the wider social and political context of her life. For myself, an understanding of the political context of my own experiences is key to my ability to live comfortably with myself and my own life. In simple terms, without that understanding I would only have half of the story. I would not be able to locate myself within a history of women. I would not have the incredible, important sense of myself as a collectively empowered part of a different future.

Politicising the issue of sexual abuse within PCT does not just change the individual woman's experiences of therapy. It changes the therapy itself, widening the focus from the distress of the individual woman to include the whole of society, and rewriting our expectations of how we should respond to that distress, whether as members of society or more specifically, as person-centred therapists. If we understand sexual abuse as an important element of the way that women experience society, we are faced with some very different, sometimes disconcerting possibilities.

Is it not possible, for example, that an abused woman's distress displays congruence with her experience, which was humiliating, frightening, and brought about a change in her concept of herself to recognise her own terrifying vulnerability, and the inescapable threat posed by other people? Is it not possible that to remain undistressed by these experiences and the realisations that they involve would actually be indicative of greater psychological denial? Thus a person-centred therapist must start from the recognition that women's feelings and behaviours may be entirely appropriate within the context of their lives. To fail to recognise this would mean that a therapist may pathologise a woman's distress in much the same way as the psychiatric system.

Could it not also be true that the fact we live in a society which tolerates the daily murder, brutalisation and abuse of women and girls is actually the greatest example of denial? That no greater example of distortion can be found than the apathy and the structural institutions of law and psychiatry which support, or at least fail to acknowledge, the normalisation of abuse within our society? Is it not psychological maladjustment to fail to acknowledge what is going on around us? And how much is a PC therapist perpetuating this denial by having therapy with individual women and not working towards changing society?

Why does PCT focus on the coping mechanisms of individual women rather than on the structures and processes which cause distress in the first place? Is it enough to seek to support women after they have been attacked and hurt? Or should we be working to prevent that hurt from occurring in the first place?

CONCLUSION

Throughout this chapter, I have illustrated how much feminism and social constructionism offer to our understanding of sexual abuse. I have drawn from both of these approaches to examine how the mainstream psychiatric response to sexual abuse has worked to pathologise and depoliticise the issue of sexual abuse. I looked at the impact this has on the individual survivor who is left feeling isolated, invalidated and disempowered—confirming, in fact, the central dynamics and consequences of sexual abuse. In contrast to the psychiatric response, I looked at how PCT might offer a more empowering, validating alternative, which meets much more closely what women say that they want.

However, I argued that the PCT response is fundamentally undermined by two aspects of its approach, both of which can be critiqued on therapeutic and political grounds:
• it sets up a hierarchy of mental health between therapist and client;
• it individualises the experience of sexual abuse.

It is simply not appropriate to see abuse as an individual issue. The sexual abuse of women and girls needs to be located within a framework of understanding of the endemic abuse and violence which is both cause and product of women's oppression in society, otherwise PCT risks repeating the same individualisation and pathologisation that characterises the psychiatric response (see Shaw and Proctor, 2004).

I described how much social constructionism has contributed to the development of feminism and the critique of psychiatry. This social constructionist/feminist approach also has much to offer PCT. In order not to impose our own frameworks of understanding, we need to know what they are. Therapists need to be aware of the gendered structures and discourses that make up systems of gendered inequality in society. We have been brought up in a heavily gendered reality and it's impossible that this will not have affected us in some way: for example, in the conditions of worth that we apply to ourselves and to other people; in the standards by which we make our judgements about what is acceptable/unacceptable; and who needs or doesn't need therapy. To deny this, or to fail to act upon this awareness, could mean that a therapist is implicated in upholding the very institutions and attitudes which have caused the client's distress.

To conclude then, my own experiences of the psychiatric response to sexual abuse serve as a powerful pointer for what is not helpful, and conversely, what is. PCT meets many of the requirements of a helpful response to sexual abuse; crucially, however, it fails to provide those things which have been central to my regaining of a sense of power and well-being. These include: a socially contextual understanding of my experiences; the opportunity to develop a political understanding of these experiences; connection with the countless other women who have shared these experiences; and the inestimable sense of empowerment in coming together with other women to enact a political response to our shared experiences. Bringing these aspects of my 'recovery' into the Person-Centred Approach to sexual abuse does not just call for change in the practice of the individual therapist. It calls for changes in the theoretical bases of the PCT approach. Ultimately, it asks the PCT movement to expand its focus from the individual to take in the whole of society, and in doing so, to ally itself with other social movements which work to address not only the impact of trauma and abuse, but also its causes. Without such a move, the efficacy of PCT therapy is limited at best and negative at worst.

REFERENCES

American Psychiatric Association (1994) *Diagnostic and Statistical Manual IV*. Washington DC: APA.

Arnold, L (1995) *Women and Self Injury—A survey of 76 women*. Bristol Crisis Service for Women, Bristol.

Breggin, P (1991) *Toxic Psychiatry: Drugs and electroconvulsive therapy—The truth and the better alternatives*. London: HarperCollins.

Burr, V (1995) *An Introduction to Social Constructionism*. London: Routledge.

Burstow, B (1987) Humanistic psychotherapy and the issue of equality. *Journal of Humanistic Psychotherapy, 27*: 9–25.

Busfield, J (1996) *Men, Women and Madness: Understanding gender and mental disorder.* Basingstoke: Macmillan Press Ltd.

Chamberlin, J (1988) *On Our Own.* London: Mind.

Chesler, P (1972) *Women and Madness.* New York: Doubleday.

Dworkin, A (1974) *Woman Hating.* New York: EP Dutton and Co.

Finley-Belgrad, EA (MD) and Davies, JA (MD) (17.2.2004) *Personality Disorder: Borderline*: www.emedicine.com.

Johnstone, L (1995) Self Injury and the Psychiatric Response, BCSW National Conference on Self Injury, 8th November.

Kelly, L (1988) *Surviving Sexual Violence.* Cambridge: Polity.

Kelly, L (1988/9) From politics to pathology: The medicalisation of the impact of rape and childhood sexual abuse. *Radical Community Medicine,* 1988/9: 14–18

Koss, M and Harvey, M (1991) *The Rape Victim—Clinical and community intervention.* London: Sage Publications.

Mackinnon, C (1983) Feminism, Marxism, Method and the State: Towards feminist jurisprudence, *Signs: Journal of Women in Culture and Society* 8(4): 635–8.

Masson, J (1997) *Against Therapy.* London: HarperCollins.

Penfold, P and Walker, G (1983) *Women and the Psychiatric Paradox.* UK: Eden Press.

Proctor, G (2004) Responding to injustice: Working with angry and violent clients in a person-centred way, in D Jones (ed) *Working with Dangerous People: the psychotherapy of violence.* Abingdon, UK: Radcliffe Medical Press pp. 99–116.

Proctor, G (2002) *The Dynamics of Power in Counselling and Psychotherapy.* Ross-onWye: PCCS Books.

Shaw, C (1999) 'This is my experience and this is important'—women who self injure and their experience of services. Liverpool Hope University, unpublished.

Shaw, C (2003) Hunger Strikers Expose Psychiatry, *Asylum, 14*(2): 18.

Shaw, C and Proctor, G (2004) Women at the Margins: A critique of Borderline Personality Disorder. *Asylum, 4*(3): 8–10.

Smail, D (1987) *Taking Care: An alternative to therapy.* London: Weidenfeld and Nicolson.

Surrey, J, Swett, C, Michaels, A and Levins, S (1990) Reported history of physical and sexual abuse and severity of symptomatology in women psychiatric outpatients, *American Orthopsychiatric Association, 60*(3): 412–17.

Ussher, J (1991) *Women's Madness—Misogyny or mental illness?* Hemel Hempstead: Harvester Wheatsheaf.

Women's Support Project (1990) *Violence Against Women Survey*, Women's Support Project, Glasgow.

TAKING CONTEXT AND CULTURE INTO ACCOUNT IN THE CORE CONDITIONS: A FEMINIST PERSON-CENTERED APPROACH

RANDALL D EHRBAR

A recent trend in psychology (Patterson, 1996), and especially feminist psychology, is attending to cultural diversity and contextual factors in treatment. This paper will examine the three core conditions of Client-Centered Therapy (congruence, unconditional positive regard, and empathic understanding) and how they relate to contextual factors such as cultural diversity. Feminist and multicultural approaches to therapy are concerned with providing treatment that is relevant, just, and useful. Client-Centered Therapy offers one way of providing such treatment. This paper is primarily an exegesis[1] of the existing client-centered theory, rather than an extension of it.

In difference based multicultural therapy (including many feminist approaches to multicultural therapy) there is the assumption that clinicians need to treat people from different cultural backgrounds differently in order to be respectful of their culture, since not doing so can reinforce existing social power structures. 'Each cultural group requires a different set of skills, unique areas of emphasis, and specific insights for effective counseling to occur' (Pederson, 1976, cited in Patterson, 1996: 229).

CONCERNS WITH DIFFERENCE-BASED THERAPY FROM A CLIENT-CENTERED PERSPECTIVE

What does client-centered theory have to say about treating different categories of people differently? Rogers (1951) proposed that 'therapy is basically the experiencing

Thanks to Dr Marjorie Witty and Dr Barbara Brodley who kindly gave copious feedback on this paper in its various drafts. An earlier version of the paper was presented at the 2001 ADPCA meeting.
[1.] A critical explanation or interpretation of a text.

of the inadequacies in old ways of perceiving, the experiencing of new and more accurate and adequate perceptions, and the recognition of significant relationships between perceptions' (pp. 222–3). He further hypothesized that 'the client will explore the areas of conflict as rapidly as he is able to bear the pain, and that he will experience a change in perception as rapidly as that experience can be tolerated by the self' (p. 222). Thus, even if the therapist knew exactly what the causes of the psychological maladjustment are 'it is doubtful that he could make effective use of this knowledge. Telling the client would most assuredly not help. Directing the client's attention to certain areas is perhaps as likely to arouse resistance as to bring nondefensive consideration of these areas' (p. 222). Bozarth's (1998) summary of the research on whether specific treatments work best for specific disorders suggests that it is not necessarily helpful to treat clients diagnosed with different disorders differently. This analogy can be extended to say there is no specific treatment X that works best with an African-American that is different from that treatment best used with a Native American.

One problem with treating clients differently based upon group membership that Patterson (1996: 229) points out is that often members of different cultural groups are portrayed as wanting or needing an 'active, authoritative, directive, controlling counselor'.

> Perhaps the greatest difficulty with accepting assumptions about the characteristics and so-called needs of clients from differing cultures is that they will lead to failure, or lack of success in counseling. The active, authoritative, directive, controlling counselor, providing answers and solutions to the client's problems, has not been considered competent or effective for many years. To provide this kind of treatment (it would not be called counseling) to clients from other cultures would be providing poor or second-class treatment. (Patterson, 1996)

To provide poor or second-class treatment to members of other cultures is discriminatory and paternalistic. On the other hand, if people from other cultures actually do need or want something different in counseling, *not* to provide it would be discriminatory and paternalistic. This is tricky, but providing treatment known to be less effective certainly is not the answer. Patterson (1996) examines the data supporting the idea that people from different cultures need something different in counseling and he finds the data to be unconvincing.

CONCERNS WITH CLIENT-CENTERED THERAPY FROM A FEMINIST PERSPECTIVE

Politically active approaches to psychology such as feminist psychology and liberation psychology, argue that it is important to address issues of oppression directly. 'It is critical that our therapeutic theorizing and systems of intervention—with girls, children of color, gay and lesbian youth—include the feminist critique, and that this critique be inclusive' (Almeida, 1998: 9). This avoids a situation arising from an unjust culture being treated as if it were a problem arising from individual dysfunction. Baker (1996) gives an example of a working-class client who injured her back, and then thought she noticed people following her. Her therapist thought that she was delusional, and had her admitted to a hospital and treated with anti-psychotic medication. What her therapist did not realize was that it is in fact common for employers to have injured workers followed (p. 18).

O'Hara (1996) raises some important points in her analysis of Rogers' work with Sylvia: she suggests Rogers' use of the term 'grown-up' (not a choice of words originating with Sylvia) as implying that Sylvia's previous sense of incompleteness was immature. O'Hara connects this word choice to 'the tendency of members of dominant groups to see dominated groups as 'children' and their behavior as immature' (p. 288). O'Hara also takes issue with Rogers' use of the word 'risk' (this time the choice of words does originate with Sylvia). O'Hara sees this as Rogers and Sylvia creating 'a shared belief that her previous sexual experience had been limited because of her own unwillingness to take risks—once again a dispositional or intrapsychic explanation' (p. 289), not taking into account cultural forces which encourage women to restrict their sexuality. This is an example that even a therapist who is very aware and sensitive (which Rogers by all accounts was) can have assumptions which he or she is unaware of play out in therapy. It is also an example of how not taking contextual factors (such as social restrictions on women's sexuality) into account can diminish empathic understanding and potentially have negative consequences.

Some authors within feminist and liberation psychology also advocate teaching the client about systems of oppression within society and how that impacts the client's specific situation. For example, in the above mentioned situation in which Rogers and Sylvia talk about her sexual experience in terms of risk, O'Hara suggests exploring 'where this sense of danger comes from, what kind of danger she envisions, and so on' (p. 289). This approach would help connect Sylvia's experience of risk to the actual external social situation rather than reinforcing a view of herself as being unwilling to take risks. O'Hara suggests that 'one of the limits of a strictly reflective, empathic therapy' (p. 290) is not making this type of educative or reframing response. Alternately such political education can be seen as unhelpful, just as it is unlikely that telling a client the source of his or her troubles will result in relief. Instead, careful empathic understanding is likely to be more helpful. In the above situation, careful empathic understanding might have included asking Sylvia what she meant by risk, not in order to enlighten her but in order to better understand her experience.

This education would be disruptive of the non-judgmental accepting atmosphere client-centered therapists attempt to create. Additionally, there is the possibility of the client experiencing this in such a way that he or she moves towards an external locus of evaluation as opposed to the internal locus of evaluation which Rogers sees as more useful. hooks (2000) articulates a feminist rejection of ideology which 'teaches women that to be female is to be a victim', pointing out that this 'mystifies female experience—in their daily lives most women are not continually passive, helpless, or powerless "victims"' (p. 45). This highlights a potential danger of viewing client experiences from an ideological standpoint.

Paradoxically the intent to instill an internal locus of evaluation in the client is directive and is thus inconsistent with Client-Centered Therapy (Brodley, 1995; Grant, 1993)! I think this is an important point, because the desire to instill an internal locus of evaluation in a client is one of the ways in which Client-Centered Therapy is said to reflect an individualistic Western cultural perspective. This is an important objection that is easily overlooked if there is an underlying '(false) premise of (Western) cultural neutrality' (Singh and Tudor, 1997: 32). It is important to distinguish between the most general form of the hypothesis of what Client-Centered Therapy does and more specific hypotheses, such as increased internal locus of evaluation and to distinguish between descriptions of possible or likely process from aims.

The most general hypothesis is that Client-Centered Therapy provides beneficial psychological conditions in which the person's own natural growth process operates more freely and that the positive effects of therapy are the result of this natural growth process (actualizing tendency). The specific hypotheses about how this actualization might manifest itself reflect a particular view of human nature. Some of the initial hypotheses Rogers (1989c/1959) proposed about changes that would happen as a result of Client-Centered Therapy reflect an individual perspective, such as the hypothesis that a client will come to have an internal locus of evaluation. That these specific hypotheses about what happens when a person becomes more freely and fully him or herself come from an individualistic perspective does not invalidate other hypotheses about this from a communal perspective. Nor does this invalidate the more general hypothesis that given certain conditions, people will tend to express their natural growth processes.

Singh and Tudor (1997) cite Nobles to point out that while Rogers' theory was originally based on an 'I' self-concept, 'it is equally applicable to a "we" concept, … a more relevant notion in many cultures' (p. 38). Schmid (2002b) argues that 'In its basic statements the PCA [Person-Centered Approach] is founded in the conviction that we are not merely a-contextual individuals, we only exist as part of a "We". Without stating it explicitly this is also inherent in Rogers' theory from the very beginning' (p. 2). A more relational or communal viewpoint might lead to the hypothesis that the client will come to have more and more mutually satisfying relationships. For example, one might just as easily hypothesize that as a person self-actualizes and gains in maturity they would develop 'trust within the context of familiarity and difference', 'interdependence within the context of multiple relationships', 'tolerance: differentiation of the self', and 'expanded identity within the context of diversity' (Almeida, Woods, and Messineo, 1998: 24), elements of a mature development proposed from a feminist viewpoint.

THE OTHER THREE NECESSARY AND SUFFICIENT CONDITIONS

Rogers (1989a/1957) proposed six 'necessary and sufficient' conditions for psychotherapy, three of which (empathic understanding, unconditional positive regard, and congruence) have become known as the 'core conditions'. Before turning to the 'core conditions', the other three conditions will be briefly examined. These are: (the first condition) 'Two persons are in psychological contact' (Rogers, 1989a/1957: 221); (the second condition) 'The first, whom we shall term the client, is in a state of incongruence, being vulnerable or anxious' (*ibid.*); and (the sixth condition) 'The communication to the client of the therapist's empathic understanding and unconditional positive regard is to a minimal degree achieved' (*ibid.*).

In the area of congruence, Rogers (1989a/1957) assumed a necessary inequality, proposing that it is necessary for the client to be in a state of incongruence, while it necessary for the therapist to be in a state of congruence. Burstow (1987) on the other hand argues that in this area, there is 'not *necessarily equality* ... neither is there a *necessary inequality* and where there is inequality it *need not* favor the therapist' (p. 13, emphasis in original). It is not true that in all therapy relationships at all times the therapist is more congruent than the client, and while Rogers sees such an inequality as necessary for change to occur (that is, at those times and in those relationships when the therapist is less congruent that the client, change is not being facilitated in the client), Burstow does not. Instead she says 'In any given case, it is *simply likely* that the therapist's coping skills will be more highly developed than the client's' (p. 13, emphasis in original). Some of the reasons why congruence on the part of the therapist is important will be addressed further below. While it is often the case that a person seeking therapy is in a state of incongruence, Brodley (personal communication, July 2003) hypothesized that this condition is not necessary but possibly reflects the influence of the psychodynamic drive-reduction model on Rogers.

The other two conditions involve psychological contact between the client and therapist and the client's perception of the therapist's empathic understanding and unconditional positive regard. Simply holding the attitudes of unconditional positive regard, empathic understanding, and congruence will do no good if the client does not perceive them and thus does not have access to them. A simple (if extreme) example of this is that there would be a definite limitation in psychological contact and communication of the core conditions between a client and therapist who do not speak the same language. Patterson (1996) points out that 'understanding of cultural differences in verbal and nonverbal behaviors (DW Sue, 1989; DW Sue and D Sue, 1990) can be very helpful' in communicating empathy and unconditional positive regard to the client, especially if the client differs from the therapist in factors such as 'culture, race, socioeconomic class, age, and gender' (Patterson, 1996: 230). An example of a nonverbal behavior which varies cross-culturally is eye-contact. In some cultures, it is a sign of respect to make eye-contact with someone when talking to them and listening to them. In other cultures, not making eye-contact is a better way to show respect and making eye contact is actively disrespectful. This is an example of how understanding cultural differences may help therapists provide the necessary and sufficient conditions.

That the core conditions need to be received to be effective points to the fact that therapy takes place within the context of a relationship. The therapist does not simply radiate empathy, congruence and unconditional positive regard in which the client is then bathed, rather there is a connection between two human beings. Rogers emphasizes the basic importance of the relationship when he says that contact is the first of his necessary and sufficient conditions for therapy (1951, 1989a/ 1957, 1989b/1958, 1989c/1959) and goes on to call it a precondition, without which none of the other conditions can exist. The relationship is again emphasized in the final condition in which the empathic understanding and unconditional positive regard of the therapist are perceived by the client. As Schmid (2002a) says, 'Presence is possible only from a We-perspective. It is the fundamental attitude which is at the root of the "core conditions", a way of being with, even more: a way of being together' (p. 33).

THE CORE CONDITIONS

Now the three conditions which have come to be known as the 'core conditions' will be examined in a feminist multicultural context. These conditions are empathic understanding, unconditional positive regard, and congruence. Vontress (1976, cited in Patterson, 1996: 229) says 'Few counselors ever ask what they can do to change themselves; few want to know how they can become better human beings in order to relate more effectually with other human beings who, through the accident of birth, are racially and ethnically different.' The discipline of Client-Centered Therapy or the person-centered approach offers an avenue through which exactly this can be done.

Empathic understanding is described as:

> the counselor's function to assume, in so far as he is able, the internal frame of reference of the client, to perceive the world as the client sees it, to perceive the client himself as he is seen by himself, to lay aside all perceptions from the external frame of reference while doing so, and to communicate some of that empathic understanding to the client. (Rogers, 1951: 29)

Accurately empathically understanding another person's frame of reference requires taking into account the context in which she or he lives. Information about a person's cultural position or context is not overly determining, that is: knowing X about a person does not automatically imply Y and Z. Rather this is just one more piece of information the counselor combines with other pieces of information shared by the client in a shifting mosaic to ever more accurately approximate the client's frame of reference.

This is consistent with a feminist approach to therapy. In discussing a case vignette, Andres Nazario Jr, a feminist therapist, said, 'We must not assume that just because Lucas is black or Shendi is biracial that we know anything about them other than what is given in those few lines ... I prefer to be curious about these issues rather than to have preconceived definitions of their realities' (Bepko et al., 1989: 56). To ignore the context in which the client lives willfully restricts understanding of the client's frame of reference and makes it less accurate. Nazario advocates 'an oppression-sensitive approach in which gender, race, ethnicity, culture, sexual orientation, spirituality, age, socioeconomic status, ability, nationality, and ecology are considered domains of existential meaning' (p. 57). Similarly, it is not possible to fully empathically understand someone without taking into account these domains of existential meaning.

> All clients ... belong to multiple groups, all of which influence the client's perceptions, beliefs, feelings, thoughts, and behavior. The counselor must be aware of these influences and of their unique blending or fusion in the client if counseling is to be successful. (Patterson, 1996: 230)

This is not possible except through understanding what the client shares of his or her experience of belonging to these groups. For example, what it means to be an American woman is not the same as what it means to be a Mexican woman, what it means to be a heterosexual woman is not the same as what it means to be a lesbian woman, is not the same as what it means to be a bisexual woman, and what it means to be born and raised as a biological female is not the same as what it means to be a transsexual woman. Each of these identities also shifts over time, as the meaning of belonging to any of these categories is different today than it was fifty years ago or will be fifty years from now. Additionally, what it means to be each of these is different for each individual.

> The theories of feminist identity that elaborate predicates of color, sexuality, ethnicity, class, and able-bodiedness invariably close with an embarrassed 'etc.' at the end of the list. Through this horizontal trajectory of adjectives, these positions strive to encompass a situated subject, but invariably fail to be complete ... what political impetus is to be derived from the exasperated 'etc.' that so often occurs at the end of such lines? ... It is the *supplement*, the excess

that necessarily accompanies any effort to posit identity once and for all. (Butler, 1999: 182–3)

That 'etc.' leaves room for lots of individual variation and for hope, because we are not completely determined by our group memberships, even though they do have an impact upon us.

Bozarth (1998) describes empathy as 'the "vessel" by which the therapist communicates unconditional positive regard in the most pure way … The action of understanding the momentary frame of reference of the client is an ultimate confirmation of the person by the therapist' (p. 46–7). O'Hara (1996) points to the relational aspects of empathy when she says 'Empathy becomes a term for how one person's life can be touched, illuminated, altered in connection with another's' (p. 297). Empathic understanding does not exist in a vacuum, rather it is part of a relationship between whole human beings.

> Person-Centered Therapy can only be done out of deference to the otherness of the other and their mystery in the sense of enigma by Levinas. It means acknowledgement instead of knowledge and is a pro-active way of being, unconditional, which can—correctly understood—be termed 'love', as Rogers did in the meaning of 'agape'. (Schmid, 2002a: 34)

Part of recognizing our clients as whole is recognizing that they live in the world and taking that into account. The recognition of ourselves as whole human beings naturally leads into increasing congruence.

Just as it is fruitful to take into account context in order to more fully understand others, it is important to take into account context in order to more fully understand ourselves. Congruence involves the therapist's accurate representation of his or her experiences, 'the self acknowledgment of the therapist's organismic experiences of any given moment' (Bozarth, 1998: 71) and especially the therapist is 'not denying organismic experiences that persisted during the client/therapist relationship' (*ibid.*). In the wider interpretation of the core conditions proposed, congruence includes the therapist's awareness of his or her own position in society and an awareness of his or her own prejudice issues (a feminist perspective is likely to assume that anyone raised in a society based on prejudice is likely to have internalized that prejudice) (Collins, 2000). Chalifoux (1996) suggests that clients are more likely to be able to trust that therapists can understand their experiences and values if 'the therapist is not only aware of their own class position and values, but is comfortable with them' (p. 33). Singh and Tudor (1997) suggest that congruence applies not only to the self but also to 'self-in-context, in relation to family, environment and culture' (p. 38). Related is Bozarth's (1998) view of congruence as a therapist's state of readiness to supply empathic understanding and unconditional positive regard. Thus Bozarth (1998: 47) cites Rogers as he suggests 'that therapists participate in activities that help them to become more genuine or more "… freely and deeply him (her) self, with his or her actual experience accurately represented by his awareness of himself"' (Rogers, 1959, cited in Kirschenbaum and Henderson, 1989).

Singh and Tudor (1997) talk about the importance of the therapist's journey 'to come to terms with their positions in their society and the predicaments of life in relation to culture' (p. 39). Recognizing one's own privilege and prejudices can be a threatening experience. This perspective is very much grounded in feminist theory. There is a strong condition of worth that people should not be prejudiced and therapists most especially should not prejudiced, particularly not with respect to their clients. At the same time if we are prejudiced but deny this to consciousness (are incongruent in this regard), we are less able to be effective therapists: 'To the extent that he/she presents an outward facade of one attitude or feeling, while inwardly or at an unconscious level he/she experiences another feeling, the likelihood of successful therapy will be diminished' (Rogers, 1956 cited in Bozarth 1998: 71). Bozarth (1998) suggests that the way to deal with this difficult and threatening situation successfully is through unconditional positive self-regard. 'For threatening experiences to be accurately symbolized in awareness and assimilated into self-structure, there must be a decrease in conditions of worth and an increase in unconditional positive *self*-regard' (Bozarth, 1998: 45).

Bozarth (1998) describes congruence as 'an attitudinal development that enables the therapist to be more able to experience empathic understanding and unconditional positive regard toward the client' (p. 46). Once again we see the intricate inter-relationship of the core conditions and how incongruence on the therapist's part leads to the therapist being less able to be empathically understanding and to provide unconditional positive regard. If a therapist does not have an awareness of any prejudice issues he or she has, or is incongruent in this respect, it is possible (or even likely) that prejudice could contaminate the therapist's unconditional positive regard. Prejudice implies that one is 'pre-judging' or judging ahead of the case. And any sort of judgment of the client will interfere with unconditional positive regard, since it is not possible to be both judging and unconditional at the same time. Also even more obviously, pre-judging will prevent empathic understanding.

Bozarth (1998) sees unconditional positive regard as 'the primary theoretical condition of change in person-centered therapy' (p. 47). This attitude can be directed inward (unconditional positive self-regard, which Bozarth sees as the basis of congruence), toward others (such as clients) and toward the context, which includes the culture itself (Singh and Tudor, 1997). When applied towards others, unconditional positive regard involves cherishing and respecting them as unique human beings. Similarly, unconditional positive self-regard involves extending this same cherishing and respect towards ourselves. When combined with the concept of the actualizing tendency, unconditional positive regard suggests that while a person may be functioning in a way which is far from optimal, his or her functioning is the result of the best available compromises under a given set of circumstances.

Unconditional positive regard toward the context or culture is a bit more complicated, but also involves cherishing the context or culture for what it is and recognizing it as influenced by past circumstances. In some ways, unconditional positive regard is similar to what Linehan (1993) calls 'radical acceptance'. She points out that 'acceptance of reality is not equivalent to approval of reality' (p. 96) and that reality must be accurately perceived and accepted before effective action can be taken to deal with it. Unconditional positive regard is a way of looking at a person or situation without assigning blame. This does not, however, mean that there is no responsibility. For example, a therapist who has internalized prejudicial beliefs is not at fault for having done so, but is responsible for dealing with them. Similarly, if there are aspects of our culture we are unhappy with, it is our responsibility to work for change. Thus Client-Centered Therapy and the Person-Centered Approach can be consistent with feminist principles of activism. In fact, Schmid (2002b) argues that 'Psychotherapy without political awareness and without political conviction is naïve and often inefficient' (p. 2).

CONCLUSION

This expanded conceptualization of the core conditions has the following implications: (1) There is no need for the therapist to 'do' anything differently based on what categories a client might fall into. Indeed, trying to 'do' therapy differently with different clients based on their ethnicity or gender, for example, leads to the possible pitfalls of being inauthentic within the therapy relationship and of offering second-rate treatment to members of certain groups. (2) As previously understood in Client-Centered Therapy, the only demands being made are of the therapist to provide the core conditions at the highest possible level, with no demands or expectations being placed on the client. (3) This does not mean that client-centered therapists need not attend to multicultural issues or contextual factors. 'Rogers himself identified experiential knowledge of cultural setting and influence as important preparation for the training therapist' (Singh and Tudor, 1997: 32). All of us are situated in contexts, and not taking these contexts into account (a) leads to the dilution of the core conditions, so that they are being provided in a lesser form and (b) might even mean that the core conditions are not perceived at all because our context impacts how we interact with others in relationships. For the therapist to provide the core conditions at the highest level possible, it is necessary for the therapist to attend to the context of him or herself (including any of his or her own prejudice issues), the client (including possible conditions of worth based on internalized oppression or prejudice) and the therapeutic relationship (including the culture in which it takes place).

REFERENCES

Almeidia, RV (1998) The Dislocation of Women's Experience in Family Therapy, in RV Almeidia (ed) *Transformations of Gender and Race: Family and developmental perspectives.* New York: Haworth Press Inc, pp. 1–22.

Almeidia, RV, Woods, R and Messineo, T (1998) Child Development: Intersectionality of race, gender, class, and culture, in RV Almeidia (ed) *Transformations of Gender and Race: Family and developmental perspectives.* New York: Haworth Press Inc, pp. 23–47.

Baker, NL (1996) Class as a construct in a 'classless' society, in M Hill and ED Rothblum (eds) *Classism and Feminist Therapy: Counting costs.* New York: Haworth Park Press, pp. 13–23.

Bepko, C, Almeidia, RV, Messineo, T and Stevenson, Y (1998) Evolving Constructs of Masculinity: Interviews with Andres Nazario Jr, William Doherty and Robert Font: Commentary, in RV Almeidia (ed) *Transformations of Gender and Race: Family and developmental perspectives.* New York: Haworth Press Inc, pp. 49–79.

Bozarth, J (1998) *Person-Centered Therapy: A revolutionary paradigm.* Ross-on-Wye: PCCS Books.

Brodley, BT (1995) Client-Centered Therapy: Not a means to an end. Unpublished manuscript, Illinois School of Professional Psychology, Chicago.

Brodley, BT (July 2003) personal communication.

Burstow, B (1987) Humanistic psychotherapy and the issue of equality. *Journal of Humanistic Psychology, 27*(1): 9–25.

Butler, J (1999) *Gender Trouble: Feminism and the subversion of identity.* 10th anniversary edition. New York: Routledge.

Chalifoux, B (1996) Speaking up: White working class women in therapy, in M Hill and ED Rothblum (eds) *Classism and Feminist Therapy: Counting costs.* New York: Haworth Park Press, pp. 25–34.

Collins, PH (2000) *Black Feminist Thought: Knowledge, consciousness, and the politics of empowerment* (2nd ed). New York: Routledge.

Grant, B (1993) Principled and instrumental non-directiveness. *Person-Centered Review, 5*(1): 76–88.

hooks, b (2000) *Feminist Theory: From margin to center* (2nd ed). South End Press Classics: Cambridge, MA.

Linehan, MM (1993) *Skills Training Manual for Treating Borderline Personality Disorder.* New York: Guilford Press.

O'Hara, M (1996) Rogers and Sylvia: A feminist analysis, in BA Farber, DC Brink and PM Raskin (eds) *The Psychotherapy of Carl Rogers: Cases and commentary.* New York: Guilford Press, pp. 284–300.

Patterson, CH (1996) Multicultural counseling: From diversity to universality. *Journal of Counseling and Development, 74*: 227–31.

Rogers, CR (1951) *Client-Centered Therapy.* Boston: Houghton Mifflin.

Rogers, CR (1989a/1957) The necessary and sufficient conditions of therapeutic personality change, in H Kirschenbaum and VL Henderson (eds) (1989) *The Carl Rogers Reader*. Boston: Houghton Mifflin, pp. 219–35. Original work (1957) published in *Journal of Counseling Psychology 21*(2): 95–103.

Rogers, CR (1989b/1958) The characteristics of a helping relationship in H Kirschenbaum and VL Henderson (eds) (1989) *The Carl Rogers Reader*. Boston: Houghton Mifflin, pp. 108–26. Original work (1958) published in *Personnel and Guidance Journal 37* : 6–16.

Rogers, CR (1989c/1959) A theory of therapy, personality, and interpersonal relationships, as developed in the client-centered framework, in H Kirschenbaum and VL Henderson (eds) *The Carl Rogers Reader*. Boston: Houghton Mifflin, pp 236–57. Original work (1989) published in S Koch (ed) *Psychology: A Study of a Science, Vol 3*. New York: McGraw-Hill, pp. 184–256.

Schmid, PF (2002a) *The person in the center of therapy: The ongoing challenge of Carl Rogers for psychotherapy.* <http://pfs-online.at/papers/pp-wcp3+lj2002-Dateien/frame.htm>.

Schmid, PF (2002b) *The unavoidable We in therapy.* <http://pfs-online.at/papers/paper-lajolla2002-coll.pdf>.

Singh, J and Tudor, K (1997) Cultural conditions of therapy. *The Person-Centered Journal, 4*: 32–46.

Sue, DW (1989, December) Cultural specific techniques in counseling: A counseling framework. Paper presented at the Southeast Asia Symposium on Counseling and Guidance in the 21st Century, Taipei, Taiwan.

Sue, DW and Sue, D (1990) *Counseling the Culturally Different: Theory and practice.* (2nd ed) New York: Wiley.

Vontress, CE (1976) Racial and ethnic barriers in counseling, in P Pedersen, WJ Lonner and J Draguns (eds) *Counseling Across Cultures*. Honolulu HI: University Press of Hawaii, pp. 42–64.

PEDAGOGICAL CROSSROADS: INTEGRATING FEMINIST CRITICAL PEDAGOGIES AND THE PERSON-CENTERED APPROACH TO EDUCATION

JEFFREY HD CORNELIUS-WHITE AND PHOEBE C GODFREY

Both feminist critical pedagogies (FCP) and the Person-Centered Approach to education (PCAE) share an ethical imperative: to empower persons. Both theories are reactions to traditional teaching practices that neglect the dignity of students. Both aim to help students move towards pro-social goals (Rogers, 1977; Gore, 1992). However, the two approaches have remained largely separate. This chapter summarizes FCP and PCAE and attempts to discuss how both may contribute to each other. (Appendix 1 provides a hypothetical example of a traditional, FCP and PCAE classroom. Appendix 2 provides internet resources for both approaches.)

FEMINIST CRITICAL PEDAGOGIES

FCP has theoretical roots in critical pedagogy and feminist pedagogy. Some forms emphasize 'a critical and social vision of education' while others emphasize 'instructional practices' begun in women's studies (Gore, 1993: 7). We define FCP as seeking to unite these diverging strands by critically exploring in theory and practice what makes education both feminist and critical. FCP try to create emancipatory classrooms, challenging individual and social oppressions, including the teacher's role, by calling for 'greater reflexivity and acknowledgement of the limitations of what "we" can do for "you"' (Gore, 1992: 69). In other words, FCP question the whole concept of education, recognizing that 'meaning is never guaranteed, fixed, or unproblematically shared among social agents' (Luke, 1996: 3). With increased ambiguity, the potential for democratic, egalitarian learning experiences likewise increases. FCP aim for collective transformation of inequalities by identifying them as manifestations of power and ideology, woven into the subjective realities of students and teachers (Ellsworth, 1992; Gore, 1992). Nevertheless there are no quick fixes in FCP, since no regimes of truth are beyond deconstruction, not even those of FCP (Lather, 1991).

CRITICAL THEORIES OF SCHOOLING: LOOKING FOR GENDER AND THE ROLE OF
STUDENT AGENCY

Critical theories arose out of the Marxist Frankfurt School, which stressed critical thinking in 'the struggle for self-emancipation and social change' (Giroux, 1983: 8). The Frankfurt School asserted that critical analyses could illuminate both 'what is and what should be', concerning societal contradictions and conflicts (Giroux, 1983: 9). Early critical theorists of schooling like Bowles and Gintis (1977) identified capitalism as an oppressive and exploitative system, depicting the multiple ways in which class inequalities were reproduced through education.

However, these critical educational theorists did not sufficiently analyze the role of patriarchy in education. For example, Bowles and Gintis (1977) explored girls and women in schools, but did not centralize gender nor question its reproduction in schools. Furthermore, they neglected issues of 'consciousness, ideology and resistance in the schooling process', (Giroux, 1983: 84) all of which form key tenets of FCP.

Many feminist critical theorists have found the classroom application of male-authored critical pedagogy highly problematic, critiquing their emphasis on teachers as having the 'power' to liberate students through critical pedagogy (Ellsworth, 1992; Gore, 1992; Lather 1991). According to Ellsworth (1992), early Giroux 'leaves the implied superiority of the teacher's understanding ... unproblematized and untheorized' (p. 98).[1] Gore (1992) agrees that such works ignored 'the context(s) of teachers' work ... [in that they] ... are constrained by, for example, their location in patriarchal institutions and by the historical constructions of pedagogy as and within, discourses of social regulation' (p. 57). Gore's critique evolves around the term 'empowerment' and its attribution of 'extraordinary abilities to the teacher' (p. 57). This leads to an over-emphasis on what students should or should not do, as opposed to questioning one's own complicity in patriarchal pedagogy, and the students' influence on teachers. Gore asserts that many critical theorists have implied that if students are not empowered, teachers (the majority of whom are female) are to blame.

Brazilian Paolo Freire (1970) developed a radically different type of pedagogy from the traditional 'banking' type of education, involving individual and collective agency. Freire's *Pedagogy of the Oppressed* introduced 'conscientization', or teaching for critical consciousness as a potential act of liberation (hooks, 1994). While he maintained a Marxist critique of capitalism, Freire focused on the ways in which

---

[1] See Giroux (Border Pedagogy in the Age of Postmodern, *Journal of Education*, vol. 170, no. 3, 1988 pp. 162–81) and McLaren (Schooling the Postmodern Body: Critical Pedagogy and Politics of Enfleshment, *Journal of Education*, vol. 170, no. 3, 1988, pp. 53–83) for their responses to Ellsworth's article 'Why Doesn't This Feel Empowering?' Also see Patti Lather (1991: 44–9) for her analysis of all three.

schools dehumanize students. To counter these oppressive tendencies, liberation pedagogy gives students a voice. Freire's conscientization together with the Frankfurt School's emphasis on critical thinking presented, 'a powerful agenda for emancipatory education' that influenced FCP (Gore, 1992: 28).

FEMINIST CRITICAL THEORIES AND PEDAGOGIES: FINDING GENDER, AGENCY AND RESISTANCE

FCP recognizes 'gender as a basic organizing principle which profoundly shapes/ mediates the concrete conditions of our lives' (Lather, 1991: 71). In bringing together the personal and the political, feminism recognizes the reciprocal influence between the researcher and the subject, showing 'a commitment to [relational] praxis' (Weiler, 1988: 63). Like Freire's notion that pedagogy must lead towards liberation, feminist theory has not looked for abstract truth, but for progressive change without assuming, as does the 'banking' form of education, how exactly that change will be accomplished.

The women's studies strand has focused on '*how* to teach and *what* to teach,' (Gore, 1993: 20) while FCP from education departments has focused on how to make pedagogical theory feminist while dismissing much critical pedagogy as patriarchal. While both strands 'similarly address classrooms', their basic emphasis remains distinct (p. 31). Our conception of FCP forms a dialectic between practice and theory, bringing the above two strands closer together by struggling to engage in the classroom on a daily basis.

Feminist educators such as Ellsworth and Lather have taken critical theories to task after implementing them into their teaching practices with mixed results. Two recurring results seem to be student resistance to being 'transformed' and teacher doubts as to what being 'transformed' means or who is supposed to transform whom. FCP are a practice in progress that may benefit from aspects of PCAE.

bell hooks stands out as representative of our view of FCP. hooks has been greatly influenced by Freire, bringing to her work a recognition of the 'interlocking systems of domination', especially racism and sexism (hooks, 1989: 22). Thus, for hooks, education for the purpose of liberation, which she calls 'engaged pedagogy', can break the cycle of oppression. As she states, 'Education as the practice of freedom [can only be achieved] when everyone claims knowledge as a field in which we all labor' (hooks, 1994: 14). In short, 'teachers' are no more authorities in the knowledge of freedom than 'students'. hooks (1994) recognizes that:

> Progressive, holistic education, 'engaged pedagogy' is more demanding than conventional critical or feminist pedagogy. For unlike these two teaching practices, it emphasizes well-being. That means that teachers must be actively committed to a process of self-actualization that promoted their own well-being if they are to teach in a manner that empowers students. (p. 15)

Resembling Rogers, hooks recognizes that change can happen if teachers exhibit genuineness: 'professors must practice being vulnerable in the class room, being wholly present in mind, body and spirit' (p. 21). However, Gore might question hooks' assertion by asking how a teacher knows if students are empowered. Unlike the critiqued works of Giroux and McLaren, hooks emphasizes the teachers own 'self-actualization'. Teachers can't really empower students, but through their own process of self-actualization, student self-empowerment becomes a possibility. Therefore, 'engaged pedagogy' goes further than conventional 'critical or feminist pedagogy,' paving the way for the integration between FCP and PCAE.

THE PERSON-CENTERED APPROACH TO EDUCATION

The basis of the Person-Centered Approach to education (PCAE) is the communication and increasing reciprocity of empathy, congruence, and unconditional positive regard (Rogers, 1951, 1959, 1969). Empathy refers to the understanding of another's perspective, congruence to authenticity or genuineness in interaction, and unconditional positive regard to an acceptance of each person. These qualities are seen as residing in the teacher and then reciprocally in the students as relationships build. The theory is in an '*if-then*' form. *If* educators manifest the above interpersonal qualities, *then* student learning and growth will emerge. No specific goal is posited in PCAE, only the general form. All students are theorized to have an actualizing tendency, which propels them to maintain and enhance their organism. The actualizing tendency is part of a larger formative tendency, whereby their social systems are also maintained and enhanced (Rogers, 1980). Hence, empowerment is based upon collaboration between students and teachers, facilitating the personal power of each student (Rogers, 1977).

In the following sections, we will explain how PCAE is more practical and validated than FCP but contains an assumption of individualism (Cornelius-White, 2002, 2003a, 2004b; Cornelius-White and Cornelius-White, (unpublished manuscript); Usher, 1989). The practicality stems from its clear methods of reifying the '*if-then*' formulation. Research from at least 42 states, 7 countries, 70,000 students, and over 48 million coded units of time lend strong support for the formulation (Aspy, 1986; Cornelius-White, 2004a). While the research and practice demonstrate that PCAE is unlikely to result in cultural bias, the theory's individual and micro-systemic premises do represent cultural-encapsulation.

Practical

PCAE acknowledges teacher content expertise as important, but the emphasis for teacher practice is on the communication of fundamental interpersonal attitudes, which all people possess to a degree and can be trained to increase (Aspy, 1986).

Before adding more of an activist agenda to Rogers' theory (Carkhuff, 1971), Carkhuff (1969) and Aspy emphasized communication skills to increase PCAE's trainability. Aspy and Roebuck's (1977) training system was found to be effective for both large and small groups.

Aspy and Roebuck's training focuses on didactic, experiential, and applied components (i.e. tell, show, and do experiences). Typically, trainers tell trainees about a theoretical concept, such as empathy. Trainers show tapes of actual classroom behavior and provide simple scales to rate empathy. Next, trainees practice empathy in their own classrooms and then play the tapes in small, supervised peer groups. Trainers model the skills throughout the training, responding empathically to students. This tell-show-do model also describes how PCAE teachers often behave. More precise examples of how a person-centered classroom is differentiated from a traditional classroom in Appendix 1.

VALID

When postulated, PCAE had little research support, being an extrapolation from person-centered counseling research. During the 60s, 70s, and 80s, supportive research for the educational theory burgeoned. Aspy (1986) showed that democratic (PCAE) classrooms were exceedingly rare. From a sample of 200,000 hours of traditional classroom instruction, 80% of class time was spent on memory behavior while 10% was spent on thinking behavior. Ten percent was affective, silence, or chaotic behavior. Student-initiated talk comprised less than 1% of the time while teachers accepted students' feelings less than 0.1% of the time. Similarly, teachers talked 80% of the time while students talked 10% of the time. Traditional teaching clearly encourages a reproduction of teacher facts rather than a production of student thinking, initiation, and feelings.

While in person-centered classrooms some teachers initially encounter resistance (Asch, 1951), students engage in more critical thinking and are more motivated (Cornelius-White, 2004a). Aspy and Roebuck's (1977) findings showed that in classrooms where teachers had undergone training in person-centered skills, elementary teachers accepted student feelings 400% more and accepted student ideas 300% more. There was also a 200% increase in student initiation. In cognitive behaviors, teachers thought and asked students to think 300% more. There was a 300% increase in non-cognitive (primarily affective) behavior and students' thinking behavior increased by 30%. Secondary teachers and students had similar but more muted results. Hence, in PCAE compared to FCP, resistance is largely transcended (Cornelius-White, 2002). Teachers follow students' experiences so the only resistance is the novelty of this experience. In PCAE, there is evidence for movement towards a critical social analysis and pro-social behavior.

The democratic interpersonal skills of empathy, genuineness and acceptance work regardless of cultural context by increasing students' mental health, pro-social behavior, initiation, attendance, IQ (grades 1–3), thinking behavior, and achievement among other factors (Aspy, 1986). In a sample of more than 10,000 participants, neither geographic location, student intelligence, gender, nor ethnicity (white, black, Mexican-American) were found to be moderators of the effectiveness of the person-centered attitudes for teachers trained in PCAE. While PCAE is effective at all age levels, the effects on elementary students and the openness of elementary educators to training are greater. Both the consistency of skill level and the average interpersonal skill were found to be predictors of the student outcomes (Aspy and Roebuck, 1977). Many of these findings have been replicated in 42 states and 7 countries (Aspy, 1986). Unfortunately, PCAE research tapered off dramatically near Rogers' nomination for the Nobel Peace Prize and death in the mid-80s and is now largely unknown.

CULTURALLY ENCAPSULATED

The Person-Centered Approach has been consistently criticized for a culturally encapsulated emphasis on individualism, whereby the Western idea that the individual is the basic unit of being human is treated as a universal truth (Cornelius-White, 2003a; MacDougall, 2002; Sue and Sue, 2003; Usher, 1989). The Person-Centered Approach has also been criticized for its lack of attention to power (Hannon, 2001; Proctor, 2002), particularly regarding gender (Waterhouse, 1993). The critiques regarding individualism and gender are usually explained with substantial misunderstandings of the Person-Centered Approach from persons who appear to have little actual practice and scholarship related to the Person-Centered Approach (Cornelius-White, 2003a). For instance, in Waterhouse's article, 4% of references were by person-centered authors while at least 80% were from feminist authors. While we applaud her attempt to compare person-centered counseling with feminism, she explains the Person-Centered Approach inadequately, leaving the reader more confused.

In a similar fashion, critical pedagogists make offhand criticisms of humanistic methods, if not PCAE directly, without adequate support. The empiricism and practicality of humanist education are replaced with complex, poetic formulations. For example, McLaren (1988) writes that critical pedagogy is 'more than the exercise of imaginative sympathy or creative compassion. It is more than the luxuriant empathy of the liberal humanist' (p. 76). He does not articulate what empathy is, explain these impressionistic dismissals, or support his assertions with empirical findings. He continues, 'Critical pedagogy does not refuse to take sides, balancing truth somewhere in an imaginary middle between silence and chaos … outside the inviolable boundaries of order in the rift between a subversive praxis and a concrete utopia' (p. 76). McLaren's references to 'imaginative sympathy or creative compassion' are lackadaisically made, serving to highlight the assumed difference between PCAE and critical pedagogy.

However, despite these poorly supported critiques, we believe that the Person-Centered Approach does legitimately have an individual bias. The central health concept of congruence postulates that persons have a salient internal reality (Rogers, 1959). The assumption of the salience of the organism is in conflict with the beliefs of some cultures and individuals who understand identity as a part of one or more systems, such as families, tribes, cultures, and environments (Sue and Sue, 2003). Similar postmodern concerns have lead to many extensions to the person-centered concept of self (see Cornelius-White and Cornelius-White, 2003). Feminist writing has challenged the individual bias and suggested starting from relationships rather than individuals (Jordan, Kaplan, Miller, Stiver and Surrey, 1991). Additionally, the individual bias can unintentionally blame students and teachers for their problems (e.g. failure, anti-social behavior, etc.) when systemic factors, such as social inequality, racism, corporate control, etc. may provide substantial contributors to the variance between persons' levels of learning. In this sense, we agree with critiques by person-centered authors that the Person-Centered Approach inadequately addresses power imbalances (Hannon, 2001; Proctor, 2002). Likewise, the very experience of students' and teachers' subjectivities may be constructed by these same power discourses (Gore, 1992). Regardless of whether subjectivities are seen as students' authentic individual experience, as part of a system, or as inherited constructions, PCAE's advocacy to empathize with and accept students' experiences as they are, explains the low likelihood of the individual bias being realized in oppressive practice.

PEDAGOGICAL CROSSROADS: INTEGRATING THE BEST OF BOTH OF FCP AND PCAE

MULTICULTURALLY APPROPRIATE, PRACTICAL AND VALID

Despite critiques about the multicultural applicability of the Person-Centered Approach, we argue that PCAE is multiculturally appropriate (Cornelius-White, 2002, 2003a, 2003b, 2004a). The facilitative attitudes are universal (Patterson, 1996) as each person also has a unique culture within (Glauser and Bozarth, 2001) and each teacher adjusts for each learner. Accurate empathy with students who don't identify with individualism requires adjustment in the educator's practice. High levels of unconditional positive regard result in acceptance of alternative identities to traditional selfhood. Though flawed in its theoretical emphasis on individualism, its practice and cross-cultural empirical support suggest that it provides a liberating and multiculturally effective methodology, as neither gender nor many ethnicities and nationalities were identified as statistical modifiers (Aspy and Roebuck, 1977). As a postmodernist writing about FCP, Gore (1992) stresses that regardless of the FCP's rhetoric, empirical or historically observed empowerment is more important than the pronouncement of liberatory practice. Hence, the empirical support of PCAE may justify it as in fact being more feminist than the pronouncements of feminism in FCP.

Cornelius-White (2002) suggested that a nondirective multicultural revision of person-centered theory could include an explicit openness to different ideas of self, constructed subjectivity, and a more broad conception of the processes and outcomes of helping relationships. In essence, to become more feminist and multiculturally appropriate, the Person-Centered Approach needs no alteration to its core or 'if' proposal, only in its 'then' form. Students can use progressive activism to learn by changing their worlds rather than only changing their own experiences. In fact, Freire (1978), like Carkhuff (1971), emphasizes that true learning includes critical thinking and action. One or the other is insufficient. Similarly, Rogers (1957) says he is concerned primarily with learning that impacts behavior in the real world. Likewise, the inverse of the proposed person-centered learning process, whereby students move away from openness rather than towards openness may allow for increased learning had students been over-stimulated and unfocused. Though empathic, unconditional teachers accommodate to these differences, the theory itself could be extended to be more inclusive of alternative outcomes, such as those advocated by FCP.

TRANSCENDING RESISTANCE FOR AGENCY

The consistent goals of FCP are 'to help liberate and empower students' and 'to make teaching vital and an act of social change'. But who is going to be changed, who is going to do the changing and how? If the teacher remains the one to change the student then it would seem that the same hierarchical relationship that is characteristic of patriarchal 'banking education' remains. What has been missing with even FCP has been a trust and belief in the actualizing tendency to learn and self-emancipate if provided with the climate to do so (Rogers, 1959, 1969). This climate opposes traditional and male-authored critical pedagogy. As Hollingsworth (1997) admits, 'For me [one of] the problem[s] of critical pedagogy hinges on ... my personal investment in having the students see things as I want them to' (p. 166). Because of the concern with deconstructing oppression, FCP want students to recognize sexism, racism, classism, homophobia ... etc. However, this poses a problem for FCP in that it sets up an ascribed agenda that might not be what the students themselves want nor what they are ready or able to do. Therefore, how can such pedagogy be empowering let alone liberating? From a FCP perspective, it may seem liberating because there is the understanding that sexism, racism, classism, homophobia ... etc. are part of the repressive economic system and have their roots in capitalism's divide-and-conquer means of exploitation, but for a white, male, upper-class straight student such 'liberating' knowledge might be difficult to identify or be empathic with. As an example, a white male student's journal—'I feel like they are telling me I'm wrong to feel the way I feel' (Lather, 1991: 141) shows students do feel judged, creating resistance. This points to the inconsistency of means and ends in FCP: teachers may tell students what to feel as opposed to understanding why they feel what they feel.

Thus, FCP have had to confront student resistance. This resistance plays a different role to the kind previously conceived where students were seen to be resisting the oppressive aspects of school (as in Black students dropping out to resist racism). Rather, students resist being turned into liberals, feminists, or any other progressive social category. Students who resist being 'liberated' become the 'problematic other that vexes the practice of critical pedagogy' (Trainor, 2002: 641). If the subjectivities of such students are not addressed, Trainor asserts that 'we risk promoting a devastating unintended consequence: the development of a conscious, essentialized, and angry white identity predicated on reactionary political values' (p. 646). As a result, she advocates that critical pedagogists should not demonize those students who have yet to deconstruct their identity. Rather, she suggests an application of Freire's pedagogy: 'we can only liberate those whom we see not as abstract categories but as persons; only those on whom we are willing 'to risk an act of love' (Trainor, 2002: 646). Or as Rogers would state, through empathy and compassion students can more likely liberate and accept themselves and others.

The struggle therefore seems to be how to better apply FCP. Gore recognizes the need for more practical and concrete solutions. She states that FCP 'need to provide better guidance for the actions of the teachers they hope to empower or they hope will empower students' (Gore, 1992: 68). We propose that PCAE provides this guidance.

REFERENCES

Asch, MJ (1951) Nondirective teaching in psychology: An experimental study. *Psychological Monographs, 65*(4): 1–24.

Aspy, DN (1986) *This is School: Sit down and listen.* Amherst, MA: Human Resource Development Press.

Aspy, DN and Roebuck, FN (1977) *Kids Don't Learn From People They Don't Like.* Amherst, MA: Human Resource Development Press.

Bowles, S and Gintis, H (1977) *Schooling in Capitalist America: Educational Reform and the Contradictions of Economic Life.* New York: Basic Books.

Carkhuff, RR (1971) *The Development of Human Resources: Education, psychology, and social change.* New York: Holt, Reinhart, and Winston.

Cornelius-White, JHD (2002) On constructing a nondirective multicultural revision of the client-centered theory of therapy (1959). Manuscript presented at Annual Conference of the Association for the Development of the Person-Centered Approach, Cleveland OH.

Cornelius-White, JHD (2003a) Person-centered multicultural counseling: Critiques, rebuttals, and revisited goals. *Person-Centered Practice, 11*(1): 3–11.

Cornelius-White, JHD (2003b) 'Teaching' Person-Centered Multicultural Counseling: Experiential transcendence of resistance to increase awareness. Manuscript submitted for publication.

Cornelius-White, JHD (2004a) Person-centered education: Preliminary results of a meta-analysis. Paper presented at the Annual Conference of the Association for the Development of the Person-Centered Approach, Anchorage AK, July 2004.

Cornelius-White JHD (2004b) Maintain and Enhance: An integrative view of person-centered and process differentiated diagnostics. Manuscript submitted for publication.

Cornelius-White, JHD and Cornelius-White, CF (2004) Diagnosing Person-Centered and Experiential Psychotherapy: An analysis of the PCE 2003 programming. *Person-Centered and Experiential Psychotherapies, 3*(3) 166–75.

Cornelius-White JHD and Cornelius-White CF (unpublished manuscript) Trust builds learning: Context and effectiveness of nondirectivity in education. Submitted for B Levitt (ed) Nondirective Person-Centered Approaches (working title).

Ellsworth, E (1992) Why doesn't this feel empowering?: Working through the repressive myths of critical pedagogy, in C Luke and J Gore (eds) (1992) *Feminism and Critical Pedagogy.* London: Routledge.

Freire, P (1970) *Pedagogy of the Oppressed.* New York: Bantam Books.

Giroux, H (1983) *Theory and Resistance in Education: A pedagogy for the opposition.* Hadley, MA: Bergin and Garvey.

Glauser, AS and Bozarth, J (2001) Person-centered counseling: The culture within. *Journal of Counseling and Development, 79*(2): 142–7.

Gore, J (1992) What we can do for you! What can 'We' do for 'You'? Struggling over the empowerment in critical and feminist pedagogy, in C Luke and J Gore (eds) *Feminism and Critical Pedagogy.* London: Routledge.

Gore, J (1993) *The Struggle for Pedagogies: Critical and feminist discourses as regimes of truth.* New York: Routledge.

Hannon, JW (2001) Emancipatory person-centered counseling: Postmodern theory for the 21st century. *Person-Centered Practice, 9*(1): 4–17.

Hollingsworth, S (1997) Feminist praxis as the basis for teacher education: A critical challenge, in C Marshall (ed) *Feminist Critical Policy Analysis I: A perspective from primary and secondary schooling.* London: Falmer Press.

hooks, b (1989) *Talking back: thinking feminist, thinking black.* Boston MA: South End Press.

hooks, b (1994) *Teaching to Transgress: Education as the practice of freedom.* New York: Routledge.

Jordan, JV, Kaplan, AG, Miller, JB, Stiver, IP and Surrey, JL (1991) *Women's Growth in Connection.* New York: Guilford Press.

Lather, P (1991) *Getting Smart: Feminist research and pedagogy with/in the postmodern.* New York: Routledge.

Lather, P (1994) Absent Presence: Patriarchy, capitalism, and the nature of teacher, in L Stone (ed) *The Education Feminism Reader.* New York: Routledge.

175

Luke, C (1996) *Feminisms and Pedagogies of Everyday Life.* Albany, NY: SUNY Press.

MacDougall, C (2002) Rogers' person-centered approach: Consideration for use in multicultural counseling. *Journal of Humanistic Psychology, 42*(2): 48–65.

McLaren, P (1988) Schooling the postmodern body: Critical pedagogy and the politics of enfleshment. *Journal of Education, 70*(3): 53–83.

Napier, MB (2004) Trusting Our Clients: The Stone Center model of therapy encounters a non-directive attitude. Chapter 10 this volume.

Patterson, CH (1996) Multicultural Counseling: From diversity to universality. *Journal of Counseling and Development,* January/February, 74: 227–31.

Proctor, G (2002) *The Dynamics of Power in Counselling and Psychotherapy: Ethics, politics, and practice.* Ross-on-Wye, UK: PCCS Books.

Rogers, CR (1951) *Client-Centered Therapy.* Boston: Houghton Mifflin.

Rogers, CR (1957, Summer) Personal thoughts on teaching and learning. *Merrill-Palmer Quarterly,* 3: 241–3.

Rogers, CR (1959) A theory of therapy, personality, and interpersonal relationship as developed in the client-centered framework, in S Koch (ed) *Psychology: A Study of Science. Formulations of the Person and the Social Context.* New York: McGraw-Hill, pp. 184–256.

Rogers, CR (1969) *Freedom to Learn.* Columbus, OH: Merrill Publishing.

Rogers, CR (1977) *Carl Rogers On Personal Power: Inner strength and its revolutionary impact.* New York: Delacorte Press.

Rogers, CR (1980) *A Way of Being.* Boston: Houghton Mifflin.

Sue, DW and Sue, D (2003) *Counseling the Culturally Diverse.* New York: John Wiley and Sons.

Trainor, JS (2002) Critical pedagogy's 'Other': Constructions of whiteness in education for social change, *College Composition and Communication, 53*(4): 631–50.

Usher, CH (1989) Recognizing cultural bias in counseling theory and practice: The Case of Rogers. *Journal of Multicultural Counseling and Development, 17*: 62–71.

Waterhouse, RL (1993) Wild women don't have the blues: A feminist critique of person-centered counseling and therapy. *Feminism and Psychology, 3*(1): 55–71.

Weiler, K (1988) *Women Teaching for Change: Gender, class and power.* New York: Bergin and Garvey Publishers.

APPENDIX 1: HYPOTHETICAL EXAMPLE OF STUDENT-TEACHER INTERACTIONS IN TRADITIONAL, FCP AND PCAE CLASSROOMS.

Please note that there is significant diversity in how traditional, FCP and PCAE teachers behave in a classroom. The following are offered as examples of how teachers and students might respond to similar statements of a male and female student. Pat, the teacher is assumed to be a white female in each case. Michael is a white student, and Mary is an African-American student. This is a 9th grade social studies classroom.

Traditional

Pat: Who can remember some of the reasons why affirmative action developed?

Michael: I hate this crap about affirmative action and women's rights. It's bogus.

Pat: Michael, you used inappropriate language. Please be respectful if you are going to be in this classroom.

Mary: I think African-Americans don't have enough opportunities.

Pat: Good Mary, this was a possible reason we discussed why affirmative action came into existence. Affirmative action was designed to …

FCP

Pat: Lets think critically about affirmative action. What do you think are the pros and cons?

Michael: I hate this crap about affirmative action and women's rights. It's bogus.

Pat: Tell us why affirmative action is bad, Michael. (No response—pause) OK, well who gains from affirmative action and who loses? (Pause)

Mary: I think African-American women don't have enough opportunities so they might gain something.

Pat: Good, what group might affirmative action hurt? …

PCAE

Pat: Who has reactions to what we have been talking about?

Michael: I hate this crap about affirmative action and women's rights. It's bogus.

Pat: You're angry because some of the programs we have been talking about don't seem fair to you.

Michael: Yeah, like why should my Dad not have a job when he is more qualified than all those African-American women working at the mall?

Pat: You're upset that your Dad is unemployed and you feel that affirmative action is to blame.

Michael: I guess. (Sulks) (Pause)

Mary: Well I can see Michael's point but I still think that African-American women don't have enough opportunities.

Pat: So in seeing how some of us differ in our reactions to affirmative action, we can nevertheless appreciate how these issues are important to us …

Student-teacher interaction is less frequent and shorter in the traditional classroom. Resistance is something to battle in the FCP classroom, here through Socratic questioning. Democratic processes are attempted in the FCP classroom but are not as prevalent as in the PCAE classroom. The teacher maintains more power over the students in the FCP classroom while students initiate more material in the PCAE classroom. In the FCP classroom, the discussion focuses more on power and appreciation for group difference, which may give more voice to marginalized perspectives and students. The PCAE classroom yields more personal growth and more interaction, including that between students. However, in PCAE societal power differentials and resulting marginalized perspectives may remain silenced without a high level of teacher empathy and an appreciation of FCP's perspective. There is more thinking and less memory in both the FCP and PCAE classrooms compared to traditional classrooms.

APPENDIX 2: RESOURCES FOR FEMINIST CRITICAL PERSON-CENTERED TEACHING

Applied Research Center/ERASE Project, www.arc.org

Center X, Institute for Democracy, Education, and Access, www.ucla-idea.org

Educators for Social Responsibility, www.esrmetro.org

Interaction Book Company, Edina, Minnesota USA (612) 831-9500

International Alliance For Invitational Learning,
     http://www.invitationaleducation.net

Mothers on the Move, www.mothersonthemove.org

National Coalition of Education Activists, www.nceaonline.org

Person-Centered Approach for Higher Education, http://elearn.pri.univie.ac.at/pca/

Radical Teacher, www.radicalteacher.org

Rethinking Schools, www.rethinkingschools.org

Teaching for Change, www.teachingforchange.org

NEW MEN? — A NEW IMAGE OF MAN? PERSON-CENTRED CHALLENGES TO GENDER DIALOGUE[1]

PETER F SCHMID

The legal equalisation of women has to be prevented under all circumstances—the Roman statesman Cato the Elder (234–149) is reported to have implored the Senate: 'Because once they are equalised they will be superior.' Some two thousand years later the traditional system still lasts, but now it is likely that male dominance will come to an end within a few generations.

There are many rearguard actions, however. Some prefer to pretend to be unaware. Others claim that they are beyond feminism already—whatever this may mean. (This was the explanation of one of the organisers of the 6th Person-Centered and Experiential World Conference in The Netherlands, to explain why they had invited only male keynote speakers. He claimed it is persons that count, not women or men.) Another method of avoidance among person-centred people is to use 'understanding' as a fatal ideology, i.e., to pretend to understand the other in order to be left in peace and keep away from confrontation.

Men not only do violence to others. They do it to themselves. The facts speak a clear language: men live shorter (5.7 years in Austria) and more dangerously (they are more often involved in serious road accidents, provide two thirds of emergency patients and three quarters of murder victims), they damage themselves more systematically (twice as many men are hospitalised due to chronic diseases) and commit suicide three times as often. The medical image of the 'typical heart attack patient' is identical to the ideal image of the 'typical man' in our achievement-oriented society. In a word: men are not only very good at the exploitation of others but also at self-exploitation. (Schmid, 1993a, b, 2002c)

This chapter examines a few considerations regarding the gender issue from a person-centred point of view developed through experience in person-centred practice, theory development and training, particularly from the perspective of men.

[1.] I am very grateful to Pete Sanders for making the text understandable to the English reader.

THERE IS NO PERSON EXCEPT AS A MAN OR A WOMAN: TOWARDS A GENDER SPECIFIC PERSON-CENTRED ANTHROPOLOGY

Carl Rogers discovered the centrality of the person, but he did not pay attention to sex and gender difference.

Although it is clear that he increasingly came to learn to perceive women-specific perspectives in the course of his life—not least through the influence of his daughter Natalie (N Rogers, 1980)—he was everything but a feminist. His merit was to emphasize the personal, the common ground on the one hand and the individuality of each person on the other hand—a decisive corrective moment in the context of his time. In addition, he definitely took leave of a uniform model of partnership (see Rogers, 1972). But some sixty years later, in the light of a new self-confidence in women, and the amount of feminist work done in the meantime, gender difference issues have become clearly apparent. They require concrete concepts and approaches to action, including in those interpersonal relations we call person-centred psychotherapy and counselling.

There is no doubt that many traditionally male concepts had already been damaged by the Person-Centred Approach. For example, the priority given to empathy and unconditional positive regard in epistemology and the practice of therapeutic understanding are things that are traditionally regarded as 'female'. This thorough paradigm change—and the development that followed in nearly all therapeutic orientations—contrasts sharply with the expert- (and thus male-) dominated classical concepts of psychoanalysis and behaviourism.

On the other hand the person-centred concept is by no means free of one-sided male thinking: the description of the actualising tendency, for example, as given by Rogers (e.g., 1959: 196, 1979: 99–100) as a directional, forward striving, expanding, transcending, increasing force, a force towards autonomy, is clearly determined by male experiencing and consciousness and formulated in male language. An understanding which is more articulated out of female experience and familiar to readers of feminist writing would possibly set out from the idea that the human being is embedded in relationships from the very beginning. Therefore human development and thus the actualising tendency would be regarded more as an unfolding and differentiating process of shaping relationships. The actualising tendency could be more accurately viewed as the force of the individual embedded in interconnectedness. As a consequence, this would stress the social nature of the person much more than it was originally conceptualised in Rogers' anthropology, although there is evidence that he gradually moved towards this understanding (see Schmid 1996a: 497, 2001a).

The actualising tendency example also shows that person-centred conceptions are open to further elaboration due to a developing understanding of the human being. This is because they are created out of experience and try to remain as close to experience as possible. The most fundamental theory in this regard is the concept of the human being as a person which underlies the *Person*-Centred Approach as a whole. Rogers used the term 'person' deliberately to characterise a particular understanding of the human being as the foundation for his view of psychotherapy and personality development. This notion embraces, equally and dialectically, both the substantial and the relational dimension; autonomy and interconnectedness; sovereignty and commitment (Schmid, 1991, 1998a, 2001a, b, c, 2002a, b). Such understanding of the human as a 'person' can be the foundation for a non-patriarchal image of the human being, an image characterised by partnership.

In order to do this it is also important to conceptualise theoretically that the human being is a person as man and woman—not sexually neutral. The human only exists as a female or a male human. What sounds so self-evident still often means, in the unexpressed consciousness of many (including theoreticians), that the human being is male, and then there is a female variant. In the meantime, many female theoreticians forcefully offered resistance and contributed to building a counter culture. Furthermore, for the moment, Rogers' focus on the respective individual, instead of the classified category, has prevailed in therapy theory and practice. Also, finally, we can no longer simply speak about 'the person', 'the man' or 'the woman', as if there was no difference, no subjective view and no history between men and women.

It is important that the dialectical understanding of the person as an autonomous being, interconnected in relationships, is not itself one-sidedly interpreted in a traditionally male sense. This always happens when the notion is grasped in an imbalanced way in respect of the substantial-individual aspect. Besides the male dominated approaches to understanding and interpretation (also still visible in Rogers' work), and the low regard for the body, the reason why gender specific aspects of being a person (particularly also in therapy theory and practice) have been almost ignored for such a long time, lies in a lack of understanding of the quality of the personal. Thus we can now see why the dimension of *autonomy* (traditionally attributed to men), stood for so long in the foreground of theory of therapies in general, person-centred therapy included, while the 'typical female' dimension of *relationship orientation* was considered to be of minor importance. There is now a growing recognition in PCT of the importance of encounter—meaning to stand 'counter' *and* to be essentially affected by the person opposite (see Schmid 1994, 1998b, 2002b). The consequence for the therapeutic endeavour is that person-centred thinking and acting can no longer be confused with a male-centred viewpoint.

The task now is to spell out, and put into concrete terms, what this means for the different areas of life. The Person-Centred Approach needs to deal urgently and intensively with the so far largely neglected areas of theoretical conceptualisation, the practice of therapy, training and supervision.

As an example I will look at two topics almost completely neglected up to now.

181

INTIMACY, TENDERNESS AND LUST
FROM SEXUALITY TO SEXUALITIES

The notably small number of relevant publications is evidence that person-centred people, in most cases, do not examine sexuality closely and thus do not make it a theoretical topic. One can no longer excuse this with regard to the necessity of putting the person as a whole in the centre of attention. There is no person without his or her sex. Whoever leaves sexuality out of consideration misses the whole all the more.

It goes without saying that sexuality can be misused as a way of having power over someone—by both men and women. Often it has been used as *the* way for men to exercise power over women, e.g., in rape or in heterosexual sex frequently being defined for the fulfilment of the man's desire. Each psychotherapist is confronted with the destructive consequences of the numerous ways of sexual violence and misuse. But the subject deserves deeper investigation.

According to person-centred anthropology and Rogers' core conditions, human sexuality can be understood in its substantial dimension as an expression of, and a striving for, *self-realization*, for pleasure, lust and satisfaction, or fulfilment. In its relational dimension, sexuality is *self-transcendence*, i.e., dedicating oneself to transcendence of one's individuality.

On the one hand it is organismic experience and self-experience (the person senses and experiences him- or herself) and thus it is the expression of one's own potency, the overall tendency of life to unfold its possibilities. It is therefore conceptually opposed to (a) the very obvious tendencies of distrust and suspicion which can be found not only throughout history in so many cultures and religions, but also in different stages of one's own life and (b) unlike other therapeutic conceptions, sexuality must be seen as a fundamentally constructive and trustworthy force. This is separating organismic experience from societal meanings and constructions of sexuality which in the main are often about domination.

On the other hand, sexuality dissolves separation and isolation, opens the human being up for the Other and, as 'body language of the person' constitutes a central form of communication, 'embodied encounter'. In sexuality, the human being 'takes a step beyond him- or herself' and may even transcend their own boundaries and limits towards the Other, which in heterosexual sex includes the possibility of the propagation of new life. In pointing at the essential interconnectedness of all life sexuality also is a decisive approach to the world.

In both dimensions it aims at self-transcendence: it is more than individual fulfilment, or completion of the one by the other, or, in a heterosexual context, for example, mutual completion of both sexes. It means self-acceptance and acceptance of the Other through dedication to the Other. As an essential aspect of being a person, sexuality is inseparably connected with personalisation—the development of the person—and thus (as an 'interface' of physical and psychological processes and as a key to the alternative 'identity versus alienation') is also central for psychotherapy.

The hasty use of clichés to label the two dimensions as 'male' and 'female' or even assign each of them to one of the sexes is a frequent trap for the downplaying of sexuality. It is an important task in the process of emancipation to free oneself from gender assignments and mixings handed down by society and to find one's personal feeling and meaning, particularly regarding sexuality. Then we can experience respective congruent symbolisation and expression of sensual, erotic, sexual feelings and experiences and develop a personal way of sexuality as opposed to just taking on what traditional role assignment and societal fashion suggest. In an analogy to Rogers' (1957) core conditions; *intimacy* (gentle empathy and temporary becoming a unity without giving up oneself), *tenderness* (non-possessive loving acceptance) and *lust* (congruence of the tension of needs and authentic activity to enhance or resolve them) can be seen as conditions for congruent, fulfilled sexuality. (This is described in more detail and with references in Schmid, 1996c.) In respect of male and female contexts of living, it goes without saying that the experiences connected with sexuality differ and it is an important challenge for each individual, woman and man (as well as their therapists), to be aware of this and to adequately symbolise it—a challenge and request to set out from the (seeming) security of traditional positions.

If sexuality is regarded as a complex interplay of biological, psychological and social factors, which actualise themselves differently in different situations and life stories, it is necessary to speak specifically and precisely. This means plurality. Therefore we need to investigate *sexualities*, particularly in person-centred contexts and when talking of the individual, or within certain sexual orientations (like attraction to same or/and opposite sex). In each of us there are different sexual inclinations, interests and potentialities. A psychotherapy oriented by person and encounter faces two important tasks: first, to deal sensitively, empathically with, and be ready to respond as a person to, these dimensions in general and with the sexual dimensions of the therapeutic relationship in particular. Second, to strictly observe sexual abstinence (because there is no sexuality without interest and therefore expressions of their sexuality, including phantasies, by the therapist always constitutes an abuse of the relationship in order to satisfy the needs of his or her own interests) (Pfeiffer, 1992; Schmid 1996a, b, 1996c).

STEPS TOWARDS EACH OTHER
NO UNDERSTANDING WITHOUT AGGRESSION

Covering up anger with alleged empathy is the beginning of what might end up in open violence. Wherever aggression is treated as a taboo or is ignored due to ideological reasons—e.g., because one thinks he or she should turn to 'the positive'—

the danger increases of encouraging destructive tendencies all the more. He or she who understands everything, understands nothing. The acceptance of a person who can accept everything is of no worth. The person who cannot stand 'counter' his or her clients, cannot 'en-counter' them. The person who ignores aggression, refuses him- or herself as a person.

Although aggression is often associated with, and experienced as, violence and although fears that violence is around the corner are realistic when encountering aggression; from a person-centred perspective, aggression is a fundamentally constructive force of the human being and an expression of the actualising tendency. From a substantial notion of what it means to be a person it is an expression of the experiencing of the person and from a relational notion it is a turn towards the Other. On the one hand, in aggression the independence of the individual becomes apparent, if he or she aims at establishing and fostering identity by differentiation (saying no, e.g., in puberty), and in this process of separation the foundation for the recognition of myself and the Other is found. On the other hand, through aggression the inter-connectedness becomes clear. This is because to be aggressive means to approach the Other ('ag-gredi' = 'make steps towards', to approach, to confront), since the Other is acknowledged as a partner in the relationship by the confrontation. In this counter-position of the con-front-ation ('frons' = 'forehead') the Other is faced, which shows that aggression is an unavoidable condition for every 'en-counter'. So, aggression is necessary for both the observance of distance and the establishment of nearness thus protecting from the loss of identity; either by merging or by alienation.

For person-centred therapy which is based on empathy, an open way of dealing with aggression and a respective therapeutic attitude of openness for conflicts is particularly important—the constructive and vital aspects of aggression may otherwise be overlooked or covered up. When denied or incomplete, incorrect or distorted aggressions can become destructive. As an example we only need to look at the aggressive and auto-aggressive parts of pity, depression or suicide. Other examples are psychosomatic suffering; where the body itself symbolizes the not-understood; or addiction, which can be seen as (auto-)aggression. Rogers, although never developing his own theory of aggression, points out that 'accepted or transparent anger is not destructive' (Rogers, 1961: 177). From a therapeutic perspective it is important to symbolise and integrate aggressive feelings and impulses as completely as possible. The ability to tolerate conflict is also crucial in terms of prevention of violence—it simply is a characteristic of maturity. Furthermore Ute Binder (Binder, 1996; Hoffman, 1990) stressed the importance of 'empathic anger' in dealing with depressive patients. (For aggression in a person-centred anthropological perspective, see Schmid, 1995, 2001c.)

The fundamental importance of aggression for gender specific identity is often underestimated. Aggression is seen as 'active' and assigned to male experiencing and behaviour (although only permitted in certain situations). Accordingly, women are then put on the 'passive' side and 'have to' suffer from aggression. Often there is only a small step from here to the cliché-like allocation of roles such as 'perpetrators' and 'victims'. Without ignoring the reality of men being so much more likely to be perpetrators of violence and women being victims, such unreflected and ill-considered allocations very often serve to disguise actual perpetrator-victim structures and prevent a differentiated understanding of ways of relationships.

Since aggression so often is associated with evil or undesirable behaviour, person-centred contexts are frequently classified and practised as soft or even weak, mild and mellow. This neglects the power of the person and the 'counter-play' of genuine encounter. To be facilitative requires aggression in terms of encountering and confronting the client with him- or herself, and to think him or her sufficiently robust. It seems that due to an inappropriate public image, often people are interested in a person-centred training who are uncomfortable with the potency of their aggression.

ON MALE POWER, ON FEMALE POWER
THE PERSON-CENTRED EMPOWERMENT CONCEPT AS
THE BASIS FOR FEMALE AND MALE EMANCIPATION

The Person-Centred Approach contrasts sharply with the traditional authoritarian understanding of psychotherapy, particularly due to its emancipatory understanding of power as empowerment (Rogers, 1977; Schmid, 1996a: 451–68). It is no surprise, then, that its anthropology serves as a foundation for feminist approaches in psychotherapy (e.g., Winkler, 1992, 2002). It builds a solid and genuine basis for new approaches of self-understanding and understanding of women in general, and in the realm of psychotherapy and counselling in particular. Women have come a long way in developing a considerable amount of sovereignty and solidarity. And along the way they shook the traditional male image of the human being—and with this, they shook men themselves.

In contrast, the emancipation of men still is pending. A free, sovereign self-understanding of men 'after' the feminist movement is still anything but obvious. It goes without saying that the ability to change nappies and sort cloths for washing machines is not enough. What does male liberation (ironically it may be called '*eman*cipation') really mean? It cannot mean simply to copy women. Neither Rambo nor Woody Allen, neither androgynous superstars nor simple house fathers, are suitable as figures for identification in the long run. Machos and softies are out. To retreat into the forest and to live only on cereal and fruit, muesli and berries is not an attractive alternative at all, and so the 'wild man' of the late eighties and early nineties did not really prevail. However, a new image of men is not yet in the offing.

Men find themselves under pressure, but this still does not mean that they have changed. It is a long way from knowing the necessity for change to actual change. The traditional image of the male is almost as strong as before; change is only superficial. For example, although a majority of men are accepting responsibility for children and the family, in a survey 60% of the men who claimed they were 'non-traditional' said women should be the first ones to be fired in a crisis situation (see Schmid, 1996b).

Men have also come under pressure (and this has forced them to either make a move or to get involved in rearguard actions), due to the waning influence of the traditional male bastions of the military, church and political parties. They no longer provide secure support as they used to do in times of unquestioned patriarchy. Again, men have had no choice but to behave more like partners. In critical situations, however, they fall back on the traditional image of men which consists of defining oneself by a role. What are men, if they are not lovers, fathers, bosses etc., but simply male human beings? Male role stereotypes no longer take effect, both in society and in the relationships between men and women. The man's world can neither go on as it is, or go back to how it used to be. And there is no immediate substitute. It's beginning to dawn on men that a new understanding of themselves and their roles must not rest on old or new stereotypes, but the creative development of new alternatives still seems a genuine mystery to men. Men might understand the necessity of their own emancipation but to really carry it out and to put theoretical insights into practice obviously proves to be very hard. Men have no choice but to turn to working for an appropriate new self-concept: the task for men is no more or less than to understand what it means to become a person.

Moreover, where relationships are concerned, men have a much harder time associating with men than women have associating with women (without ignoring that there are also difficulties for women associating with women due to, for example, heterosexual competition for men). The experienced threat has led to new forms of male bonding. There is a great temptation to turn back the hands of time or to take countermeasures by grouping in traditionally male associations or unions. This encourages crypto-fascist and homophobic patterns of thinking and acting and is clear in recent developments in Europe and North America with the present political shift to the right. One particular issue is the still widespread, and not reflected, latent and deep seated anxiety about homosexuality fed by many sources. It all too clearly shows the difficulties men encounter when dealing with both their equals and themselves. The development of new models for social relations of men with their fellow men, for male friendship and for communities of men is largely in abeyance.

This insecurity in men is evident particularly in psychotherapy and counselling training programs. To a great extent psychotherapy and counselling is regarded as a 'typical female' profession. Often in a minority, male trainees find themselves in a defensive position. This becomes particularly evident when women challenge the men, for example, in encounter and self-development groups to express their view of the relationships between men and women. When so challenged, men are often speechless. Experiences like these reveal that men have become conscious of their incongruence, but the path to new congruence seems to be a long one.

The task is not to simply react but to create. When stimulated or 'disconcerted' by women, men are challenged to find out what being a man is all about and to develop a new self-understanding. This must happen in dialogue with women. The objective is neither new male chauvinism nor a feminisation of men or society. The aim is not that men roam about in penitential robes or set out to play the roles of victims themselves. A retreat from dealing with the conflict cannot be the solution either. However, a temporary retreat may be an important and necessary step. Men must take responsibility for their own solutions, not expect women to teach them. So whilst self-experience in all-male groups is important, it is insufficient for emancipation, if taken as the sole action; it rather indicates being stuck in a puberty-like position of denial. And as it is clear that male emancipation cannot mean that men become what emancipated women think they should become, it is also clear that dealing with women is crucial as a starting point for dialogue. It goes without saying that it needs political work—together with the women.

A new male image cannot be foisted but must rest on a new feeling of self-worth, the source of which is neither guilt feelings nor defensiveness. On the basis of an understanding of power as empowerment and potency as potentiality, men can find the possibility for a new self-understanding in dealing with each other and with women. After taking leave of the traditional patriarchal allocation of role and power, both men and women, can, in the end, only together develop new approaches to same and different sex partnerships and the intrinsically connected therapeutic and political implications.

Much unused potential of men goes to waste. From a person-centred point of view the question of what a male human being might look like 'before' all role expectations and assignments, can only be answered with respect to the primacy of the experience and the importance of self-understanding. The untapped potential of sensitivity, partnership and capacity to love, waits for its actualisation. This will not happen by demonising rationality in favour of emotionality or by creating new taboos in areas where formerly men were justly blamed for over-emphasising their importance; potency, rivalry, the power of self-assertion, achievement, toughness, etc. They need to be balanced in their importance and value, not to be devalued completely. Only on such a basis new self-esteem can grow that does not rest on being directed against somebody—against women, against fathers, etc. Rather it discovers and develops authentic male tenderness, male desire and desirability, male body language, male dedication, a new culture of conflict resolution among men and with women and self-confidence without striving for dominance etc. This of course means to be challenged: to give up securities and embark on the path of risks.

The task of person-centred therapists must be to facilitate such processes of development by congruently bringing oneself as a man or a woman into play. This means that men and women develop their respective self-understanding in sovereignty and solidarity—as male and female persons—instead of falling into new stereotypes, new false adaptation and appeasement, or being fixated on fights against the other sex, and therefore not being aware of the possibility of mutual enrichment. As always, in a genuinely person-centred approach, therapeutic support does not happen by keeping oneself out but rather by engaging in the therapeutic relationship which includes transparency as a man or a woman. Therefore it must be the task of person-centred training to actively further such an attitude by first of all bringing the subject up and paying attention to it during the training programme. Then the experience might be possible where a meeting and encounter of gender specific images of the human being will not only be fight and drama; it might well be fun and provide pleasure and delight.

Men have the difficult task of facing up to what should also be the enjoyable challenge of developing a new, previously unfamiliar, non-dominant male system of values instead of cultivating defence strategies. This means nothing more or less than to face the challenge of developing a new image of oneself. These systems and images will not be the only ones that enjoy the power of definition and carry social relevance. There will be a paradigm change of tremendous impact which has already begun and will continue to be work for some more generations. This requires dialogue between and within male and female human beings on different levels (from talking about sex to research, from exploring one's own world of experiencing to empathising with the world of the other)—in a discourse no longer dominated by men. The task is to co-create a new self-understanding. Such dialogue promises to enhance the quality of life (as can be seen from the statistics mentioned at the beginning) in terms of health and life expectancy but also in terms of excitement and lust.

REFERENCES

Binder, U (1996) Empathie und kognitive soziale Perspektivenübernahme, in C Frielingsdorf-Appelt, H Pabst, and G-W Speierer (eds) *Gesprächspsychotherapie: Theorie, Krankenbehandlung, Forschung*. Cologne: GwG, pp. 131–43.

Hoffman, ML (1990) The contribution of empathy to justice and moral judgment, in N Eisenberg and J Strayer (eds) *Empathy and Its Development*. Cambridge: Cambridge University Press.

Pfeiffer, WM (1992) Gesundheitsförderung, Vorsorge und Begleitung im Rahmen der Sozialarbeit, in U Straumann (ed) *Beratung und Krisenintervention*, Cologne: GwG, pp. 84–99.

Rogers, CR (1957) The necessary and sufficient conditions of therapeutic personality change. *Journal of Consulting Psychology, 21*(2): 95–103.

Rogers, CR (1959) A theory of therapy, personality, and interpersonal relationships, as developed in the client-centered framework, in S Koch (ed) *Psychology: A Study of Science. Vol. III: Formulations of the person and the social context*. New York: McGraw Hill, pp. 184–256.

Rogers, CR (1961) *On Becoming a Person: A therapist's view of psychotherapy.* Boston: Houghton Mifflin.

Rogers, CR (1972) *Becoming Partners: Marriage and its alternative.* New York: Delacorte.

Rogers, CR (1977) *On Personal Power: Inner strength and its revolutionary impact.* New York: Delacorte.

Rogers, CR (1979) The foundations of the person-centered approach. *Education, 100*(2): 98–107.

Rogers, N (1980) *Emerging woman: A decade of midlife transitions.* Point Reyes Station: Personal Press.

Schmid, PF (1991) Souveränität und Engagement: Zu einem personzentrierten Verständnis von 'Person', in CR Rogers and PF Schmid *Person-zentriert: Grundlagen von Theorie und Praxis.* Mainz: Grünewald, pp. 15–164.

Schmid, PF (1993a) Neue Manns-Bilder? Auf dem Weg zu einer Emanzipation der Männer. *Diakonia* 3: 145–50.

Schmid, PF (1993b) A New Image of Man: Toward male emancipation. *Theology Digest, 40,* 3: 217–20.

Schmid, PF (1994) *Personzentrierte Gruppenpsychotherapie: Ein Handbuch. Vol. I: Solidarität und Autonomie.* Cologne: EHP.

Schmid PF (1995) Auseinandersetzen und Herangehen: Thesen zur Aggression aus personzentrierter Sicht. *Personzentriert* 2: 62–94.

Schmid, PF (1996a) *Personzentrierte Gruppenpsychotherapie in der Praxis: Ein Handbuch. Vol. II: Die Kunst der Begegnung.* Paderborn: Junfermann.

Schmid, PF (1996b) Sexualität: Selbstverwirklichung und Selbsttranszendenz. Der anthropologische Befund. *Diakonia* 4, 222–32.

Schmid, PF (1996c) 'Intimacy, tenderness and lust': A person-centered approach to sexuality, in R Hutterer, G Pawlowsky, PF Schmid and R Stipsits (eds) *Client-Centered and Experiential Psychotherapy: A paradigm in motion.* Frankfurt/M: Peter Lang, pp. 85–99.

Schmid, PF (1997) Personale Macht: Thesen aus personzentrierter Sicht. *Brennpunkt* 67: 5–20; 70: 29–32.

Schmid, PF (1998a) 'On becoming a person-centered approach': A person-centred understanding of the person, in B Thorne and E Lambers (eds) *Person-Centred Therapy: A European perspective.* London: Sage, pp. 38–52.

Schmid, PF (1998b) 'Face to face': The art of encounter, in B Thorne and E Lambers (eds) *Person-Centred Therapy: A European perspective.* London: Sage, pp. 74–90.

Schmid, PF (2001a) Authenticity: the person as his or her own author. Dialogical and ethical perspectives on therapy as an encounter relationship. And beyond, in G Wyatt (ed) *Congruence.* Ross-on-Wye: PCCS Books, pp. 217–32.

Schmid, PF (2001b) Comprehension: the art of not-knowing. Dialogical and ethical perspectives on empathy as dialogue in personal and person-centred relationships, in S Haugh and T Merry (eds) *Empathy.* Ross-on-Wye: PCCS Books, pp. 53–71.

Schmid, PF (2001c) Acknowledgement: the art of responding. Dialogical and ethical perspectives on the challenge of unconditional personal relationships in therapy and beyond, in J Bozarth and P Wilkins (eds) *Unconditional Positive Regard*. Ross-on-Wye: PCCS Books, pp. 49–64.

Schmid, PF (2002a) Presence: Im-media-te co-experiencing and co-responding. Phenomenological, dialogical and ethical perspectives on contact and perception in person-centred therapy and beyond, in G Wyatt and P Sanders (eds) *Contact and Perception*. Ross-on-Wye: PCCS Books, pp. 182–203.

Schmid, PF (2002b) Knowledge or acknowledgement? Psychotherapy as 'the art of not-knowing'—Prospects on further developments of a radical paradigm. *Person-Centered and Experiential Psychotherapies, 1,* 1&2: 56–70.

Schmid, PF (2002c) Neue Manns-Bilder? Personzentrierte Heraus-Forderungen zu einem Dialog der Geschlechter, in C Iseli, W Keil, L, Korbei, N Nemeskeri, S Rasch-Owald, PF Schmid and P Wacker (eds) *Identität—Begegnung—Kooperation: Person-/Klientenzentrierte Psychotherapie und Beratung an der Jahrhundertwende*. Cologne: GwG, pp. 65–91.

Winkler, M (1992) Du Tarzan—ich Jane. Geschlechterdifferenz in der therapeutischen Interaktion, in P Frenzel, PF Schmid, M Winkler (eds) *Handbuch der Personzentrierten Psychotherapie*. Cologne: EHP, pp. 193–205.

Winkler, M (2002) Das Private ist politisch: Aspekte Personzentrierter Feministischer Therapie, in C Iseli, W Keil, L, Korbei, N Nemeskeri, S Rasch-Owald, PF Schmid and P Wacker (eds) *Identität—Begegnung—Kooperation: Person-/Klientenzentrierte Psychotherapie und Beratung an der Jahrhundertwende*. Cologne: GwG, pp. 66–78.

MAKING SENSE OF MONSTERS : WORKING THERAPEUTICALLY WITH WOMEN AND CHILDREN WHO HAVE EXPERIENCED SEXUAL VIOLENCE

MARGARET BIRD AND EDNA DAVIS

Grappling with the monsters of the world, trying to understand and make sense of them is often what we find ourselves doing as feminists and as therapists. In thinking about our work as practitioners with women and children who have experienced sexual violence[1]—and in thinking about writing this chapter, we both felt that the concept of monsters was a meaningful way of exploring the issues involved in working from a person-centred approach and with feminist consciousness.

INTRODUCTION

Both of us work therapeutically with women who have experienced sexual violence in adulthood and/or in childhood, and who, having managed to survive, are attempting to recover. From our individual and group work with women we hear from them how frequently their experiences contain elements of meeting monsters and experiencing monstrosities—without and within. Edna's therapeutic work in the playroom illustrates how frequently children who have been similarly victimised will use the ideas of monsters very naturally—to make meaning of their experiences of being abused sexually, physically and emotionally. They may use this concept to deal with their terror, to show how they have been hurt, to find ways to survive psychologically and recover. We often see some kind of a process happening which can include meeting the monsters, facing them, making sense of them and then separating from them.

The theme of monsters is present throughout the writing—how these concepts affect us as people, as clients and as therapists and how they may be acknowledged

---

[1.] It should be said that the vast majority of our experience is of working therapeutically with White women and children.

and used in the therapeutic space. Briefly we also consider the wider picture—the monsters of oppression operating on a global scale and the disempowerment of groups and communities—the monsters magnified.

What follows is an exploration of our attempts to apply the core conditions of a person-centred approach in our therapeutic work with women and children who have experienced sexual violence. Alongside this, we strive to bring our knowledge and awareness of the structural realities of power inequalities and to stay open to learning more of how they impinge on the lives and experiences of those we work with—and on our own too. We aim not to replay the power dynamics that exist outside the therapy room—but acknowledge that inequalities of power still exist within it. We try to create a space where the client has total control of their world—where they can make sense of it for themselves.

A feminist understanding informs our approach as we work with victimised women and children in dealing with the damage that has come from the abuse of power by mainly male perpetrators.[2] We also stay alert to the damages that arise from the often additional layers of oppressions by more powerful groups. We think here about how these values underpin the work we do and how we translate and apply these to therapeutic settings. Case material and personal reflection illustrate our points.

MEETING THE MONSTERS

WHAT ARE THE MONSTERS?

Monsters can be things which we may fear to talk about although we know about or sense their existence. We may think about them and have memories of coming face-to-face with them and harbour a terror of meeting them again. Monsters may change and shift shape. They may trick us into thinking they aren't really monsters. They may appear in one guise, but underneath be something else. They may inhabit our thoughts, feelings, dreams and physical sensations. They may speak to us in voices. We may hear their voices inside ourselves.

The monster here represents a complete abuse of power. The still popular media slogans of 'sex beast', 'dangerous stranger', 'sick pervert' and so on, allow and encourage us to distance the monstrous behaviour of perpetrators of sexual violence. We know though that a 'monster' can be and often is taking part in everyday life, living within a family, a member of a household, part of any group, profession or community. Sexual violence in private still benefits from validation by a wider public environment in which women and children are frequently objectified, reactions to women and girls are casually sexualised and where being female is often negatively

---

[2.] A small minority of those we work therapeutically with have experienced sexual violence by women; a useful exploration of these issues can be found in Liz Kelly (1996).

depicted. Moving along this continuum of oppression, women and children are sexually harassed, attacked, physically and sexually abused, raped, brutalised, killed—more often than not by those they know and in private spaces. This is monstrous behaviour committed by human beings. Most often this behaviour is perpetrated by men. Gender and power are entwined. Feminism helps us by focusing on the distribution of power between men and women and analysing the workings of inequality. Our aim here is not to wonder at how and why things got like this, but to look at how they are—to face the monster—and hear what women's and children's experiences tell us about survival, recovery and the effects of sexual violence.

The oppressions of sexism and sexual violence, racism, homophobia, poverty and low status in so many forms become internalised in ourselves. This process embeds within us the destructiveness that has come from elsewhere.

> In complying with brutalization, we brutalize ourselves. We experience ourselves, or parts of ourselves as the Enemy ... The enemy self becomes in us something we try to destroy or contain, and at the same time, something we fear for and protect. We hate the monster and yet carefully protect it from exposure behind the barriers we erect, like the walls of ancient citadels, to guard us from the world. Whatever is in us that we have been taught is bad, wrong, unacceptable—our anger, our intense feelings, our sexuality, our bodies—becomes monstrous. (Starhawk, 1987: 141)

MONSTERS OF GLOBAL PROPORTIONS

The expanded picture includes communities as well as individuals who have been victimised and terrorised. In particular women, children and others positioned with the least amount of power in society. The magnified external monsters operate globally, socially and collectively. It is difficult to escape the fact that these monsters continue to flourish and grow in a world where global power and influence is still firmly held by men and by White dominated societies. We see them in the ongoing thrust of world markets where vast profits are sought and made to benefit a minority, in the allocation of immense amounts of resources to the promotion and use of force, violence and war, in the waste of human lives and potentials, in the destruction of the environment and of the livelihoods of marginalised communities to further the needs and the agendas of the rich world.

Arundhati Roy writes of the embracing of the nuclear bomb by India as a final act of betrayal by the ruling class of the country's people, hundreds of millions of whom lack formal education. The horror of this she describes as: 'The orbits of the powerful and the powerless spinning further and further apart from each other, never intersecting, sharing nothing' (Roy, 2002: 34–6).

This primacy given to domination, violence, and the means to wage war also includes the power of using sexual violence, where individual acts are part of the bigger picture of institutionalised sexual violence. We know that rape is a weapon of war and that sexual violence has long been used to keep women and other oppressed groups in a powerless position, economically, culturally and socially. Angela Davis talks about the slave owners who encouraged the terroristic use of rape in order to put Black women in their place. If Black women had achieved a sense of their own strength and a strong urge to resist, then violent sexual assaults—so the slave owners might have reasoned—would remind women of their essential and inalterable femaleness and therefore their inevitable powerlessness (Davis, 1982).

We may face this brutalisation, deal with it as best we can and make some recovery within ourselves. If we are able to face the damage we may become more resilient and accept ourselves. If we're not able to, or if we have to continue to accommodate and survive in hostile or dangerous conditions we will carry the damage done to us.

> The patterns in our minds reflect the patterns of power in our culture, as surely as our architecture, clothing and work reflect those patterns. Outwardly and visibly. Power-over reproduces itself inside the human psyche. The structure of our inner being is like a landscape peopled with events, beings, plots, and stories that we take in from the culture around us. The patterns of patriarchy become literally embedded within us. We are possessed. (Starhawk, 1987: 96)

What is it that permits these things to happen and to keep happening? What is it that muffles or silences the voices of dissent? How does feminism and a person-centred approach relate to these issues?

As therapists if we begin with unconditional regard and accept something as it really is, it means that we may face the monsters; if we have empathy and attune wholly to another in their process of making meaning, it means that we can be alongside someone in her struggle to make sense of the monster. If we are congruent and acknowledge our own thoughts and feelings, it helps us to hold our authenticity and humanness in the process of grappling with monsters within ourselves and others and outside in the world. Carol Wolter-Gustafson notes that 'these three core conditions make Rogers' theory a brilliant match for the process of hearing women's experiences directly' (Wolter-Gustafson in Fairhurst, 1999: 205).

FOCUS ON SEXUAL VIOLENCE

Sexual violence towards women can be seen as existing on a continuum reflecting the extent and range of behaviours that women experience as abusive, some of which could not wholly be identified within current legal definitions. This concept has been particularly explored by Liz Kelly who has defined sexual violence as 'any physical, visual, verbal or sexual act that is experienced by the woman or girl, at the time or later, as a threat, invasion or assault, that has the effect of hurting her or degrading her and/or takes away her ability to control intimate contact' (Kelly, 1988: 41).

The model of sexual violence as a continuum has at its heart the experience and perception of the individual woman or girl; it principally acknowledges her point of view. It does not define from an outer so-called 'objective' standpoint, from a legal standpoint or from a male standpoint. It clarifies the reality of the power relationship in sexual violence. It is based on integrity of experience and not on myth.

Myths persist powerfully around women and sexual violence and have been well documented in feminist literature including that from the rape crisis movement (London Rape Crisis Centre, 1988). We need to understand the power and impact of these on our inner and outer worlds to comprehend the workings of sexual violence. These myths are rooted in a system where 'power-over' others underpins the mainstream culture and where power is held and exercised as if by right. Therefore, those who speak out about or question this misuse of power are subject to blame and punishment. Newspaper and other media reporting still divide women into deserving and undeserving of sympathy and justice. Sue Lees wrote of her findings researching women's experiences of the legal process in taking cases of rape to court in the UK. She showed how male norms are institutionalised at every stage of the criminal justice system and how the law is defined and operates in male interests. She noted that it is not unusual for women going to court to face threats of retaliation and death, and to be stereotyped as 'sluts' (Lees, 1996: 4–5).

Children and young people who have been sexually abused have been labelled as 'responsible', 'collusive' or 'provocative'. These are glimpses of the collective grooming process which perpetuates these beliefs in wider society. Germaine Greer writes of the powerful propaganda machine aimed at young girls in Britain indoctrinating them and inciting them to be sexual with males:

> To deny a woman's sexuality is certainly to oppress her but to portray her as nothing but a sexual being is equally to oppress her. No-one doubts that teenage boys have peremptory sexual urges, but they are never depicted as prepared to accept any humiliation, endure any indignity, just to get close to some, any, girl. Nor are they pushed to spend money on their appearance or to dress revealingly or to drink too much in order to attract the attention of the opposite sex ... the British girl's press trumpets the triumph of misogyny and the hopelessness of the cause of female pride. (Greer, 2000: 410–11)

In such a culture, the beliefs and actions of the perpetrators of sexual abuse acting either alone or with others (such as in paedophile networks, internet child pornography, women portrayed on 'page 3') are continually reinforced and validated by other men. For many, it is still more comfortable to deny the possibility of routine horrific and cruel acts and see them as the product of someone's imagination, rather than face the pain, fear and disruption that comes from acknowledging what happens behind closed doors. This 'blaming the victim' (or the therapist) again serves to divert attention from the real focus of concern.

> Within patriarchal society, women who are victimised by male violence have had to pay a price for breaking the silence and naming the problem. They have had to be seen as fallen women, who have failed in their 'feminine' role to sensitise and civilise the beast in man. (hooks, 1989: 89)

And when there is a safe space, free from the monster, there are narratives and stories that as women we share amongst ourselves, about terror, pain, despair and courage. There are psychological battles to stay one step ahead, to identify and track the new mutations of the monster. There are ways that women have to manage, to survive. Some of these are complicated. Some of them take a lot of disentangling. Some of us are devastated or eventually killed by the monster. And how do we respond internally? Sometimes we internalise the monster, tell tales to ourselves that it is us who are monstrous. We hurt ourselves and possibly others with this belief. How do we work this all out?

SURVIVING CHILDHOOD ABUSE

One minute he's alright and then the next he's like a monster ... A very nice father. He really cares for his children ... But then suddenly he's a different man.
(Mama in Hanmer and Itzin, 2000: 48)

Judith Herman believes that repeated trauma in adult life erodes the structure of the personality that has already formed. Repeated trauma in childhood 'forms and deforms' (Herman, 2001: 96) the personality as the child is trapped in an environment of abuse and has to find a way to adapt and survive. She notes that this childhood environment of abuse forces the development of extraordinary capacities, which can be both creative and destructive and fosters the development of abnormal states of consciousness in which ordinary relations to the body and mind, reality and imagination, knowledge and memory, no longer hold. Many people survive the trauma of child sexual abuse by internalising the hostile perpetrator and may be full of self-loathing. The internalised perpetrator will be judging and analysing the vulnerable child, who will be afraid and feeling powerless, and will be filled with self-loathing driven by the constant critic (Miller, 1991; Bass and Davis, 1991; Cappachione, 1991). Anna Salter suggests that just as the victimised person survived by internalising the hostile perpetrator in order to cope with the trauma, so she has the capacity to internalise the therapist's view of her. The implication therefore is that the therapeutic *relationship* is the most important aspect of the healing. Therapy presents the child or adult with a place where intimacy does not lead to abandonment, punishment or betrayal (Salter, 1995).

WORKING WITH CHILDREN

When children are referred to me for therapeutic work, they often arrive together with a whole group of what I hope are well-meaning people, all of whom usually have their own adult agenda. If I am not careful, the child's agenda can easily become lost in the needs of the adult world. Therefore my approach to working with children is primarily child-centred and my therapeutic work with the child is non-directive. I encourage the child to lead the way towards healing—by accepting the child, by reflecting rather than teaching, by being non-directive and interpreting only rarely. I encourage the child to find self-expression and self-value, anchoring therapy in reality by providing limits.

Theorists such as Cattanach (1992) and Gil (1991) propose that for children lost in the maze of abuse, there are three stages in the therapeutic process. The first stage involves the beginning or the establishment of the therapeutic relationship—the creation of a safe place—a time when children decide how they are going to play. The second stage involves 'meeting with the monster'. This stage sees the child and the therapist engaging in a more focused way to help integrate and make sense of the terror of the past—the stage of the monster. The third and final stage involves becoming visible and begins to witness the development of self-esteem and an identity that is not so bound up in abusive relationships of the past. As a child-centred therapist working with what emerges from the child's process, this theory appears to often make sense.

Following children's agendas in working with sexual and physical abuse issues over the years has shown how powerful these metaphors are as ways of making sense of children's experiences.

CREATING SAFE SPACE

Much has to be done before meeting the monster. To communicate empathic understanding, authenticity and positive regard in ways that the client experiences as non-threatening is a principal task. Working in a non-directive way with children we first need to establish a safe space. So as a therapist working with a child, we would together establish boundaries or rules around the play—this would include agreements about keeping safe, not hurting or harming each other, how often we would meet, and how long we would meet.

MEETING THE MONSTER

The examples below are concerned with what could be seen as the middle phase of the therapeutic process in working with a child, having established a safe therapeutic relationship. (All identifying details in the examples that follow have been changed to protect anonymity.)

> Lucy's agenda was 'I want to get out of my head what is in my head'. Lucy's play was totally spontaneous as she prepared to meet with the monster. Special dolls and toys had been selected to help her meet the monster. She had selected the happy/angry doll as an auxiliary or therapeutic aide, and placed the doll with angry face to the fore in a high place where she could survey the playroom and witness all.
>
> The angry face seemingly represented the angry part of Lucy. She was creating a picture of her inner process or creating metaphorical representation of her inner feelings (Hoey, 1997). The doll was to witness all of Lucy's work in the playroom and was to be a witness to her abuse and her healing. Lucy worked with the 'monster' over many weeks. A crash doll was selected to take on the role of the monster. She could take the doll apart, dismantle arms and legs, disorientate the doll by moving body parts around or make the doll limbless. Lucy was in control as the doll was tossed around the room and all the while the angry self sat on the shelf and witnessed everything.
>
> Lucy was working in 'surplus reality'—it is seen as 'a dream land state in which painful tasks are finished by the gesture of a hand or by a smile, scenes in life which endure for days are here reduced to a minute' (Moreno, 1972 in Kellerman, 1992: 212). In these moments Lucy took control. In reality her father had been her oppressor. He had physically, sexually and emotionally abused her—but Lucy was no longer feeling powerless; she was in control. As the work progressed Lucy selected other dolls as additional auxiliaries, babies who were nurtured and taken care of, while the monster resided in bits in the fireplace and the angry self witnessed all.

Monsters can take on many forms. This was particularly significant for Peter and Stephen, who prepared to meet their monster by taking on the roles of numerous 'superheroes'.

> In the playroom they were afraid of nothing and battled with snakes and other strange animals as they prepared to meet the monster. A character called 'Changing Man' emerged in this play. This man was not all that he appeared to be. He looked OK and was kind to everyone

but then suddenly started to steal things. A gun appeared and threatened a special child. Superheroes rescued the special child who was wrapped in cloths of silver and gold and taken to a safe place. During a later session, the 'devil' visited the playroom, but 'god' came and banished the 'devil' forever.

We have noticed in our work with children during therapeutic play, that they may often take on stereotypical roles, which can be reinforced by carers and other professionals working with the child. A female child may often take on a socially 'acceptable' role of nurturer and carer. A girl or young woman who breaks the mould for whatever reason and expresses anger is still often labelled 'mad', 'bad' or the 'monster'. Male children often take on the role of superheroes who hold the power to deal with the monster. Armed with guns and knives, they kill the monsters in an 'acceptable' way that reinforces male power and control. Children who fall outside society's dominant norms of 'male' and 'female' behaviour are often viewed as 'damaged' by what has happened; their sexuality is questioned and negated if they fail to fit into heterosexist stereotypes. In the playroom we can see further manifestations of the oppressions of patriarchy.

MAKING SENSE OF THE MONSTER

Creating a safe space means that the monster may be faced and dealt with in which ever way makes sense for the child:

John was seven years old and had been physically, emotionally and sexually abused by his father. John had also witnessed his father's abuse of his mother and sister. For John there had been no escape. In our early sessions he only created Chaos in the playroom, re-creating the world of the monster. Windows were blacked out, lights went out, people were terrorised and the playroom was wrecked. Nothing in the playroom remained untouched. John could hold no boundaries as his eyes rolled around in his head—he was the monster and was terrorising me. John's task appeared to be to separate off from this monster that had terrorised everyone and everything in sight. John worked this way for weeks until gradually his world became calmer and he became more able to hold boundaries. John then began to use role-play, working with the different parts of self. He would move from 'caring parent' to 'monster' to 'child'; life was never predictable as I began to get a clearer picture, to understand and begin to make sense of the world that John had lived in. Children were locked in bedrooms and monster would come in the night and scare the children, scream and shout and throw things around the room. And the room would rattle and shake and furniture would get thrown around the room when the monster entered. No one was safe. John is still battling with the monster but it seems to be getting weaker (sometimes nice things happen in the playroom) as John becomes stronger.

The separation process here illustrates that the child can detach herself from the struggle which has taken place within. For some children the monster can emerge in the guise of a giant:

> Katy used the concept of magic to prepare to meet the monster ... After weeks of working Katy sat me in a chair and told me I was not to move. I was to be a witness to something special. Katy began wrestling with herself and told me that this was a giant; she struggled then fell to the ground and then climbed over the sofa to the other side. I asked Katy what had happened and where she was. She told me that the giant was dead—and now she is in heaven. When I asked Katy what heaven was like she told me 'oh it is fine here, god is there, and there are flowers'. Katy had found a safe place to be. She had wrestled with the giant, separated from the monster and was now in heaven.

WORKING WITH WOMEN

The most common rapists are current and ex-husbands or partners.
(Rape Crisis Federation)

Every week two women are killed in a domestic violence situation.
(Women's Aid Federation)

The concept of creating a safe space is equally important in our groupwork with women. The groups we refer to are confidential, women-only groups, set up to work therapeutically with the issues of domestic/sexual violence. The formation of such groups has been in response to expressed needs usually via voluntary sector organisations. The attention to setting—such as creating a woman-only space which can be voluntarily entered into—is therefore significant. It comes from a feminist understanding of power relations between women and men, and acknowledges the dynamics of gendered violence against women. We know there is a need to have woman-only spaces so that we can work with women on issues related to domestic/sexual violence. This principle has been applied successfully for many years in work with women, for example the Rape Crisis and Women's Aid movements. Our aim is to be woman-centred; the group and therefore the space belong to the women. They work out what they want to use it for. Some women have not been in such a group before. We try and make our agenda transparent as facilitators, so that the experience of participants may be as empowering as possible and we attempt to demystify what we are doing.

At the beginning we offer different ways of working—a response to the reality that everyone's most fluent language may not be verbal. We mention psychodrama and other creative methods (such as using drawing and painting, stones, cushions, toys, writing, clay, etc.) as possible ways of working with what comes up for group members. We let the group know how we work and basically what that means. In working with a person-centred approach we are placing paramount importance on the woman's own interpretation of herself. So her own inner story, her language, is translated and communicated by herself. Psychodrama and other ways of expression offer a concretisation of this process. We aim to trust in the group and in ourselves. Safety and trust only begin to develop when we are able to be authentic ourselves in our responses and ways of being.

We aim to help create a space where terrifying and painful realities may be faced and acknowledged. In these situations, as facilitators in the group we will initiate a discussion of the issues of safety and work with group members to put together an agreement that helps participants feel safe in the group. We see this as a proactive and empathic response to the fear and anxiety that women frequently show in the first session. It is also one way of explicitly addressing feelings and experiences of powerlessness. In this process we acknowledge how difficult and frightening it may be for them to come to the group, given their past and current experiences and what they are having to manage as a result. We acknowledge and make visible the process that is going on—that it is so frightening to be there.

MEETING THE MONSTER

Men with power, dominant father figures and abuse by men are issues that continue to be powerfully present in the groups we work with and are common themes for all the women we work with.

Unprocessed experiences into adulthood may further develop into themes of monstrousness, evil and dirtiness—experienced by women as residing inside themselves. From our practice we know that this brutalisation may manifest itself vividly through the experience of hearing voices.

Often in group sessions and individual work, soft toys are available and may be used by clients to concretise their experiences or their feelings about themselves. A soft red devil toy may for example become a representation of someone's internal struggle. The 'devil' in a woman's head may be a way of explaining the internal voices she hears. For many women that we have worked with who hear voices, they have recognised the voices readily as their perpetrators. Many of these voices can be abusive and urge self-destruction. It seems that the notion of these voices being the internalised messages from the women's abusers is not usually given acknowledgment by psychiatric practitioners. Some women may be given medical diagnoses of psychosis and paranoid schizophrenia, and their experiences not listened to or validated. We have worked with many women and children who have experienced similar atrocities and who also deeply believe that they are bad and to blame, and who take on an immense burden of responsibility and self-hate. By sharing this in the group settings many women express feelings of great relief that they are not alone in hearing voices.

> A woman was curled up in a childlike position in the group and appeared to be functioning around the age that she was when her abuse possibly began. She took a pencil and drew childlike pictures of blood and killings, pictures of children being locked in cupboards, being beaten and abused by men and women. There was no safe place for her to be. Monsters and the devil inhabited her world.

She had used the space in the group to be as she needed to be. Paint and drawing materials were available to be used. Through this media she was able to externalise her internal processes and used drawings to show not only what had been done to her as a child but also her feelings. She externalised her experiences of abuse and her feelings of deep rage both as a child and as an adult.

> A child is beaten and sexually abused; a mother is beaten and sexually abused—subjected to years of rape within a marriage and she is then seen as 'the problem'—as the one who didn't protect her child. This was what she herself felt and believed. This was her internal struggle. She was forced to flee her home and leave everything, because those who had particular positions of power and influence in the community she lived in were supporting the man that abused her son and subjected her to years of physical and sexual violence. She was the 'bad one'— this must be the truth she said, there must be something wrong with her; she felt like 'the devil' because she wanted her perpetrators to burn in hell. She is filled with anger and rage that she can't express, for fear of being seen as the 'mad' woman. In the group sessions she painted dramatic and powerful representations of hell.

In the context of the group, this woman was supported and acknowledged in her fight to gain protection for herself and her child from violent perpetrators, some of whom held powerful positions in the community. Her sense of hopelessness and exhaustion in her continuing struggle was heard, as was the terror evoked from proximity to her abusers. This woman had used psychodrama and art techniques to externalise her abuse in the group. She used 'surplus reality'[3] to talk to one of her perpetrators about what he had done to her and how she felt about it. Both women were able to successfully use action methods and creative techniques, painting vivid pictures of what had been done to them as children. Rogers' core conditions were consistently offered throughout the life of the group. This created a holding container and a climate of safety that was enabling for all of the women.

The strength of this is evident in the women's evaluation of the group experience. One woman said that the group had helped her to face up to things and that doing psychodrama had helped her put her perpetrator out of her life completely—and that she knew now that it wasn't her fault. The group had helped her feel safe and she had learned to laugh again. She said that one of the best things about the group had been meeting people in similar situations, making friends, feeling safe and not being criticised by others.

> A woman talked about her anger with her mother for not supporting her and for keeping the secret from her father about her abuse by a paternal uncle. She used the medium of psychodrama to explore why her mother had wanted to protect her father from knowing about the abuse. It was only then that she realised that her deeper anger was towards her father.

We saw this piece of work as a reflection of the power dynamics that continue to exist. In order to 'protect' the father from the pain and anger he was expected to feel, this woman's mother stayed silent and powerless. As a man in the family his feelings were of paramount importance. In staying silent, the daughter's abuse was denied. We see again patterns repeating—women's roles seen still as carers, nurturers and existing to meet the needs of men; women being given a primary role of responsibility for men's emotions; once again women's voices not being heard.

A woman-centred approach and feminist approach in therapy prioritises women's own definitions of themselves and their experiences; it acknowledges the external and internalised oppressions that so often create a climate of silencing. So such an approach addresses not only individual women's perceptions but also their collective experience.

The feminist tradition of consciousness-raising groups is a space where women can begin to understand their experiences from a wider perspective through making links and finding commonalities. We would see women-only therapy groups as part of this tradition.

Allowing a process to unfold at an individual woman's pace and being aware of

---

[3.] The dimensions of alternative past, present and future events that are a 'reality' in the imagination, if not in the outside world (Moreno, 1965).

how that process relates at individual and collective levels to the situation of women can be seen as an intersection of the Person-Centred Approach and feminism.

CONCLUSION

It is clear throughout our work with women and children that the monster that is called patriarchy is alive and well, and continues to exist in our world. A world where women and children continue to be socialised to meet the needs of men and the powerful western culture. Monsters become a metaphor for the oppression and brutality which impacts on women and children at an individual, group and societal level. Monsters surround us and continue to exist alongside us just as they always have. 'Good' and 'evil', 'god' and the 'devil', monsters that come in the night and many others, help us to distance from the real monsters. The real monsters change and shift in shape just like the 'Changing Man' that appeared in Peter and Stephen's work. They can groom us, silence us and convince us that they are safe and want to help. They may become a 'pillar of our community', then hold the power to control all of our lives. Alternatively they can control us through brute force or render us emotionally helpless and totally dependent on them for our existence.

The global monsters that wage war, invade and exploit other countries, brutalising already powerless populations, can convince us that this is what is needed—that a complete invasion of someone's space, destruction and death will be beneficial; that to deny and redefine a person's reality is 'for their own good' just like the exploitation of children (Miller, 1991).

Our work with women finds them struggling with external monsters as well as the monsters that they have internalised in order to survive in the world. Some of them are living in a kind of 'middle ground'—a transitional place neither in one world nor the other. Individually they may hold incongruent feelings towards the abuser and themselves in the midst of the abuse. They are also expected to be a 'nurturer', they blame themselves, they feel responsible. They have to manage their own incongruence and the incongruence that exists in the world. One woman in the group described herself as a 'buffer' who was carrying the weight of the trauma in the world.

Our experience of the therapeutic struggle is that some of the women and children feel they become the monsters that have abused them, grappling with monsters who have hurt them and battling with giants, monsters and devils. Experiencing flashbacks and reliving their abuse, women may use at times self-harming behaviours as a way to cope. Women often tell us that they think that they are going 'mad' and mental health services may sometimes reinforce this thinking as psychiatric diagnoses are made, women are medicated and are seen as the problem. Equally women surviving rape and sexual assault in adulthood struggle with and suffer frequent injustice and powerlessness within the criminal justice system (Lees,

1996). A low and declining conviction rate reinforces the powerlessness they have already experienced.

A feminist perspective combined with a person-centred approach means creating a safe therapeutic space in conjunction with the women and children we work with, to make a place for voices to be heard. It is a space for them to challenge society and address the power dynamics and oppressions that continue to exist. We trust in the group's capacities to hold and positively value the differences between each other. By offering congruence and unconditional positive regard we aim to help them move towards a more congruent place within themselves and within the world. When we try to hold our own power, to stand in our own skin and to be all that it is to be ourselves, that is when we are at our most positive as facilitators. As person-centred therapists we aim to follow the woman's and/or child's agenda—to work with their reality and their perceptions; to enter their world and to walk alongside them as they make their journey. We aim to start at their beginning and end at their ending.

REFERENCES

Bass, L and Davis, E (1991) *The Courage to Heal.* New York: Harper and Row.

Cappachione, L (1991) *Recovery of Your Inner Child.* New York: Newcastle Publishing.

Cattanach, A (1992) *Play Therapy with Abused Children.* London: Jessica Kingsley Publications.

Davis, A (1982) *Women, Race and Class.* London: The Women's Press.

Gil, E (1991) *The Healing Power of Play.* London: The Guilford Press.

Greer, G (2000) *The Whole Woman.* London: Anchor.

Herman, J (2001) *Trauma and Recovery: From domestic abuse to political terror.* London: Pandora.

Hoey, B (1997) *Who Calls the Tune.* London: Routledge.

hooks, b (1989) *Talking Back.* London: Sheba Feminist Publishers.

Kelly, L (1988) *Surviving Sexual Violence.* Cambridge: Polity.

Kelly, L (1996) Feminist perspectives on violence by women, in M Hester, L Kelly and J Radford (eds) *Women, Violence and Male Power.* Bristol: Open University Press.

Lees, S (1996) *Carnal Knowledge: Rape on trial.* London: Hamish Hamilton.

London Rape Crisis Centre (1988) *Sexual Violence.* London: The Women's Press.

Mama, A (2000) Violence against black women in the home, in J Hanmer and C Itzin *Home Truths about Domestic Violence—Feminist influences on policy and practice.* London: Routledge.

Miller, A (1991) *Banished Knowledge.* London: Virago.

Moreno, J (1972) cited in P Kellerman, (1992) *Focus on Psychodrama.* London: Jessica Kingsley.

Moreno, ZT (1965) Psychodramatic Rules, Techniques, and Adjunctive Methods. *Group Psychotherapy 18*(1–2): 73–86.

Rape Crisis Federation (1991) Wales and England, Statistics, www.rapecrisis.org.uk

Roy, A (2002) *The Algebra of Infinite Justice*. London: Flamingo.

Salter, A (1995) *Transforming Trauma*. London: Sage.

Starhawk (1987) *Truth or Dare*. San Francisco: Harper and Row.

Wolter-Gustafson, C (1999) The power of the premise: Reconstructing gender and human development with Rogers' theory, in I Fairhurst (ed) *Women Writing in the Person-Centred Approach*. Ross-on-Wye: PCCS Books.

Women's Aid Federation of England, (2002) Domestic Violence Statistical Factsheet, www.womensaid.org.uk

MAKING CONNECTIONS: DOMESTIC VIOLENCE, FEMINISM AND PERSON-CENTRED THERAPY

SOPHIE SMAILES

INTRODUCTION

Embarking on a chapter which reflects on therapeutic engagement with women experiencing domestic violence (DV) feels complex. Part of my intention within this chapter is to unravel some of the elements involved in this work, including focusing on aspects of women's lives, which are specifically located and informed by historical, political and social contexts. So I want to professionally and personally place myself within this exploration, as well as interweaving women's narratives within the discourses of person-centred therapy (PCT) and feminism.

I will be exploring two 'scenarios' which are an amalgamation or synthesis of work with clients. The process and context of this work will be discussed, highlighting issues of power, diversity and social constructs as being intrinsic to this exploration (Walker, 1990; Marecek and Kravetz, 1998; Seu, 1998). Integral to this discussion will be the incorporation of my own ongoing process and reflections.

Both scenarios concern heterosexual relationships, reflecting the largely gendered nature of DV and the fact that it is overwhelmingly male-on-female (Radford, 1987; Hague and Malos, 1999; Maynard and Winn, 1997). Same sex and extended family DV also occurs and I am neither assuming that issues around heterosexual relationships exclude these relationships but neither am I presuming a complete overlap. I have tried to explicitly and implicitly illustrate how feminism and PCT work together, and in conflict, on issues of DV. While I have fore-grounded the aspects of my work which relate to DV, this is not everything that we worked on nor is it everything these women are. Highlighting a particular element can run the risk of rendering whole lives as invisible, privileging the violence as the only way of identification.

WHO ARE THE WOMEN?

Firstly, these 'scenarios' represent an amalgam and reflection of women I have worked with—so more that one woman's story is integrated within each scenario and all identifying personal details have been removed. Secondly, they are all from at least two years ago, so I am relying on a mixture of detailed case notes and retrospective reflections. Thirdly, all the women were contacted and permission given to 'write' their stories. Respecting and honouring my clients' lives and voices is informed by my therapeutic, personal and feminist allegiances. It feels vital to engage with these clarifying processes as I am committed to giving women a voice and a voice with which they choose to engage. At the same time I want their stories to be as unrecognisable as possible. The risk here is that I could present a generalised picture rather than individual frameworks and lives. Throughout this chapter I will try to balance the need for anonymity with the need for specificity. My abiding concern is for the welfare and well-being of these women and finding a way of working with these knotty issues of power, confidentiality and representation.

WHO AM I?

Professionally I am both a person-centred counsellor and an academic. My academic work is largely located within a health care studies department of a large metropolitan university. I have worked there, as a lecturer, for about seven years and while working part-time, trained to be a counsellor. I have counselled in both statutory and voluntary organisations and am presently counselling with one voluntary organisation in particular. I have been interested and involved in issues around domestic abuse and violence for over 20 years. More recently I have researched areas around DV with minoritised populations as well as worked therapeutically with women who have experienced (or are experiencing) DV. I am a White, middle-class woman which locates me variously in positions of both privilege and minoritisation. Who I am, my beliefs and attitudes, is intimately tied up with how I work therapeutically with my clients. Acknowledging diversity and difference forms part of how I move in my world, and both feminism and PCT form part of my identity.

A BRIEF LOOK AT FEMINISM

Definitions of feminism are by no means unified, nor are they static—they are an area which is both contested and evolving. However, rather than go down the route of endeavouring to classify feminisms, and mine in particular, I hope that elements of my perspective will emerge through the scenarios. At its heart is the recognition that women's lives are politically, socially and culturally situated, informed by patriarchal and socially constructed norms. This affords women inferior status and constructs their meaning as being in relationship to, and less than, men. Interlinked with these meanings is that of other diverse constructs, e.g., race, class, sexuality, religion, culture, etc., which have further implications for women's lived experiences and positioning.

MY TAKE ON PCT

Rogerian counselling has at its heart a commitment to the client's internal frame of reference. Integral to this is a belief in the essential trustworthiness of the client, informed by the conviction that all individuals move instinctively towards realising their full potential (Colledge, 2002; Dryden and Mytton, 1999; Mearns, 2003). A respect and honouring of the client's understanding and experiencing of their world further informs the process of the therapeutic engagement. Rogers emphasised the importance of the therapist's ongoing self-awareness, seeing the therapist as 'the companion to the clients on their journey as they enter into and explore their inner worlds' (Dryden and Mytton, 1999: 78). Thus, for me to be able to provide an environment in which the client can experience themselves, their world and our relationship, there has to be a commitment on my part to provide the 'attitudinal conditions' (Nelson-Jones, 1996) for this exploration.

MEANINGS OF DOMESTIC VIOLENCE

There are a variety of perspectives which traditionally inform our understanding of DV. Not least of these is the historically informed notion of women being men's chattels, their belongings, to do with what they willed. Discourses of social construction and feminism consider that our understandings of gender, and gender relationships, are 'built', i.e., socially defined, as opposed to essential, i.e., determined by biology. Essentialism, however, often seems to have dominance when considering the 'hows' and 'whys' of DV. For instance DV (within reason) was historically considered as a manifestation of (essentialist) beliefs around masculinity in response to femininity—a natural expression of power, dominance and control over a subordinate being. Thus, domestic abuse is hinged on 'patriarchal norms and practices which lay the groundwork for violence to occur and permit one group (men) to dominate and control another (women)' (Sharma, 2001: 1408).

While ostensibly there is now less overt acceptance of DV and an increasing recognition of it as a serious social problem (Mooney, 2000) it shows little sign of abating. It is well known that DV is widely under-reported (Dobash and Dobash, 1992; Mooney, 2000) and that the true extent of DV is unknown. Added to this has been the privileging of the physical aspect of violence (with its often clear 'evidential' characteristics) while other more incipient manifestations e.g., sexual, financial, emotional and psychological, have gone unacknowledged (Batsleer et al., 2002).

The advantages of violence as a method of control for establishing/maintaining power are commonly recognised (Hanmer, 2000; Hearn, 1995) and linked with how heterosexual relationships can be played out. Masculinity is often personified by control, power, rationalisation and strength, while femininity's personification is one of submission, nurture, vulnerability, weakness and subservience. These seemingly static and fixed essentialist notions may result in heterosexual relationships where complimentary discourses of domination and subordination reveal themselves in terms of DV. So in this instance DV may be explained as an 'understandable [if not always justifiable] response to another person's actions' (Radford, 1987: 143) leaving the way open to victim blaming and the 'why doesn't she leave him?' school of thought.

A WORD ABOUT AGENCY

Finally before engaging with the scenarios I want to briefly look at the idea of agency—that is being the main actor in your own life. I feel this concept has a great deal of influence on how we may respond to DV, from both Rogerian and feminist perspectives. Agency, a Westernised liberal concept, locates power and choice with the individual—believing in the autonomous and private self that can somehow stand apart from history and culture (Marecek and Kravetz, 1998). This individualising of women's experiences outside the social context runs the risk of expecting them to act divorced from the oppressive system in which they are positioned. This leads to dichotomous beliefs around women either being considered agents of their own destiny (and, therefore leaving) or victims (and staying) (Mahoney, 1994; Waterhouse, 1993). PCT, it has been argued, is built on assumptions of free choice and self-determinism, based on individualistic notions of agency (Marecek and Kravetz; 1998) which assumes that personal control and choice is a universal ideal and possibility. Feminism on the other hand has emancipatory goals and a history of 'consciousness-raising' built on beliefs of what women should and could be like. The potential here could be to equate 'change' with feminist ideals as opposed to working with the diverse value systems which clients can bring. Women's agency, therefore, may become constricted by the very frameworks which are intended to 'free' her.

Feminism works with the explicit premise that a woman's experience and response to DV are informed by these societal power imbalances (Sharma, 2001; Burstow, 1992; Walker, 1990; Waterhouse, 1993). However, this focus can render invisible the other hierarchies of power (Marecek and Kravetz, 1998) and the diverse ways in which women assert themselves in response to the violence (Mahoney,

1994). At the same time PCT can honour women's individual understanding of DV, while potentially decontextualising it from its genderised framework (Waterhouse, 1993; Lyddon, 1998).

Farzana

> A Pakistani Muslim young woman, 19 years old who has been married for two years, with one baby girl. Farzana lives with her husband's family and the violence (physical, mental and sexual) comes from her husband, whom she came over to England to be with. While English is not her first language she can communicate; but initially 'chose' to have a translator for more complex reasons than just 'translation'. Her husband and his family wanted her to come to counselling as they see her weeping and depression as her inability to acclimatise to a new environment and be a 'good wife'.

Working with Farzana epitomised the value and difficulty of working with PCT and feminist constructs. PCT and feminist theory emphasise the importance of working within a woman's frame of reference, validating and acknowledging the way in which she constructs her world and (in the case of PCT) reflecting that world back to her (Hawtin, 2000; Dryden and Mytton, 1999). Conflict can arise when in endeavouring to be a 'companion' to Farzana's journey I neglect to work with the impact and influence of my own gendered, racial and social situation on the therapy itself.

In terms of working with Farzana there were two immediate difficulties: the first was that she had brought a family friend as a translator, and secondly that she had been 'told' to come by the very person who was abusing her! This latter particularly reverberated for me in many ways. It reflected the feminist stance about DV which acknowledges how the multifaceted nature of abuse often manifests itself in 'blaming the woman' for whatever transpires (Kelly, 1987). This was the case with Farzana. It was not the problematising of the abuse itself which was her desired focus but rather how she was 'mis-managing' the isolation and bewilderment of her new life. The client believed that the abuse was deserved or a result of her inadequacies as a woman, wife and mother. This is clear example of how our understanding of male violence is often filtered through notions of the man's violent behaviour being either aberrant or 'understandable' (Stanko, 1985) and 'the fiction that violence is exceptional is fundamental to stereotypes that portray battered women as helpless, dependent, and pathological' (Mahoney, 1994: 63).

Added to this is the potential to typify Farzana's experience as being a characteristic of her cultural background. Both Batsleer et al. (2002) and Sharma (2001) discuss the risk of locating abusive behaviour within cultural norms rather than individual culpability and response. Thus, stereotyped assumptions that race is the primary identity of an individual can act as a filter for understanding Farzana's experience. The importance of transcultural work requires us to work with the fluidity and variety of cultural, religious and gendered standpoints rather than presenting monolithic voices of representation (Marshall et al., 1998). At the same time to negate the importance of race, culture and religion in terms of client's lived experience would be equally problematic.

Both aberrant and 'understandable' perspectives locate the violence in terms of a response to women's deviations from their appropriate roles (Stanko, 1987; Maynard and Winn, 1997). So for me the core condition of acceptance needs to acknowledge these hugely influential constructs on how I may respond to my clients. Rogerian theory has often been criticised as ignoring these political constructs in favour of an idealised and value-free unconditional positive regard (Lyddon, 1998; Biever et al., 1998). Feminist theory, on the other hand,

> ... urges therapists to take into account society's belief system concerning accepted role patterns and behaviours that have been prescribed for males and females. (Biever et al., 1998: 165)

Staying with Farzana's 'here and now' experiencing of the dislocation and discordance in her world formed an important part of the work. My sense was she had had little opportunity to do this before. It felt vital to honour and respect her world without mythologising it and placing it within some stereotypical world of 'this is what happens in South Asian families and to South Asian women'—thereby making invisible her own understanding and response to her world. My own fear was that I might unwittingly colonise (take over in terms of 'reading' her experience through my Westernised world) her experience, rather than recognising her in all her complex individuality as opposed to being representative of a group to which she belongs or to which she has been assigned (Gordon, 1996).

I worked hard to empathically accompany Farzana on her journey of telling, gradually finding myself getting to 'know' her rather than feeding my sense of her through particular constructs of meaning. Again this is where PCT with its non-analytical framework and its emphasis on the core conditions comes into its own.

I found working with a translator difficult. It felt like Farzana's and my processing was restricted due both to the 'act of filtering' which translation can take as well as the prior relationship between the translator and Farzana. PCT works very much with the empathic response and sensing of the client's process. Reflection plays a big part in this, where clarification of content can be pivotal in gaining a clear insight into the sensed world of the client. Having a third person translating both the literal meaning as well as her interpretation of what Farzana and I were saying often obscured what was being said. My sense was that Farzana's and the translator's relationship also served to further 'monitor' the work. I was able to reflect this back (albeit rather awkwardly) to Farzana and, indeed, by association, the translator. However, while from my Rogerian perspective the creation of space in which a client feels safe and respected enough to explore was being restricted, for

Farzana this was not initially her expressed experience. The presence of the translator had enabled and supported Farzana to come to counselling. It was here that conflicts between person-centredness and feminism were further highlighted. At a very basic level here we were a group of women, with the opportunity to share our gendered and racialised experiences. We could have engaged in a more cooperative activity, where personal experiences could have been linked to a larger system of inequality, hierarchy and control. Space could have been made to discuss how we might unconsciously collude and conform to these systems. While this may seem somewhat facetious there is a strong feminist commitment to highlighting:

> ... personal problems [as] both created and exacerbated by societal power imbalances. Helping women make the connections and resist is a key to what feminist [theory] is about. (Burstow, 1992: 40)

The conflict arises when it seems that the focus is taken away from the woman's felt experience and the feminist commitment to 'enlightenment' is given precedence. Thus, instead of 'identifying and honouring a woman's belief structure and view of reality and then joining her there unjudgementally' (McClosky and Fraser, 1997: 437) I would be asking her to join me within my feminist framework. This would have set me up as the 'expert', a role which conflicts with my Rogerian beliefs around trusting the client's own authenticity. So my acceptance of the translator had to be on Farzana's terms and not my own.

Initially we stayed with Farzana's distress around her continued sense of dislocation in terms of being away from her country of origin. The distress was located as her inadequacies as a mother and wife. Feminist frameworks which acknowledge the influence of these socially proscribed roles in terms of women's sense of value were useful in this instance as they placed her experience within the construction of motherhood and heterosexuality. Working from both a Rogerian and feminist perspective facilitated the validation of her experiences within a non-judgemental and empathic framework. So the Rogerian process of the reflective, minute-to-minute empathic response and the feminist stance of working from the woman's own voice provided a space for Farzana to begin to have a sense of her own experiencing. The painfulness, for me, was her insistence in working with her 'wrongs' as isolated and pathological problems as opposed to being located in contextual frameworks. By choosing not to highlight these structures to her, I felt sometimes collusive in her abuse and her sense of being in the wrong. However, at the same time Rogerian theory rightly places emphasis on the unconditional positive regard of the client's framework. This includes walking alongside Farzana's distress and further enabling therapeutic conditions where she could feel accepted and respected. The struggle for me, at times, was to accept her framework and not see it filtered through my feminist ideologies. I needed to trust that her actualising tendency would enable her to be more accepting of herself—in her own time and way and not through imposing my own understanding (Dryden and Mytton, 1999).

We continued to work with the translator for some time until one day Farzana came without her. She was both excited and pleased about her decision while I felt hugely moved. She had been able to utilise the very way in which she had been located by her husband and his family to her advantage by saying that her shame was too great to bear a translator. Her acknowledgement of subverting oppressive frameworks of shame and blame emerged as we continued our work. The feminist notion of agency was interwoven with the importance of her family and community. We worked with our differences, clarifying that while in Western cultures individualism and self identity are part of our philosophical construction of self, her response to her cultural norms construct the self more in terms of community and family (Choudry, 1996; Sharma, 2001). At the same time feminist theory emphasises the importance of being aware of diversity and commonalties, challenging the 'homogenized conceptualisation of "Asian" and [acknowledging] instability of ethnic boundaries and practices' (Marshall et al., 1998: 125)—so not fixing meanings into a static and prescriptive stereotype. Similarly Rogerian personality theory considers that personal realities and perceptions are informed by past experiences, opinions and responses, in particular 'conditions of worth' (Rogers, 1959). While these perceptions are very real to us in the moment they are not static and can change over time and place (Dryden and Mytton, 1999).

The decision not to have a translator was a turning point for Farzana. She began to experience a sense of self-worth and acceptance. In this the non-acknowledgement of the abuse could also be explored, with the implicit understanding that leaving was not an option. The difficulties of leaving, particularly for some minoritised women involve the obstacles of finances, housing, transport and childcare but for Farzana there was also the issue of language and immigration laws. The 'one-year' (two years as of April 2003) rule stipulates that women who have entered the country as spouses of British citizens have neither recourse to public funding nor leave to stay, should the marriage break down within that time (Batsleer et al., 2002) unless they can 'prove' DV to the satisfaction of the Home Office. There is also the fear and possibility of having a child/children taken from the mother and bringing shame and dishonour to her family back home (Choudry, 1996; Sharma, 2001; Batsleer et al., 2002), again fears which have much veracity. Farzana's agency or pursuit of self-worth was to be developed from within her relationship emphasising the many ways that women will work with the abuse in their life and challenging the popular belief that it is only through leaving that women assert themselves (Mahoney, 1994).

The step-by-step work of clarification, reflection and acceptance enabled her to engage with a sense of self and reduce some of the ways in which she experienced her distress as 'her problem'. PCT, which values the individual organismic self, worked well with some of the feminist constructs of gender, sexuality, race and class. Farzana could not be taken out of these milieus but neither could I assume some hegemonic understanding of how these contexts influenced her. The conflicts arose when I either negated the influence of these constructs on how I responded to Farzana or forefronted my feminist ideologies as a way of explaining Farzana's world. While I did not always shy away from challenging her individual pathologisation of her experiences, the balance between placing myself in the role of the expert and trusting her authentic self was sometimes hard to maintain.

Jessica

A white heterosexual woman, in her thirties who identifies as middle-class. She has lived with her partner for three years and works in public relations. They have no children. Jessica has recently been feeling bewildered, confused and lost. Both incomes are controlled by her partner and she is often forced to have sex with him to keep the peace. She is constantly told that she is stupid and ugly. These moments are interspersed with moments of remorse, and subsequent deep happiness and fun, with a good social life. No one knows of the abuse and she describes herself as deeply ashamed and embarrassed. We worked together for about seven months and she specifically wanted to explore her relationship.

The focus of our work together in the initial stages was her bewildered disbelief that this was happening. 'Violence, especially from those who are apparently to be trusted, is a deep and terrible assault on the self' (Walker, 1990: 145). Trying to equate her experience of the abuse with her understanding of love was a huge struggle (Waterhouse, 1993; Jackson, 2001; Towns and Adams, 2000). By drawing on feminist theories of heterosexual and romantic love I was able to contextualise her confusion rather than individualise it as being completely separate from popular cultural messages. The influence of discourses of 'perfect love' as a way of silencing women's talk about the violence (Jackson, 2001; Towns and Adams, 2000) needed to be considered. I was able to reflect the confusion being experienced regarding meanings of love and how it felt proscribed with various characteristics. This, I feel was both a way of working with my congruent/empathic sense of Jessica as well as highlighting some of the potentially restrictive ways we may understand romantic love.

What became clear as we progressed was that she did not at first consider his behaviours to be DV but rather indications him being 'screwed up'. This feeds into a number of discourses which consider how women, in trying to resolve the love/abuse dilemma, will explain it as the boyfriend being messed up, having anger problems or having had a hard life (Jackson, 2001).

As with Farzana I often felt torn between feminist 'consciousness-raising' commitments and my Rogerian commitment to working with her conceptualisations. I struggled to work with my conflicted self by engaging with her process, step by step. Immersing myself within her framework enabled me to engage more empathically, accepting and working with her journey. This did not mean that I self-abdicated but rather I was able to give space to my struggle without it taking over Jessica's own struggles. The two were not mutually exclusive but rather interwoven in ways which emphasised the persistence of unchallenged media and mainstream-fed conceptions of heterosexual relationships. This creation of an accepting, non-judgemental space in which Jessica could explore the conflicts in her life was fundamental. My belief in her trustworthiness could enable me 'to vacate the position of expert and instead work to enable the client to realize [her] own resources and self-understanding' (Hawtin, 2000: 172).

Having said that, when Jessica reached a point where she recognised her experience of the relationship as abusive, at some unwelcome level I felt vindicated and am aware that despite all my best intentions I was still harbouring elements of a belief of 'knowing better'! Writing this down is uncomfortable and highlights how sometimes feminism and PCT can clash, blocking my ability to work without judgement.

Empathising with her sense of betrayal and hurt was painful and fundamental to our therapeutic engagement. Being able to engage with the Rogerian belief in the authenticity and actualising tendency of the client seemed so helpful to her process. It meant that the space was created for Jessica to explore without being told what and how to feel. Emerging from this stage in the process was her shame. Shame is often a very powerful and stultifying response to DV and can keep women immobilised (Walker, 1990; Sharma, 2001; Jackson, 2001). This is linked with DV, as discussed before, being seen as a reaction to women doing something wrong. So the shame in not being a good enough woman/wife feeds into this belief as does the shame of being a 'victim' which is often characterised as irresponsible and self-pitying (Jackson, 2001).

Caught up in this was her belief that this 'sort of thing' didn't happen to people from her background and class. Again it was important to work both with the societal stereotype which places DV as a working-class phenomenon without losing site of Jessica's own understanding of what was happening. For Jessica the maintenance of the introject that 'it shouldn't happen to women like her' resulted in her working hard to find explanations for the violence that fit this belief. Rogerian theory discusses how we will endeavour to maintain an introject particularly when it is challenged, until we are ready to renegotiate our understanding (Colledge, 2002; Thorne, 1992). We stayed in this uncomfortable space for some time; feeling congruently stuck with what was happening, and what should be happening. It formed a significant stage where Jessica was able to name her partner's behaviour as abusive—thereby validating her experiencing. Once the abuse was 'named' the work seemed to speed along. While the sense of shame remained she was able to confide and seek support from close friends and family, enabling her to feel less isolated within her abuse.

The staying with and clarifying her sense of unreality and conflict was a constant part of our process. In conjunction with this, Jessica came to her own understanding of how the moral responsibility for the success of a heterosexual relationship often resides with the woman, which in turn means when it fails the failure is often felt to be hers (Mahoney, 1994). Staying with the hurt and anger, while uncomfortable, was a rich space in which we shared the difficulty of being angry and a woman. I found myself often feeling furious and energised by her experiences and at some level wanting to grab her by the hand and flee. My own framework sometimes struggled to allow her the space to experience the denial. My desire for her to 'see' her experiencing as abusive was often very strong. It is at times like this when I try to work very closely with the core conditions of congruence, empathy and acceptance. Their value lies in the belief that working with the client's framework cultivates therapeutic growth and self-realisation. I have a great deal of commitment and belief in the vitality of the empathic engagement with the client and this enables me to [mostly] stay with the client rather than prioritise my own feminist frameworks. However, this belief does often struggle with my own sense of the oppressive frameworks which seek to maintain control and encourage conformity. While I felt able to reflect on the struggles in response to Jessica's process, I am also aware that my own idealism was itching to get loose! I know I was not always successful in accepting Jessica's own understanding and this, for me, is the constant dilemma in terms of working with both PCT and feminism.

CONCLUSION

What I have hopefully illustrated in this chapter is the value, and difficulty, of working with PCT and feminism. The scenarios I have explored clearly demonstrate the chaotic and multifaceted nature of DV and that there are no easy answers. It is about focusing on where the woman is in her life and working with her in her framework and her world. For me it is also about acknowledging that the process of 'becoming a person is made difficult by internal factors [which] may be impeded by external, social and political constraints' (Waterhouse, 1993: 64). The world of DV can be hugely distressing and even debilitating when entering into it with the woman. The potential for Rogerian counselling with its open, accepting and empathic approach to provide space for the women to 'be' is clear. The trusting of the client's world takes nothing away from her, nor does it try to control her process but rather walks alongside her experiencing.

Feminism also honours the woman's individual reality and her understanding of her world. It places this meaning within a political and social context which is defined and controlled by patriarchal norms and values. Thus, a framework for 'understanding' women's experience of DV is given, linking it to notions of masculinity, femininity and power relations inclusive of racial, cultural, sexuality and class positions. The strength of combining PCT and feminism lies in being able to contextualise both my own and my client's responses to DV. Instead of placing the individual outside the political arena, which PCT can do, it locates them within it. Thus, women can begin to make connections with their experience with some of these discourses instead of individualising them as their isolated problems. The conflict arises when either feminism takes precedence over the individual experiencing of the client or PCT minimises informing contextual frameworks other than the family. While at some level this is about feminist theory itself, it is also about me and how I respond and feel in relation to narratives of domestic abuse.

The balance for me then is to be able to acknowledge my feelings and to consider my feminist beliefs as a way of underpinning and potentially informing the therapeutic process. On reflection, what I think sometimes happened with these two scenarios was that I latched onto feminist theory as a way of managing my own sense of helplessness in response to their distress. So perhaps, at the core of this chapter is an emphasis on the need to be flexible and responsive with both approaches, using them together but always giving the centre stage to the client's therapeutic process.

REFERENCES

Batsleer, J, Burman, E, Chantler, K, McIntosh, HS, Pantling, K, Smailes, S and Warner, S (2002) *Domestic Violence and Minoritisation—Supporting women to independence.* Women Studies Research Centre: Manchester Metropolitan University.

Biever, J, De las Fuentes, C, Cashion, L and Franklin, C (1998) The social construction of gender: a comparison of feminist and post-modern approaches, *Counselling Psychology Quarterly, 11*(2): 163–79.

Burstow, B (1992) *Radical Feminist Theory: Working in the context of abuse.* London: Sage.

Choudry, S (1996) *Pakistani Women's Experience of Domestic Violence in Great Britain.* Home Office Research and Statistics Directorate No. 43.

Colledge, R (2002) *Mastering Counselling Theory.* Basingstoke: Palgrave.

Dobash, RE and Dobash, RP (1992) *Women, Violence and Social Change.* London: Routledge.

Dryden, W and Mytton, J (1999) *Four Approaches to Counselling and Psychotherapy.* London: Routledge.

Gordon, P (1996) A fear of difference? Some reservations about intercultural therapy and counselling, *Psychodynamic Counselling 2*(2): 196–208.

Hague, G and Malos, E (1999) Homeless children and domestic violence, in P Vostanis and A Cumella (eds) *Homeless Children: Problems and needs.* London: Jessica Kingsley, pp. 68–82.

Hanmer, J (2000) Domestic violence and gender relations: contexts and connections, in J Hanmer and C Itzin (eds) *Home Truths About Domestic Violence.* London: Routledge, pp. 9–23.

Hawtin, S (2000) Person-Centred Counselling and Psychotherapy, in S Palmer (ed)

Introduction to Counselling and Psychotherapy. London: Sage, pp. 172–85.

Hearn, J (1995) Policy Development and Implementation Seminars: *Patterns of Agency Contacts with Men Who Have Been Violent to Known Women, Research Paper No 13.* Research Unit on Violence, Abuse and Gender Relations, University of Bradford.

Jackson, S (2001) Happily Ever After: Young women's stories of abuse in heterosexual love relationships, *Feminism and Psychotherapy, 11*(3): 305–21.

Kelly, L (1987) The Continuum of Sexual Violence, in J Hamner and M Maynard (eds) *Women, Violence and Social Control.* Basingstoke: MacMillan, pp. 46–60.

Lyddon, W (1998) Social construction in counselling psychology: a commentary and critique, *Counselling Psychology Quarterly 11*(2): pp. 215–22.

Mahoney, MR (1994) Victimisation or Oppression? Women's lives, violence and agency, in M Albertson Fineman and R Mykitiuk (eds) *The Public Nature of Private Violence: The discovery of domestic abuse.* New York: Routledge, pp. 59–92.

Marecek, J and Kravetz, D (1998) Power and Agency in Feminist Therapy, in IB Seu and MC Heenan (eds) *Feminism and Psychotherapy.* London: Sage, pp. 13–29.

Marshall, H, Woollett, A and Dosanjh, N (1998) Researching Marginalised Standpoints: Some tensions around plural standpoints and diverse 'experiences', in C Griffin, K Henwood and A Phoenix (eds) *Standpoints and Differences.* London: Sage, pp. 115–34.

Maynard, M and Winn, J (1997) Women, Violence and Male Power, in V Robinson and D Richardson (eds) *Introducing Women's Studies* (2nd ed). Basingstoke: Macmillan, pp. 175–97.

McClosky, KA and Fraser, JS (1997) Using feminist MRI brief therapy during initial contact with victims of domestic violence, *Psychotherapy, 34*: 433–66.

Mearns, D (2003) *Developing Person-Centred Counselling* (2nd ed). London: Sage.

Mooney, J (2000) Revealing the hidden figure of domestic violence, in J Hanmer and C Itzin (eds) *Home Truths About Domestic Violence.* London: Routledge, pp. 24–43.

Nelson-Jones, R (1996) *The Theory and Practice of Counselling* (2nd ed). London: Cassell.

Radford, J and Stanko, E (1996) Violence against women and children: the contradictions of crime control under patriarchy, in M Hester, L Kelly and J Radford (eds) *Women, Violence and Male Power.* Buckingham: OUP, pp. 65–80.

Radford, L (1987) Legalising Woman Abuse, in J Hamner and M Maynard (eds) *Women, Violence and Social Control.* Basingstoke: MacMillan, pp. 135–51.

Rogers, CR (1959) A theory of therapy, personality and interpersonal relationships, as developed in the client-centered framework, in S Koch (ed) *Psychology: A Study of a Science. Volume 3: Formulations of the person and the social context.* New York: McGraw-Hill, pp. 184–256.

Rogers, CR (1962) The interpersonal relationship: The core of guidance. *Harvard Educational Review 4*(32): 416–29.

Seu, IB (1998) Change and Theoretical Frameworks in Feminist Therapy, in IB Seu and MC Heenan (eds) *Feminism and Psychotherapy.* London: Sage, pp. 203–18.

Sharma, A (2001) Healing the wounds of domestic violence, *Violence Against Women, 7*(12)

December 2001: 1405–28.

Stanko, E (1985) *Intimate Intrusions.* London: Routledge and Kegan Paul.

Stanko, E (1987) Typical Violence, Normal Precaution: Men, women and interpersonal violence in England, Wales, Scotland and the USA, in J Hamner and M Maynard (eds) *Women, Violence and Social Control.* Basingstoke: MacMillan, pp. 122–34.

Thorne, B (1992) *Carl Rogers.* London: Sage.

Towns, A and Adams, P (2000) 'If I Really Loved Him Enough, He Would Be Okay', *Violence Against Women,* 6(6): 558–85.

Walker, M (1990) *Women in Therapy and Counselling.* Milton Keynes: OUP.

Waterhouse, RL (1993) 'Wild Women Don't Have the Blues': A Feminist Critique of 'Person-Centred' Counselling and Psychotherapy, *Feminism and Psychotherapy,* 3(1): 55–71.

WOMAN-CENTRED PRACTICE

MONICA HILL

I have been involved in Bradford Rape Crisis Group (BRCG) for over 20 years. My experience has been that from our earliest beginnings we have been putting into practice both feminist and person-centred principles and values. These values apply not only to the services we provide to our callers and clients but also to the way we manage the organisation, train ourselves and others and relate to each other within the group.

What follows is clearly my individual experience of one organisation and cannot be taken as representative of other Rape Crisis (RC) groups or as representing the views of everyone in BRCG.[1] In writing this piece I have been aware of a constant tension between 'I' and 'we'. When am I speaking only for myself, when is it legitimate to speak on behalf of my colleagues, my clients and of 'women'? This reflects the struggle we have as an organisation to meet individual needs, to recognise the uniqueness of every woman and her experience and yet to recognise the commonality of our experience of sexual violence and our collective need for change in a society where rape of women is still condoned, denied or minimised.

Whilst writing this piece, I asked other members of the organisation for their thoughts and experiences—their replies are included here.

WOMAN-CENTRED PRACTICE

I use this term to describe what I see as a synthesis of feminist and person-centred

---

[1] The organisation is now known as Bradford Rape Crisis and Sexual Abuse Survivors Service, including Project Jyoti (working with Black and Asian women) and New Hall Counselling Service (working with women in prison). I use BRCG to describe the group of women, paid and unpaid, who are involved in any part of the service.

values and theory, which informs our clinical practice. We do not require our counsellors or therapists to be trained or identified as person-centred but we do ask that they consider how their practice may or may not be congruent with certain values which include, for example, that the client is the expert on her own life. Women working as helpline and support workers are not usually trained counsellors but their in-house training includes an exploration of the person-centred core conditions and their relevance to working in an empowering way. Our focus is on the whole woman, rather than problem-focused. Our experience in working with survivors shows that sexual violence reaches into every aspect of women's lives leaving little or nothing untouched. It is impossible to say where the effects of rape and child sexual abuse begin and end. We do not offer a prescribed recovery programme or a set view of what the healing journey looks like. We work with each client at her own pace, and to the depth and breadth that she chooses. Much of our therapeutic work with women is long-term, where clients are exploring the whole of their life experience and relationships.

The term 'woman-centred' does not mean 'person-centred' for women. Instead it implies an understanding of what it is to be a person that takes into account that we are gendered human beings. Our self-concept and our conditions of worth are at all times heavily influenced by our gender and other factors such as 'race', colour, class and culture(s). Central to feminist practice is a commitment to work with both commonality and difference; without acknowledgment of difference, whole groups of women are marginalised and any hope of real equality is lost. 'Woman-centred' does not prescribe a certain kind of womanhood. Instead it recognises the political implications of a therapy that aims to allow women to become themselves in ways that go beyond gender roles, expectations and stereotypes. As women become more fully human, men too can step outside the straitjacket of 'masculinity'.

TRAINING

The organisation was set up by women for women, from the ground up. There were no professionals involved at the beginning, though some of us have gained professional qualifications along the way. Our starting point was our own responses and experiences of sexual violence. Not all of us had been raped (this is an assumption made by some) but sexual violence had impacted on us all in some way. All women have experienced the fear of rape and we all have to accommodate or deal with this fear in our daily lives. Rape and the fear of rape affect the way every woman lives her life and the choices she makes—this may not always be in awareness. In Bradford in the late seventies and early eighties it was brought sharply into awareness for most. Peter Sutcliffe, also known as the Yorkshire Ripper, was murdering women. Part of the media response was to focus on women's responsibility to keep themselves safe by never going out alone without a male escort for protection. Ironically, at the same time, feminists were discovering that women were most at risk of rape and violence from men that they knew.[2] It was clear then that as well as being a devastating attack on an individual woman, sexual violence is a means by which all women are socially controlled. It was in this climate that Bradford Rape Crisis Group was created.

In preparing ourselves to offer a service to other women—long before any of us undertook any formal counselling training—we met as a group and explored our own feelings and experiences. London Rape Crisis sent us their helpline training manual and we sat in a circle taking turns to read to the group, argue and discuss. I don't think any of us, at that stage, had heard of Rogers; we didn't see ourselves as an encounter group, but looking back that is exactly what we were doing. We set out to put feminist theory into practice; without knowing it we were putting into practice person-centred theory too. For many of us, from the beginning and still today, being part of a Rape Crisis group has been a life-changing experience on many levels. (See also Cameron 1997 and Wood 1995.)

> My placement with BRCG has opened a door into a place where I am enjoying the work and being with people who have changed and enriched my life. (G., volunteer counsellor and management group member)

I think respect, empathy and genuineness were mentioned in those early training notes and were easily taken on board by us because they fitted with the way we wanted to relate to each other and our feminist commitment to equality. We saw no division between our future clients and ourselves; we were creating something for ourselves. We were offering not so much therapy as solidarity. 'We turned the best part of ourselves toward the best part of our colleagues in order to accomplish something of lasting value that neither could have done alone' (Wood 1995: 23).

In recruiting staff, volunteers and students on placement we place a much higher value on particular attitudes and openness to experience than on formal qualifications or level of training. In common with client-centred therapy training we consider personal development to be perhaps the most crucial element in the development of a counsellor/therapist. Developing self-awareness, personal growth and self-care remain central to our in-house training. Trainees are encouraged to develop a high level of responsibility for themselves and the group.

Autonomy, so highly valued within a person-centred approach, raises particular issues for women. Our society praises and celebrates men's self-actualisation whilst denigrating or punishing women's. Where men are 'driven', women are 'selfish'. We can compare and contrast media views of men with those of women who have been successful in business or sport and those who take risks to achieve a personal goal. For example, Alison Hargreaves, the first woman to climb Everest unsupported by

---

[2.] This continues to be the case. 1998 and 2000 British Crime Surveys show that strangers were responsible for only 8% of rapes.

Sherpas or oxygen, who died on an expedition to K2, was vilified for her irresponsibility in leaving behind her two children with their father while she attempted dangerous climbs. (Observer Magazine 30/3/03)

We recognise the weight of social conditioning that often compels women to care for others, neglect themselves and gain power or control over others by caring. These kinds of introjected conditions of worth that may or may not be in awareness have to be confronted before we are able to offer our clients a fully respectful and more equal therapeutic relationship. As girls, later to be women (both clients and therapists) we learn to get our own needs met through attending to others. Our mothers may prepare us for disappointment at the same time as teaching us the rules of the femininity game—we learn to look 'dependent' on men, at the same time knowing that our deepest needs will not be recognised or met. We may learn to deny that the need exists, to ourselves, and others. We learn to submerge our own needs under the cloak of caring for others, giving away what we most want for ourselves, and silently feeling shame for wanting. This has a complex effect on our relationship with ourselves, and each other, in a service by women for women.

Our experience echoes that of the London Women's Therapy Centre as described by Eichenbaum and Orbach:

> ... far from the popular belief that women were dependent on others, in fact women strongly protected themselves against showing their dependency needs. Women expressed feelings of shame and self-dislike for having these needs in the first place. Time and again we heard our clients assuming that they should not and could not expect care and attention from anyone else. (1984: 13)

For most of us as girl children, our main carer was a woman and this leads to some highly contradictory messages, for example: 'be like me, but don't be like me.' (Walker, 1990: 45) The complexities of a mother-daughter relationship can be replayed in other relationships between women. Women often rely on each other for support yet at the same time we are taught that as part of growing up we must separate from mother and learn to rely on, whilst taking care of, men. We are taught to compete with each other for male attention and to put each other down in the process. Women often come to therapy with an idealised self and an idealised view of the therapist, which sometimes masks an internalised hatred of self as woman.

Deep longing, deprivation, envy, anger and competition are themes that emerge and re-emerge during therapy, training, supervision and working together. If we neglect to nurture and develop our own positive self-regard as women therapists, the prizing of our women clients is compromised and contradictory. Unlike men we are not expected to take or demand power but to gain it, if at all, through manipulation, or by the back door. This sexist conditioning has an impact not only on the therapeutic relationship between two women but also on the dynamics of a women-only group. We tend to have high expectations of each other as women and we have had to work through great pain and disappointment when (inevitably) we fail to live up to the high standards we set for ourselves, and each other.

STRUCTURE

For many years we operated as a collective with weekly meetings. Reluctantly we moved to a different structure with a management group as, in common with many similar organisations, we found that most volunteers were not willing to take on the responsibilities of being employers. In addition there has been the pressure from funding bodies to 'professionalise'. However we have maintained an open, democratic and largely non-hierarchical structure where although there are different areas of responsibility, everyone has a say and decisions are made by working for a consensus, not by voting. I see much common ground within feminist and person-centred approaches to organisation particularly in terms of commitment to working in a collaborative style that equalises power and responsibility and a valuing of every member of the group.

> The absence of hierarchy allows everyone to give of their best, and integrity is paramount. There is room for volunteers to grow, and to initiate events. (G.)

Despite criticism and sometimes hostility we have continued to be an organisation run by women for women. Perhaps this hostility is rooted in the expectation that women will take care of men's needs. Women-only provision with an explicit focus on women's needs challenges this assumption. In mixed organisations women's needs and perspective are easily lost. As well as providing a safe and appropriate space for women to heal, this also keeps us focused on a woman-centred understanding of sexual violence and working therapeutically. It also seems to have a profound effect on how women working in the organisation come to feel about themselves:

> The satisfaction I have felt about being a woman is something I have never really experienced up until I started working here ... society, culture and the media had taught me that I wasn't enough ... I wasn't equal ... We as women need to learn to value ourselves to understand that we are of worth and importance and the best way and the only way we can ever achieve this is if women themselves take the responsibility to value themselves and each other. (H., Project Jyoti worker)

> I value being part of a rare female-owned, run and catering for women organisation. I think we are a model of good practice for the wider voluntary sector and I'm sure some statutory services. The service we offer to women is a vital lifeline, somewhere safe to go, to help them make sense of the pain and abuse they've

225

> endured; we expose the abuse, we don't normalise it. I don't do direct sexual abuse work with women any more, but the training and ethos of working within BRCG has given me greater awareness generally and affects how I treat others. (E., ex-volunteer, ex-worker, currently management group member)

> The organisation I feel values what and who I am, my sexuality, my experiences, my spirituality. I feel that the members of the organisation understand oppression ... Being a lesbian myself I want my sexuality to have a visibility where I work. This is true of our organisation. (e., volunteer counsellor).

Many feminists like myself, working in women-only organisations, are delighted to see men setting up their own survivors' groups and services—taking care of their own and other men's emotional needs. We are also interested to note that they do not face criticism for being men-only groups. I believe there is still a need for women to organise separately in order to confront sexism and truly empower each other.

> It is important to stress that persons exist as women and men, to delve into sex- and gender-specific issues and to celebrate diversity in this regard. (Schmid 2002: 67)

WOMAN-CENTRED THERAPY

Just as the client-centred approach challenged some of the traditional orthodoxy around therapy, the political view of many women involved in RC groups has been highly critical. We have seen the ways that therapy has been used to keep women in their place or 'adjust' to second-class status.

Too often therapy and therapeutic technique have been shrouded in mystery, held onto by experts. A key aim of ours has been accessibility, not just of therapy itself but also information and understanding about therapy and how it can help. We recognise the very real limits on women's power and choices, whilst at the same time working to enable women to find the power they do have and discover their capacity for self-healing. This includes sharing information, resources and sometimes 'techniques' or 'tools' for self-care, self-awareness or self-development. These are offered, never imposed; the woman's right to choose is paramount. As a general rule we do not take referrals and we always check out whether a client has chosen to come to us or if she's under pressure from someone else.

As feminists we are critical of any theory that has been developed largely by men, in a patriarchal society, including person-centred theory. 'Gender-neutral' or non-political approaches are likely to simply reinforce the status quo. (See also

Shaw, Chapter 12, this volume.) For some of us this is one of the difficulties with 'non-directiveness':

> One issue for me is the tension between the person-centred focus on the individual, and the reality of the client's relational and social disempowerment. This tension was made particularly evident for me by a client who spoke of her sadness that she couldn't have children because she carried the belief that all people who are abused will themselves become abusers, given the opportunity.
>
> Whilst I felt it was valuable to challenge this client in a person-centred way, inviting her to look at her sense of her own capacity to give love and keep a child safe, I also gave her the information that made it clear that her belief didn't fit with the bigger picture of abuse and abusers as shown by the statistical evidence. My approach with this client was also informed by my awareness of her perceptual bias towards self-blame, and how this was continually reinforced through her experience of relating to others within a framework of shared patriarchal assumptions. To the extent that I was bringing in information that was external to the client, and consciously seeking to foster the awareness that would help empower her, I feel I was stepping out of the person-centred ground of non-directiveness. (S., volunteer/student counsellor)

We look for what is useful in a theory and rethink or adapt it to our own reality and experience. Many of us feel that there is much common ground to build on person-centred and feminist theory but feminists have also made a huge contribution (perhaps under-recognised) to advances in analytic and psychodynamic theory and other therapeutic approaches such as Gestalt. At BRCG we have deliberately chosen not to restrict our counsellors and therapists to one theoretical model, unlike many women's therapy services that are aligned to one (usually psychodynamic) approach.

In common with the Person-Centred Approach, we never seek to pathologise our clients. Rape is one of the ultimate tools of a patriarchal society that seeks to deny women freedom and power. Just as Rogers saw every person as always seeking actualisation—though that may be expressed in bizarre or apparently distorted behaviour—we have understood that a woman struggling to reclaim her power may behave in self-destructive ways. We view this self-destructiveness not as pathology but as internalised oppression. Similarly the rapist is not suffering from some kind of pathology and rape cannot be understood in this way—as the act of a sick individual. Rape is both the cause and effect of male power and pornographic lies about women. It is the logical outcome in a society that says women are 'lower', that our sexuality is 'dirty' and that our role is to service men. We see women's and men's psychology as socially constructed. We also see a society that has deeply contradictory values around sex and around violence.

We aim not to be restricted by the limits of the therapy room. We did not set out to be a counselling service only and we think carefully about the barriers that different women face in getting support around issues of violence. This has included working in schools, youth groups and community centres, using the places where women already meet and doing outreach work. We have set up a specific project for Black and Asian women—Project Jyoti—and a service within a women's prison.

As a feminist therapist and Rape Crisis trainer, I work within the following system of core beliefs and values. I see some of these beliefs and values as grounded in both feminist and person-centred theory, some are based more on feminist theory and practice and may present a challenge to person-centred practice, if not to theory.

- The client is the expert on her own life. The therapist's expertise lies in creating the conditions where the client can find her own path, her own healing.
- Equality: this must be worked for rather than assumed. Being willing to recognise and address both commonalities and differences between myself, my clients, and my colleagues. Recognising my role responsibility and my personal power and working in ways that enable rather than disable others.
- The personal is political. In some ways this is similar to Rogers suggestion that what is most individual is most universal. The significant difference is perhaps the word 'political', which implies issues of power. It is women's very personal experience that provides the information about power relations in society. The point has been made that one way to judge a society is to look at how those with less power are treated. Look again at the reaction when those with less power begin to take power or resist oppression.
- Balance rather than competition between opposites—this does not mean 'having it all' but I think it relates well to the idea of congruence—allowing ourselves to be more fully human, unrestricted by gender stereotyping. It also means valuing both 'feminine' and 'masculine' attributes and ways of thinking. It means a move away from the patriarchal model of dominance and submission as a way to deal with conflict and difference. It implies less competitive, more collaborative, non-hierarchical thinking. (See also Chaplin, 1988: 7–10.)
- Recognising oppression and its different effects. Understanding and awareness enhance and deepen empathy. Sexism could be seen as the model for other forms of oppression—the distortion of, the dehumanising of the 'other'—racism, homophobia, disablism, abuse of children. It is no coincidence that rape is routinely used as a weapon of war and has only recently been recognised as a war crime.
- Recognising that women's (and men's) psychology is socially constructed. Conditions of worth are created not just by primary caregivers and the family but by the child's wider community and culture. Gender splitting is deep-rooted and insidious; it may not always be in awareness. (See also Natiello, 1999: 163–7 and Proctor, Chapter 11, this volume.) Being congruent raises particular challenges for women when it comes up against a self-structure, and a self-concept that have been formed in a sexist world.

• Awareness of both subjective and objective realities. As a feminist therapist, both aspects are important; clients are struggling often with both internalised oppression and external barriers to their fully becoming persons. Clients are attempting to manage not just their own, but society's incongruence. (See also Shaw, Chapter 12, this volume.)

• Recognising the particular issues that may arise for women around dependence/ independence. We may have difficulty recognising our needs, expressing them and having them met.

• The right to autonomy and self-determination. Woman-centred practice includes an awareness of the particular tensions that arise for women and for people in communities where the 'self' is always 'self-in-relation-to-others'.

• Individual acts or behaviour either perpetuate or challenge existing power relations. Rape is an abuse of male power that acts as a form of social control of women (and children). It is one of the most basic attacks on a woman's right to be, her autonomy, self-determination, freedom and personhood.

A feminist perspective on women's psychology and sexual violence need not detract from a commitment to stay close to the client's moment-to-moment experiencing. I believe it does sensitise me to possible elements in the client's experience and enables my awareness of what is unspoken or assumed. My frame of reference will inform and influence my empathic response, just as it will in a therapist with a different perspective. (See Villas-Boas Bowen, 1996: 90.) Bringing a feminist perspective into client-centred practice does not reduce my commitment to being non-controlling nor my respect for the client's autonomy—I would argue instead that it enhances it and that therapists who have not considered a feminist perspective are likely to unintentionally reinforce sexist expectations of men and women in their work with clients. This perspective and understanding also helps me to stay present with a client when I'm feeling frustrated or stuck. It informs my values, my respect and my acceptance both of myself, and the women I work with. It helps me to reconnect with my capacity for empathy and trust when I'm feeling overwhelmed, drained or disheartened.

Taking the step from individual therapy towards a social therapy. (Schmid, 2002: 68)

As women committed to the struggle against violence, we are all committed to one another; that is, to a worldwide community of women. (G.)

From the beginning we set out to be a campaigning organisation as well as supplying a much needed service. However the demands on the service have been so great and the resources so small that we have been forced to prioritise so that now our involvement in campaigning has almost disappeared and even our public education role has been greatly reduced. We have quite rightly prioritised the expressed needs of women contacting the service for individual help but other important projects such as raising awareness in schools and therapeutic group work have been greatly reduced or lost. I feel both politically frustrated as a feminist and personally frustrated as the mother of two young boys that we are not doing more to challenge the beliefs, attitudes, values and power structures that perpetuate sexual violence.

When I ask myself 'how did we get here?' I can answer that we have quite rightly been 'client-led', putting individual women survivors first and responding to what they most wanted from us. I could also say it's about funding; government and local government generally want services not campaigns. I can also say we have been part of a wave focused on individual solutions that both feminism and the Person-Centred Approach must challenge.

> Taking the human seriously as a social being, as a person in a group, results in a re-evaluation of the indication for single and group therapy. The question arises of how far the group is the therapeutic place to be chosen first, as opposed to the 'pathology' of over-emphasizing single therapy ... ' (Schmid 2002: 67).

I see working in groups as highly valuable for both clients and counsellors/therapists. It helps us to place our personal experience in context as well as breaking down isolation, enabling mutual support and experiential learning. One member of an in-house supervision group said:

> We learnt about unconditional positive regard and being non-judgemental at college. It always felt like just theory there but here I feel I've really experienced it. (T., student on placement)

Another says:

> I'd like to acknowledge and celebrate the way I'm able to experience myself through being part of the group of workers at BRCG. I feel there is a genuine commitment to holding the core conditions in the way we relate to each other, and the resulting ethos is one of empowerment. I've found myself able to be very open and honest, and to speak out effectively when I've been unhappy about something—which is totally new to me in a work environment. I've also been able to experience making mistakes as part of an acknowledged process of learning, which has directly challenged my usual process of self-blame and shame. Best of all is the quality of the support I have received here, and my new found ability to ask for it when I need it. (S., volunteer/student counsellor)

Individual perceptions of need are partly socially constructed. Whereas in the late 1980s I was running two survivors groups a week, in more recent years survivors contacting the service are more likely to see individual therapy as the best path to healing. We have become providers of a professional service but that does not have to mean we lose what we set out with—a sense of solidarity. As a feminist organisation and as feminist therapists I think we have been swept along by the wave but also waving (not drowning!): trying to hold onto some broader view, some collective power, some change beyond individual healing.

RADICAL BECOMES MAINSTREAM OR DOES IT?

Both feminist and person-centred theories are revolutionary in that they challenge conventional wisdom and traditional power relationships. It could also be said that both approaches have been, to some extent, taken on or absorbed into mainstream thinking—a victory of sorts but with inherent dangers. Just as the PCA has changed the language used in therapy, e.g. client instead of patient, so feminists have changed the language around sexual violence, for example 'survivor' instead of 'victim'.

In the 1970s and 80s, feminist research and feminist organisations working with survivors, such as ours and other Rape Crisis groups, succeeded in highlighting the prevalence and the nature of child sexual abuse. However our work has been largely appropriated and transformed by the therapy industry and statutory organisations. The social meaning and context of sexual violence is lost and the arena has become one of:

> ... increasingly individualised frameworks and practices. Sexual violence has become the vehicle for the production of a multitude of syndromes and disorders, all of which require 'treatment'.
> (Hester, Kelly and Radford, 1996: 11)

As a feminist therapist, I find myself in a double-bind. I recognise that labels and 'syndromes' are rarely empowering for the client and from a person-centred perspective they do little to enhance my capacity for empathy with an individual client. At the same time, other professionals seem to respond with greater compassion and understanding when medical terms are used to describe some of the common responses to rape and child sexual abuse that women experience. It would also be true to say that some women will feel reassured by the idea that they are suffering from 'post-traumatic stress disorder' and it beats being labelled as 'mad'. (See also Proctor, Chapter 11, this volume). However this focus on the 'victim' and what she is suffering from completely avoids the issue of why rape happens and the power context in which it thrives and goes unchallenged.

Feminists, like myself, have difficulty with a view of power that is focused purely at a subjective, individual level:

> A central tenet of post structuralism is that material power does not reside primarily in structures of contemporary western society,

> such as the patriarchal relations of oppression and subordination, class relations of capitalism or the racism of post colonial societies. Instead power is represented as diffuse, infusing all social and personal relationships. Being everywhere, but nowhere in particular, it dissolves in complex and confusing ways within the subjectivity of unique individuals. (Hester, Kelly and Radford, 1996: 9)

There is a danger with all therapy, including Client-Centred Therapy, that a focus on individual, subjective experience neglects, denies or minimises the significance of structural power. So individuals are helped to recover, but power and abuse of power continues unchanged and unchallenged. A purely political response is also limited in that it neglects individuals' need for support and a safe place to become all that they can be.

I have often experienced clients moving from 'I' to 'we', from a position of 'how can I get through this' to a position of 'how can I help others to get through this?' or 'how can I give something back?' Whilst this can be understood as evidence of the 'fully-functioning person' who becomes more fully herself and more socialised, I have a note of caution. This may also be an expression of the introjected condition of worth 'I must give more than I take'. Women often feel deeply unentitled to the service and will minimise or trivialise their own experiences of violence, sometimes offering to end therapy early 'because there must be others who need your service more than me'. Again this echoes the experience of the London Women's Therapy Centre, as described by Eichenbaum and Orbach:

> This need to give and the difficulty with receiving was such a feature of each woman we encountered that we began to see it as central to the development of women's psychology. (1984: 13)

As women we often have difficulty balancing our own needs with those of others. As a feminist therapist I aim to hold a perspective that includes both the wood and the individual trees, the outer as well as the inner reality of our lives, the personal and the political power relationships which shape us.

CONCLUSION

I hope that I have demonstrated that woman-centred practice embodies the values of the Person-Centred Approach both in how we do therapy and how we organise ourselves. It is possible to put both feminist and person-centred values into practice in therapy, in training, in working together and in organising. I believe that the Person-Centred Approach can be enriched by feminism that offers a wider understanding of what it means to be women and men, as well as an understanding of how our life experience and our self-concepts are shaped in part by our place in societies that still accord different status, power and understandings to individuals based on existing power relations. Who is seen as 'normal' and who is seen as 'other', different or deviant is still largely framed and determined by those existing power relations. We are still limited by gender splitting, racism and other deeply ingrained power relations.

The tension I described in my introduction between the 'I' and the 'we' is alive and well in the therapy room, the person-centred group and feminist organisations like BRCG. For feminists there is no individual liberation without political and social change. A person-centred approach informed by feminist understanding holds out a possibility for managing this tension in creative, challenging and empowering ways that go beyond the therapy room.

REFERENCES

Bowen, M Villas-Boas (1996) The myth of non-directiveness: The case of Jill, in B Farber, D Brink and P Raskin (eds) *The Psychotherapy of Carl Rogers.* New York: Guildford Press.

Chaplin, J (1988) *Feminist Counselling in Action.* London: Sage.

Cameron, R (1997) The personal is political: Re-reading Rogers. *Person-Centred Practice* 5(2): 16–20.

Eichenbaum, L and Orbach, S (1984) *What do Women Want?* London: Fontana.

Hester, M, Kelly, L and Radford, J (eds) (1996) *Women, Violence and Male Power: Feminist research, activism and practice.* Buckingham: Open University Press.

Natiello, P (1999) The Person-Centered Approach: Solution to gender splitting, in I Fairhurst (ed) *Women Writing in the Person-Centred Approach.* Ross-on-Wye: PCCS Books.

Schmid, PF (2002) Knowledge or Acknowledgement? Psychotherapy as 'the art of not-knowing'—Prospects on further developments of a radical paradigm. *Person-Centered and Experiential Psychotherapies* 1(1 & 2): 56–70.

Walker, M (1990) *Women in Therapy and Counselling.* Milton Keynes: Open University Press.

Wood, JK (1995) The Person-Centered Approach: Toward an understanding of its implications. *The Person-Centered Journal* 2(2).

THE EDITORS

Gillian Proctor. For as long as I can remember, I have been incensed by the oppression and social injustices in this world. Constantly questioning taken-for-granted authority, I have always been intrigued by different responses to the mad world in which we live, and how we survive this madness in creative ways. Following my natural curiosity about people and survival in varying circumstances, I have always loved to travel and this book collaboration is one result of my travels. I am a Doctor in Clinical Psychology, currently working as part of the mental health therapy team for North Bradford Primary Care Trust and an honorary lecturer with the Centre for Citizenship and Community Mental Health at Bradford University, West Yorkshire, UK. Being paid to indulge my curiosity about people is a privileged position to be in, and I take the responsibility that comes with my position very seriously. My particular interests are in ethics and power, and my exploration of power in therapy resulted in *The Dynamics of Power in Counselling and Therapy: Ethics, politics and practice*, PCCS Books, 2002. Whilst the Person-Centred Approach helps me to concentrate on the uniqueness and potential for growth and creativity of each individual, feminism brings my focus to the commonalities within dominant and marginalised groups and the effects of socially constructed positions and limitations on people.

Mary Beth Napier, PsyD, MPS. Imagine my delight when I was able to combine my two passions in one book! I am a clinical psychologist, supervisor of therapy students, teacher and conduct neuropsychological assessments. In each of these areas, feminism and client-centered principles guide my actions and attitudes towards others. I feel privileged to share my life with my partner of 14 years and to have the opportunity to add writer and editor to the list of activities that give me life. In previous years I have been a campus, youth and music minister and a spirited camp counselor. All of these activities have taught me to listen carefully, to love passionately and to work diligently to create connections between people and between ideas. I hope that this book can bring together individuals to continue this dialogue of empowerment.

THE CONTRIBUTORS

Gay (Swenson) Barfield, PhD, LicMFT was a member of the Center for Studies of the Person (CSP) based in La Jolla, California, for nearly 30 years, where she helped create one of the first Women's Centers in San Diego and the 'Living Now Institute', among other national and international events. In 1984, she and her long-time colleague, Dr Carl R. Rogers, became Co-Directors at CSP of the Carl Rogers Institute for Peace, a project to apply person-centered principles to real and potential crisis situations. She has received numerous honors from organizations recognizing outstanding women, and in 1992 received an award from the County of San Diego for 'improving human relations', particularly for a series of cross-cultural 'Living Room Dialogues' on inflammatory US/Mexican border issues.

She strongly believes in working to increase mutual respect within and across genders, so that we may become more effective and constructive members of all our diverse forms of family, social, political and spiritual systems. For her, combining feminism with Rogers'

Person-Centered Approach, both central to her own best personal changes, makes that more possible. In Hilo, Hawaii, where she now lives, she offers women's groups, counsels individuals and couples, and loves training and 'mentressing' young therapists through what she sees as 'an inspirited Rogerian gender egalitarian lens'. Currently she is writing about her experiences as a gatherer, social activist and idealist over the past 30 years.

Margaret Bird. I have worked with women for a number of years around issues of sexual violence and violence in domestic settings. My training and approach is person-centred and I practise as a counsellor, psychodramatist, groupworker, trainer and supervisor. My work is informed by feminism and at the same time it continually helps to develop my feminist understanding. What I hear and witness always affects me. I make connections with my own thoughts, my own feelings, my own identities, my own experiences of being a woman in the culture I live in, being a woman in this world. I reflect on my relationship to power—when I misuse power and when power is misused over me. As I make connections, I learn more about the workings of power and the effects of powerlessness. For me, feminism offers parallel struggles and rewards with a person-centred way of being—both continue to be empowering and challenging for me, a way of reaching to my true power-within.

Jeffrey HD Cornelius-White, PsyD is an assistant professor of psychology at Texas A&M International University. He teaches primarily in a Master's of Counseling Psychology program and is an activist, cyclist, and husband. Jeff is the managing editor of the *Person-Centered Journal* and an associate editor of the *Renaissance*, the journal and newsletter of the Association for the Development of the Person-Centered Approach, respectively. His scholarly and community work have been primarily concerned with person-centered multicultural counseling, education, and social reform.

Edna Davis. I have been working with children, young people and families surviving sexual violence for 18 years and often wonder what my life was like before my therapeutic training began and before I moved into this area of work. This period of my life has been a time of great richness, growth and learning. Learning not only about me and my life but also about how it sometimes is for women and children who exist in a world that does not always value their 'presence', allow them to exist in their own right or recognize them as human beings. I have applied a person-centred approach to my practice and have tried to integrate creative techniques such as art, drama and psychodrama.

Randall D Ehrbar, PsyD. Dr Randall Ehrbar is a post-doctoral fellow at the University of Minnesota Program in Human Sexuality. He is very interested in client-centered therapy and diversity issues in general. Other interests include human sexuality broadly defined, including: issues of sex, gender, sexuality, and couples relationships. He became interested and aware of issues of difference, justice, and oppression at an early age, as they have been relevant in his own life in a variety of ways. When he was introduced to Client-Centered Therapy, he was immediately drawn to it because of the deep respect for people inherent in this modality and because it fit well with his feminist ideals.

Phoebe C Godfrey, PhD is an assistant professor at Texas A&M International University. She teaches graduate and undergraduate sociology in a manner that attempts to combine feminist critical pedagogy and person-centered education. She is very committed to empowering students in her classrooms as well as working towards progressive social change in her community and throughout the world.

J Wade Hannon, EdD, is an Associate Professor in the Counselor Education Program at North Dakota State University, Fargo, North Dakota, USA, and lives in Moorhead, Minnesota. He is contemplating what it means to be 50 years old when no one over 30 can be trusted. To him, feminism and the Person-Centered Approach both are 'ways in which to enable people to overcome the shackles of oppression and live as liberated human beings'.

Monica Hill. I picked up a copy of Spare Rib (women's liberation magazine) in a newsagent, when I was 16 and felt I finally belonged somewhere. Two years later I moved to Bradford and became a feminist activist. I have been a member of Bradford Rape Crisis Group ever since. When I began training as a therapist, it was the Person-Centred Approach that seemed to me to fit best with feminist politics and practice.

Rosemary Hopkins. As white, heterosexual, able-bodied, educated, and financially secure, I value and celebrate my privileges, my freedoms, and my responsibilities. As a woman in a male dominated and unbalanced world, I strive to live myself fully as wife, mother, grandmother, sister, friend, therapist, community builder, and activist for peace and justice. I welcome dialogue and discussion—<emoyeni@hopkins.net>. Feminism is the 'how' of my *being* myself, as well as part of a global community. Feminist principles nurture me and provide the solidarity that is fundamental to my well*being*. PCA embodies the chosen values of the 'how' of my *doing* all that I do.

Maureen O'Hara. Dr Maureen O'Hara is the President of Saybrook Graduate School, San Francisco. Working with American psychologist Dr Carl R. Rogers, she and several colleagues working in collaboration developed the Person-Centered Approach to psychotherapy and group process. More recently her writings have examined the relationship between large social change and internal psychological adaptation. She has presented nationally and worldwide at events such as the World Psychotherapy Conference in Vienna, World Future Society, OD Network and APA conferences. She is a Distinguished Clinical Member of the California Association for Marriage and Family Therapy, Fellow of the World Academy of Art and Science, Fellow of the American Psychological Association, Fellow of the Meridian Institute on Governance, Leadership Learning and the Future, member of the International Futures Forum at St Andrews University, Scotland.

She writes: 'For me PCA is fundamentally an orientation that trusts that there is an evolutionary principle in all of nature, including human nature, and seeks to align individual actions in accord with that principle. Feminism aligns itself with the same principle and focuses on identifying barriers to the self-realization of women that are created by attitudes and structures of sexism.'

Peter F Schmid is Associate Professor at the University of Graz, Austria, and Faculty Member of Saybrook Graduate School and Research Center, San Francisco; person-centered psychotherapist; practical theologian and pastoral psychologist; founder of person-centered training and further training in Austria; director of the *Academy for Counseling and Psychotherapy* of the Austrian *Institute for Person-Centered Studies (IPS of APG)* and Board Member of both the World Association (*WAPCEPC*) and the European Network (*NEAPCEPC*). He has authored and co-authored eleven books and numerous articles about the anthropology and further developments of the Person-Centered Approach in German and English. He is co-editor of *Person-Centered and Experiential Psychotherapies*, the journal of the World Association, and of the international German language journal *PERSON*. He is also webmaster of *The Person-Centered Website* at <www.pca-online.net>. His main interest is in the genuine development of the Person-Centered Approach and its anthropological foundations. Due to his pursuit of the philosophical notion of 'person' as the underlying foundation in PCA he became convinced that gender issues including the feminist approach need to be paid more attention to in PCA. Thus one of the main priorities of his training programme is gender issues. Homepage: <www.pfs-online.at>.

Clare Shaw. I'm an anarchist first and foremost, which means that I have a deep belief in people's ability to live according to the principle of co-operation rather than competition or co-ercion. Consequently, I am actively committed to challenging hierarchies of power and status in individual relationships and wider society; hierarchies which include those structured around gender, 'race', class and other differences. My own experiences of the psychiatric system have given me a great passion for challenging the profound power differences which characterise that institution; and for working towards meaningful alternatives based on mutuality, co-operation and friendship. My interest in the Person-Centred Approach springs not only from my experiences of therapy and my academic interest in all things 'mental health', but also from an early conversation with Gillian Proctor in which she described Rogers' principles and philosophy, and I concluded that the man must be an anarchist. I think I was wrong now.

Sophie Smailes. I am a practicing person-centred counsellor and a lecturer and researcher in the Health Care Studies Department of Manchester Metropolitan University. The areas of interest I have include issues of diversity, constructs of the self and the counselling relationship. I have co-written one book *Domestic Violence and Minoritisation* and written a number of articles on issues of domestic violence, minoritisation and power (within and without the counselling relationship).

Both the Person-Centred Approach (PCA) and feminism inform who I am and how I work. They are concerned, in varying degrees, with the recognition of the individual's frame of reference and the understanding, and meaning, we have of our lives. I believe we are informed by political, social, familial, gender, cultural, sexual, racial and class norms and constructs. These have implications in terms of our conditions of worth and life experiences. PCA's regard for the individual's experiences as being unique to them endeavours to make no assumptions of meanings while feminism acknowledges that we are part of larger picture which is imbued with inequalities—the potential for these two approaches to compliment each other as well as conflict are what I explore within my chapter.

Deb Steele is a Senior Lecturer in Counselling and Psychotherapy at Nottingham Trent University and is also a British Association for Counselling and Psychotherapy (BACP)

Accredited counsellor and a supervisor in private practice. The core values of feminism and the Person-Centred Approach are a fundamental part of her being, as is the experiencing of life as essentially a spiritual journey.

Carol Wolter-Gustafson, EdD. They say 'the truth will set you free', but whose truth are we talking about? Questions like that have been puzzling me for as long as I can remember. The emancipatory power of feminism and the Person-Centered Approach have nourished me personally, politically and intellectually. We offer a pathway out of the 'us-versus-them' territory and rhetoric that fuels violence locally and globally. Our shared radical assertion that each voice must be heard is literally life-giving.

I first met Carl Rogers at a nine-day residential workshop on Long Island in 1978, while I was a graduate student in the Department of Humanistic and Behavioral Studies at Boston University. Our department chair Paul Nash shared power, challenged hierarchy, and cultivated a person-centered, multinational, interdisciplinary program. I was fortunate to have these profound and innovative experiences early in my career. I later taught philosophy and human development to prospective teachers at Lesley College, and I continue to maintain a private psychotherapy practice in Boston. I am now concentrating on writing and exploring the role of movement and non-verbal communication in the fully-functioning person.

INDEX

CARL ROGERS COUNSELS A BLACK CLIENT

RACE AND CULTURE IN PERSON-CENTRED COUNSELLING

EDITED BY ROY MOODLEY, COLIN LAGO AND ANISSA TALAHITE

Foreword by Clemmont E Vontress

ISBN 1 898059 44 6
234x158mm   pp. 296
£17.00

'*This is an ambitious and courageous book ... Though the starting point of the book is two brief interactions between two individuals, its scope is as broad as humanity. The book itself is a case study of intellectual honesty and racial sensitivity. It is the most important discussion of race, culture and ethnicity in the context of person-centred therapy ever written.*'

Tony Merry, University of East London

This book investigates and explores the issues of race and culture in a single case study of one of Rogers' own demonstration films: *Carl Rogers Counsels an Individual. Part 1: Right to be Desperate. Part 2: On Anger and Hurt*, in order to generate multiple meanings of how person-centred therapy can be more inclusive of Black and ethnic minority clients. The films show a young Black man in a state of remission from leukaemia, in therapy with Carl Rogers.

CONTRIBUTORS
Michele Baldwin, (USA); W. R. Selwyn Black, (N. Ireland); Debora C. Brink, (USA); Barbara Temaner Brodley, (USA); Khatidja Chantler, (UK); Mary Charleton, (UK); Jean Clark, (UK); Christine Clarke, (UK); Shukla Dhingra, (UK); Graham Falken, (South Africa); Gary Foster, (Canada); Michael Goldman, (Canada); William A. Hall, (USA); Susan James, (Canada); Colin Lago, (UK); Courtland Lee, (USA); Germain Lietaer, (Belgium); Melanie Lockett, (UK); John McLeod, (Scotland); Sharon Mier, (USA); Roy Moodley, (Canada); Josna Pankhania, (Australia); Catrin S. Rhys, (N. Ireland); Gella Richards, (UK); Debra Rosenzweig, (USA); Shauna Savage, (N. Ireland); Richard Saxton, (UK); Geraldine Shipton, (UK); Will Stillwell, (USA); Anissa Talahite, (Canada); Clemmont E. Vontress, (USA); William West, (UK); Stephen Whitehead, (UK); Marge Witty, (USA)

www.pccs-books.co.uk
tel. +44 1989 770 707
fax +44 1989 770 700

Women Writing in the Person-Centred Approach

edited by **Irene Fairhurst**   ISBN 1 898059 26 8   £16.00

Irene Fairhurst writes:
'… in the field of counselling and psychotherapy, on person-centred training courses, women outnumber men by between seven and nine to one, yet in our literature the opposite is the case. In the volume *Client Centered and Experiential Psychotherapy in the Nineties*—the book of papers presented at the first conference on Client-Centred and Experiential Psychotherapy in 1988—of the 52 authors of papers, 7 are women.'

Women Writing in the Person-Centred Approach both redresses that balance and presents the reader with a uniquely themed collection of work in the person-centred tradition.

Irene Fairhurst is co-founder and past President of the British Association for the Person-Centred Approach. Her further involvement in the person-centred approach includes founding the Institute for Person-Centred Learning and working with Carl Rogers in Europe and the UK.

www.pccs-books.co.uk
tel. **+44 1989 770 707**   fax **+44 1989 770 700**